Health Economics in India

Health Economics in India

Edited by
Himanshu Sekhar Rout
Prasant Kumar Panda

New Century Publications
New Delhi, India

NEW CENTURY PUBLICATIONS
4852 / 24, 1st Floor,
Ansari Road, Daryaganj,
New Delhi – 110 002 (India)

Tel.: 011-4101 7798; 4358 7398; 98112 66355
E-mail: info@newcenturypublications.com

www.newcenturypublications.com

Editorial office:
4800 / 24, Bharat Ram Road,
Ansari Road, Daryaganj,
New Delhi – 110 002

Edition: 2026

ISBN: **978-81-7708-141-1**

Published by New Century Publications and printed at Milan Enterprises, New Delhi.

Designs: Patch Creative Unit, New Delhi.

First Published: 2007

PRINTED IN INDIA

About the Book

Health economics as an independent scientific discipline is about 30 years old. This field is now so well established that it has appeared in the curriculum of most universities. Although, health economists are mainly found in medical departments, the connection to economics proper is being strengthened. In India, scanty literature is available on the concept of health and health economics. This book provides the much needed material on health related topics.

Health is an important aspect of human resource development. Good health care facilities and services are essential for creating healthy citizens and society that can effectively contribute to social and economic development. With increased urbanisation, industrialization and the changing environment, health related issues and problems are being emphasised and have become a great concern for the contemporary world.

Over the years, though the researchers, academicians and governments have tried to find ways and means to this, many issues and aspects of health, viz. provision of quality services and an effective delivery system, managing health expenditure and its financing and adequate expansion of service network to rural and tribal areas to achieve equity in access to health care, are yet to be completely resolved. Little attention has been paid to the micro aspects of health economics by the researchers, government, policy makers and the development planners.

The present volume, containing 16 papers, covers different aspects and issues related to health with empirical evidence. It is an initiative to partially address these issues and draw the attention of government functionaries and health planners.

The main themes which the volume covers are: health status and development, tribals' health, determinants of health, health care service delivery and health sector financing and reforms.

The volume will provide immense inputs and help to the academicians, health researchers, policy makers, health planners and government officials.

EDITORS' PROFILE

Himanshu Sekhar Rout was awarded Ph.D. in applied economics, M.Phil (A and A Economics), M.A. (A and A Economics), M.A. (Public Administration) and M.Ed. from Utkal University, Bhubaneswar and APA from NIIT, Tezpur, Assam. He has attended 11 training programmes/short-term courses/summer schools/winter schools at various institutions like IIT Delhi, Karolinska Institute Stockholm, IIT Kharagpur, IIT Kanpur, ISI Kolkata, IGIDR Mumbai, IIM Kolkata, VVGNLI Noida, CSER Mumbai and CSS Surat. He has 12 years of teaching/research experience in various organisations like Xavier Institute of Management, Bhubaneswar, Institute of Business Administration and Management, Bhubaneswar, Lal Bahadur Shastri National Academy of Administration, Mussorie, Kendriya Vidyalaya Sangathan and Department of Economics, Utkal University, Bhubaneswar. He is presently involved in both teaching and research at P.G. Department of Economics, Dr. SRK Government Arts College, (Government of Puducherry), Yanam, India. His areas of teaching and research interest include, economics of health and education, environmental economics, gender studies, rural development and tourism economics. He is a life member of Indian Economic Association, Indian Labour Economic Association, Indian Association for Research in National Income and Wealth and Orissa Commerce Association.

Prasant Kumar Panda is presently working in the Post-graduate Department of Economics, Dr. SRK Government Arts College, Yanam, Government of Puducherry. Earlier he had worked in Orissa University of Agriculture and Technology, Bhubaneswar and Silicon Institute of Technology, Bhubaneswar. His research interest includes public finance and public policy, health economics and gender studies and rural development. Besides teaching, he has been constantly contributing research papers to national and international Journals.

EDITORS' NOTE ON THE BOOK

Health is an important aspect of human resource development. Good health care facilities and services are essential for creating healthy citizens and society that can effectively contribute to social and economic development. Over the last three and half decades, health economics has been considered as an independent scientific discipline and is included in curriculum of most universities. With increased urbanisation, industrialisation, changing environment and the changing nature of health aspects, the health-related issues and problems are emphasised and have become a great concern for contemporary world.

Over the years, though the researchers, academicians and governments have tried to find ways and means to this, many issues and aspects of health, viz. provision of quality services and an effective delivery system, managing health expenditure and its financing, and adequate expansion of service network to rural and tribal areas to achieve equity in access to health care are yet to be completely resolved. Again, little attention has been given to the micro aspects of Health Economics by the researchers, government, policy makers and development planners.

In a spirit of optimistic empathy for the health needs of the people, particularly the poor and under-privileged, it had been hoped to provide 'Health for All by the year 2000 AD', through the universal provision of comprehensive primary health care services. In retrospect, it is observed that the financial resources and public health administrative capacity which it was possible to marshal, was far short of that necessary to achieve such an ambitious and holistic goal. Presently, India's health sector is characterised by the western model of health services, urban bias, favouring to the haves, over-weighted in favour of curative programmes, prevalence of commercial physicians, inappropriate policies, poor governance structure and inadequate financial arrangement. The presence of private sector in the provision of health services and its delivery need to be properly analysed.

The present volume, covering different aspects and issues related to health with empirical evidence, is an initiative to partially address these issues and draw the attention of government functionaries and health planners.

This volume has emerged from the research papers contributed by research scientists and academicians from different parts of the country selecting specific health problems and issues from different states in particular and the country in general. Both primary and secondary data have been used by the authors to analyse the problems and conclude with suggestions. The main themes which the volume covers are: health status and development, tribals' health, determinants of health, health care service delivery, and health sector financing and reforms.

We hope that the volume will provide immense inputs and help to the academicians, health researchers, policy makers, health planners and government.

All the contributors have been selected for their direct knowledge and recent experience of working in health economics and for their ability to illuminate the ways in which economic concepts and techniques can be, and are being, applied to health and health services.

Health economics as an independent scientific discipline has an age of about 30 years, in the sense that the specific treatment of topics related to the economics of the health care sector has become more and more common. The field is by now so well established that it has appeared among in the ordinary curriculum of most universities, and even if health economists are mainly to be found in the medical departments, the connections to economics proper are being strengthened, and the methodology applied refined. In India, scanty literature is available on the concept of health and health economics. This book, it is hoped, will provide much-needed material on health-related topics.

Subject matter of each of the research papers included in this book is set forth below.

Himanshu Sekhar Rout and Narayana Chandra Nayak have explained extensively the concept of health and health economics in their paper entitled **Health and Health Economics: A Conceptual Framework.** They defined health economics as the study of how scarce resources are allocated among alternative uses for the care of sickness and the promotion, maintenance and improvement of health, including the study of how health care and health-related services, their costs and benefits, and health itself are distributed among individuals and groups in society. Health economics is likely to be of increasing significance in the developing world because of an economic climate where resources are extremely scare and decisions on priorities are crucial but difficult; a growing appreciation among health professionals and policy makers that health economics and economists can help them to formulate policies and make decisions; the increasing maturity of the sub discipline of health economics; and the growth of interest among economists and other in applying their economic skill to health issues.

In his paper entitled **Health Scenario in India: Progress and Challenges**", Mihir K. Mahapatra and Rajesh Raj S. N. make an attempt to analyze the health scenario in India during the pre-reforms and reforms period taking 15 major states. To assess the performance of health indicators, attempt has been made to examine the growth of expenditure on medical and public health across major states in India. They found that there has been considerable improvement in the health sector during the last few decades in India but there is a long way to go to meet the target stipulated in the Millennium Development Goals and to be on par with some of the Asian Countries. A comparative analysis of health status during pre-reforms and reforms period reveals that performance is not encouraging during the latter period. It can be partly on account of erosion in growth of social sector expenditure especially Medical Health and Family Welfare. With the substantial rise in current consumption primarily on account of implementation of the fifth Pay Commission recommendations, persistence of high interest payment and improvement in life expectancy at birth; the major states in India failed to sustain high growth of social sector expenditure. Again, there has been widening of disparity in revenue expenditure on public health during the 1990s and onwards. To ensure improvement in Human Development Index (HDI), social sector need to be prioritized and adequate investment to be made so as to improve equity in access to health care. On account of resource constraint, there is a need to explore avenues for public-private partnership so as to develop health infrastructure, attract and retain skilled manpower. This necessitates introduction of user fee.

Inappropriate policies, poor governance structure and inadequate financial arrangement in the supply side and high incidence of poverty, ignorance and traditional practices and cultural factors operating at the demand side influence health outcomes. Financing health care being an important element, in his paper entitled **Fiscal Reforms and Health Care Spending: An Inter-state Analysis**, Sarit Kumar Rout seeks to examine the pattern of public financing of health care in 14 major non special category states of India during 1990-91 to 2005-06. It is observed that out of 14 states, 13 states have reduced the share of budgetary allocations to health sector during the post crisis period. The poor states particularly Bihar, Uttar Pradesh which have a significantly lower human development index in comparison to Kerala and Gujarat have reduced the health expenditure more. West Bengal makes highest budgetary spending towards health sector. The average share is 5.68 percent during the study period against 3.08 percent for Haryana which is the lowest in the country. The high income states like Punjab, Haryana and Gujarat allocate relatively lower share of state expenditure towards the health sector in comparison to poor states like Bihar, Orissa and Uttar Pradesh.

The regional inequality measured in terms of co-efficient of variation among different states is widening over the years. During the process of reforms the gap between the poor and rich states is rising indicating the poor states are not in a position to allocate more and more resources towards health sector. There exists a negative correlation between ratio of health care expenditure to Gross State Domestic Product (GSDP) and GSDP for 14 major states of the country during the period of analysis. So increasing GSDP doesn't contribute to the rise in health care expenditure in case of Indian states. It is not the allocation alone rather the service delivery mechanism may be improved to translate the outlays to health outcomes. The long route of accountability that exists in the service delivery chain may be broken. In order to improve the quality of delivery of services, the states may put efforts to transfer power to the Panchayati Raj Institutions (PRIs). The states are required to design policies to increase efficiency of public expenditure and maximize the benefits of every rupee spent for public purpose. This needs well integrated policies and political commitments.

There is a growing concern about the status of tribal health, particularly women and children, in India which is marked by all the negative features that one can find in terms of persistent morbidity and high mortality, lack of personal hygiene and environmental sanitation, malnutrition and undernourishment, low coverage of preventive measures and vaccination and absence of proper health education and awareness. In their paper entitled **Health Status of Tribals in India: Evidence from Andhra Pradesh**, Prasant Kumar Panda, Atulya Bhoi, Yoginder Singh and K. Sankaraiyah have tried to critically evaluate the health status of tribals in Andhra Pradesh (AP) on the basis of different determinants and health indicators and their access to different forms of health care services. The study shows that the health status of tribal population in AP is better than that of all India average of tribals but it is not satisfactory if it is compared with the non tribal population of AP. There exists a wide gap in the health indicators between tribal and non tribal areas which is mainly due to uneven provision and utilization of heath care services at the both areas. Infant mortality and maternal mortality are very high among the tribals.

Due to early marriage, lower acceptance to contraceptives, and low rate of sterilization, the fertility rate among STs is much higher than the same in Non-tribals. Tribals prefer more to the traditional form of medicines and practices than the health care facilities available in private run clinics and PHCs for healing their diseases. The distance of PHCs from the tribal location, frequent absenteeism of doctors, poor infrastructural and health care facilities, the lack of awareness and illiteracy, and moreover tribals' apathy to modern form of practices and the approach of the practitioners are the main reasons why they are ignoring the PHCs services. It is not only quantity of health care facilities but also the quality and approach of service delivery are important to promote health services in tribal areas. A multi-pronged approach with the active participation of Government, NGOs and public is essential to promote tribals' health. Up-scaling and extending the health care facilities into tribal areas including non-revenue tribal villages, proper mechanism to deliver the services and more importantly dedicated service attitude by the doctors and officers posted in the tribal areas will help in this regard. They also emphasize on a well coordinated and integrated health policy for tribals.

Old age is a natural part of human life. It has been seen as an opportunity for intellectual development, as the elderly persons constitute the storehouse of knowledge of both past and present and have the ability to predict the future. They play an important role through volunteer work, transmitting experience and knowledge and helping the families with caring responsibilities. Their experience and accumulated wisdom are essential assets in child-rearing and for other adults in the family. Older people are a resource for their families and for the society at large. The efficient use of this (elderly people) capital would benefit the family and the society as a whole, even after their regular employment has been ceased. A. Balasubramanian, in his paper entitled **Health Status of the Elderly in India** studied the health status of the elderly in India, by using 1995-96 cross-sectional data of NSS 52nd round health care survey. The health capital conceptual framework developed by Grossman as an extension of Becker's theory of household economics was applied to study the factors determining the health conditions of the elderly. Health capital is measured by a self-assessed categorical measure of overall health status, and an ordered probity model is used to estimate the demand for health equation. The results are consistent with the theoretical predictions and show that the demand for health increases with income (proxy by expenditure), employment status (Wage rate) and education and decreases with age, other demographic and health characters like region, being single, household size, number of children's, physical immobile, risk factors and health problems have influenced the health status of elderly.

To prevent delay to access the health facility at the time of emergency, the Government of India had initiated a scheme called "Referral Transport Scheme" (RTS) under the Reproductive and Child Health (RCH) Phase I in 1999-2000, to promote access of women with obstetric emergencies to the first referral units. The basic model prepared was with the main objective for providing transport facilities (not only the fund for transport) but also to make arrangements for transport at the local level for the women who were in need. Assessing the **RTS for Emergency Obstetric Care under Reproductive Child Health (RCH) - Phase I in Rajasthan,** Manisha Chawla found that lack of clarity related to guidelines of the scheme among the stakeholders; lack of Knowledge related to the scheme in the community; and lack of Monitoring and Non- availability of health providers at headquarters, the scheme was a failure, therefore, it was withdrawn from RCH-II, but Government of India has recently announced Janani Suraksha Yojana (JSY) which is a safe motherhood intervention under the National Rural Health Mission (NRHM) being implemented with the objective of reducing maternal and neo-natal mortality by promoting institutional delivery among the poor pregnant women. JSY is a 100 per cent centrally sponsored scheme and it integrates cash assistance with delivery and post-delivery care. The success of the scheme would be determined by the increase in institutional delivery among the poor families which is to be monitored under the scheme. Although, the overall structure of JSY seems quite satisfying, the scheme can be further evaluated on the factors identified as bottlenecks in this study.

The paper **Health and Development Inter-Links in India** of Neena Malhotra and Shweta, attempts to study the pattern of public health expenditure in various states of India and analyses the extent to which states are fulfilling its responsibility in providing public health facilities. The inter-state disparities in per capita public health expenditure (PCHE) have not changed much during 1991-2001. There is no major change in the ranking of states in terms of PCHE during the same period. Interstate analysis shows states like Orissa, Madhya Pradesh, Uttar Pradesh, Bihar, are low performing states where as Kerala, Maharashtra and Tamil Nadu are better performing states in the health outcomes. The study shows that life expectancy both for male and females has positive and highly significant relation; and IMR, CBR, and CDR have negative relation with per capita net state domestic product. Therefore, there is a strong interlink between health and economic development. The authors suggest that to improve health indicators, the state governments will have to spend more on public health as well as education.

In their paper **Health-Development Interface in the Context of Malaria in Orissa**, Nirmal Chandra Sahu and Santosh Kumar Bali formulated a research problem from a surmise that the reciprocity between health and development is not always true. While good health has positive effects on development, it's contrary is not true everywhere. Unless well-focused policies are in place, economic development may not imply better health status for the people. This proposition is examined in the context of Malaria in Orissa and proved. From a simple time series analysis of incidence of malaria and increase in income of Orissa, it is evident that economic growth could be insensitive to health problems. For development to be helpful to health, well-focused political commitment to social sectors is necessary.

Human resource is a key factor in development. The foundations of man's physical, mental and social development are laid in early childhood. Today's child is the nation's future economic asset. The quality of our future human resource is determined largely by the investment for the development of our child production. Healthy and literate children are not only assets but also the stepping-stones to build a strong and prosperous nation. The morbid or diseased children are not only a burden on their family members, but also on the society where they live in as well as on the nation. Evaluating Integrated Child Development Scheme (ICDS) in Coimbatore City, Tamil Nadu, in her paper **Determinants of Nutritional Status of Children in Urban Households**, A. Sugirtha Rani proved that mother's labour force participation has a positive impact on nutrition and health status of children by taking 483 households (242 were working mothers and 241 were non-working mothers), having children in the preschool age. The ICDS scheme provides supplementary nutritious food and it is not a substitute for household care for children. Availability of public supported childcare nutritious programme should be encouraged for the strengthening future human resources of the country. Even though mother's earning has a positive effect on nutrition and health status of children, it could not be said, to improve the maximum level. But at least it helps to meet the minimum requirement for the household. Because already the household is in poor economic strata and the income earned by husband is not sufficient to meet the family expenditure.

In her paper entitled **Status of Health and its Determinants in North East India**, Keya Sengupta examines the health status of the people of the north eastern region of India. The study seeks to make a detailed analysis of the various indicators affecting health condition of the people of the region across different social, religious, and linguistic groups, in view of the significant inter-state, rural, urban and group differential in standard and quality of life characterizing the region. The study is based on primary data collected from the sixteen districts of the various states of the region (Six districts from Assam, two each from the smaller states except Manipur), through multistage stratified sampling method. The Sample Size is 350. She claims that the present paper is perhaps for the first time that such a microscopic study on health condition of the people of the region is conducted. The study reveals that some districts of the region, some income groups and certain special groups, perform much better than the all India performance level, whereas the record of the others is much below the national average, and may take several years, before they can reach the national average.

Among the religious groups, the Buddhists have the highest IMR, which is as high as 11 per thousand followed by Muslim, Christians and Hindus. Among the social groups, the scheduled caste (SC) group has the highest rate of IMR followed by schedule tribe (ST) group. Muslim community has the highest life expectancy of 60 years, followed by Christian community (59 years), Hindus (57 years), and Buddhist (54 years). Among the social groups; the general category has the highest life expectancy followed by the ST, OBC and SC groups. The author urges to raise the health status of the population of this region, it is necessary to tackle these problems differently at different socio-economic levels. As far as provision of government health services at the supply side is concerned, some kind of uniformity may not be undesirable for all socio-economic and economic groups.

On the demand side however, tackling the problem at a heterogeneous level is called for. Provision of health services by the state uniformly irrespective of any groups or community is extremely essential particularly in some districts of the region. In view of the remoteness of some of the districts of the region, and the extremely sensitive nature of the tribal population who occupy a dominant place in the region, policy action cannot be like the rest of the country. Minute and careful variation is called for, even within the region itself.

In his paper entitled **Health Care Delivery System in Orissa**, Rabi N. Patra, analyzes the health care delivery system, examining the issues of accessibility and financing health services and spelling out their implications for policy making and programme implementation in the context of Orissa, India. The study is based on both primary and secondary data. He is satisfied with the functioning of two programmes of government of Orissa, i.e., '*barefoot doctors*', '*Panchavyadhi Chikitsa Vyabastha*' for the improvement of health of rural people. But he is more concerned about the poor state of health care system in Orissa.

Firstly, the Public sector health care facilities are inadequate, inappropriate, and not less expensive in comparison to the private providers and by the criterion of quality they are worse. Treatment of serious patients on the floor is a naked scene in the public hospitals. The quality of care in the private sector is not very encouraging either.

Secondly, the private alternative has undermined the public system and in view of preferential treatment to the relatively well to do in the latter, inequality in access to health care facilities is increasing.

Thirdly, concern for health has increased and hospitalization has become quite costly pushing many to debt trap and poverty.

Fourthly, people are willingness to pay even for public health services on quality considerations. However, the economically weaker sections exhibit a low willing to pay compared to the better off.

Fifthly, cost recovery through user fees hardly amounts to one per cent of public expenditure on health and there is no mechanism to review user charges and to ensure its utilization. In this situation, he suggested that, there is an urgent need to improve the quality of public health care services as well as putting the private providers under regulatory cover. Moreover, there is an urgent need to reorient the health sector of Orissa. In this connection, the government may earmark at least six per cent of net state domestic product for the health sector and think of alternative sources of financing public health. Thirdly, the onus of improving the health care system lies with the government, the civil society and the people themselves. But given the type of political economy and the nature of governance which we have, reforms in the health sector are really a Herculean task and our aim of providing 'Health for all from womb to tomb' is difficult but not impossible.

In her paper **Use of Primary Health Care Services among Rural Population**, R. Annapoorani studied the organization and management of a selected primary health centre (PHC) in Perumanallur village, Tirupur block, Coimbatore district in Tamil Nadu. She also assessed the beneficiaries and measures the efficiency of the PHC. She urged that the health care sector should be accorded the status of a core sector. To reduce the demand and supply gap with regard to primary health care, it is necessary to increase the number of doctors, nurses and health assistants in the primary health care unit. Due to free treatment, free accessibility of doctors and nearness to the place of residence, low income people made use of primary health care as compared to high-income group. With improvement in income, people shift their health care to other private hospitals.

In their paper entitled **Health Care and Awareness among Urban Educated Females**, Shweta Upadhyay and A. K. Jain tries to assess the health care and awareness among urban educated females. The study based on primary data collected from 100 girl (Arts) students of University of Allahabad, Uttar Pradesh, India. With regard to awareness about health care, 36 per cent girls of Undergraduate classes, 18 per cent at postgraduate level, 16 per cent at D.Phil. level girls were aware of the need for health care and they do meditation, yoga, physical activity, diet control and health checkup for their health. A large section of girls were not aware and so they were not doing anything for their health care. Only 28 per cent girls regularly consult doctors for their health problems where as 72 per cent girls are casual. This shows a lack of proper health care awareness. For group health insurance scheme only 48 per cent girls are agreed where as 52 per cent girls are not in favour of it. In this connection they suggested that, necessary direction should be provided to increase awareness regarding health and maintain good health through proper health care. The educational institutions should generate health awareness amongst the students through appropriate campaigns regarding the benefits of good health as well as the drawbacks of ill health. Health camps should be organized where free or subsidized health check-ups can be made to identify any ailments especially regarding hemoglobin, iron content, glucose along with routine pathological tests.

In his paper **Determinants of Health and Medical Care in India**, Dastageer R. Myageri examines the performance of healthcare system as a whole by measuring the trends of health indicators, determinants and the effect of the determinants of health status on each of the health indicators. The public expenditure on health and family welfare has increased during the year 1980-81 to 2004-05. The trends of pre-reform and reforms period revealed that, the central and state government spending on public health much higher during reform period, than pre-reform period. The allocation for health rises as GDP increases. Regression analysis revealed that there is an inverse relationship between public health expenditure and birth rate both in the pre-reform and reform period. Access to hospital facility also plays a significant role in reducing the birth rate. Expenditure on medical and public health, number of hospitals and hospital beds per lakh population have influenced the death rate negatively, leading to decrease in the death rate. The increased per capita income and expenditure on public health, ensured better medical and health services and supply of medicine reduce the death rate. The number of hospitals and beds per lakh population contributed significantly to reduce the death rates during pre-reform and reform period. Health expenditure and IMR are inversely related but not significant. However, IMR decreases significantly as hospitals and beds per lakh population increase.

In his paper entitled **Rural Primary Health Centers (PHCs) in Andhra Pradesh,** explained the status of health infrastructure and public health expenditures pattern in A.P. Examining the utilization and functioning of the PHCs in Khammam district, he suggested that public health expenditure may be increased from present 0.9 per cent of GDP to at least two per cent. Such increases are vital to make public health services more accessible and effective. However, increase in expenditure must be accompanied by better utilization of resources with emphasis on preventive and primary health. Secondly, necessary steps may be taken by the *Panchayat Raj* Department for continuous supply of drinking water by identifying problem affected areas. Thirdly, government control and regulation over private/corporate hospitals is required so that the medical help will be with in the reach of a common man with reasonable charges, that the common man is free from institutional victimization. Fourthly, effective public education, counseling, replacement therapies and treatments should be standardized to suit the requirement of each region and group. Fifthly, it would be better if the PHCs are provided with the test for the AIDS as it has become hazardous in the present time. It is also necessary to keep oxygen operator at the PHCs as to meet the needs of the emergency cases.

This book emerged from the research papers contributed by economists and academicians from different parts of the country. We express our deep sense of gratitude to all paper contributors who have accepted our request and put their hard work in preparing and sending the papers in a short span of time.

We would like to extend our sincere thanks to Mr. Sandeep Sury, Chief Executive, New Century Publications, New Delhi for accepting our proposal to publish this volume and perpetuating his active cooperation at each stage to bring the volume in its present form.

We would be failing in our duty, if we do not thank our family members, teachers, colleagues, friends and students, whose constant motivations and inspirations are propelling force behind all our research works including this volume.

Yanam
June 4, 2007

Himanshu Sekhar Rout
Prasant Kumar Panda

List of Contributors

Annapoorani, R.	Professor in Economics, Avinashilingam University for Women, Coimbatore.
Balasubramanian, A.	Department of Economics, Bharathiar University, Coimbatore.
Bali, Santosh Kumar	Department of Economics, Berhampur University, Berhampur.
Bhoi, Atulya	Lecturer, P.G. Department of Commerce, Dr. SRK Government Arts College, Yanam.
Chawla, Manisha	Assistant Professor, Indian Institute of Health Management and Research, Jaipur.
Jain, A. K.	Professor, Department of Economics, University of Allahabad, Allahabad.
Myageri, Dastageer R.	Center for Multi-Disciplinary Development Research (CMDR), Dharwad.
Mahapatra, Mihir K.	Assistant Professor in Economics, Goa Institute of Management (GIM), Goa.
Malhotra, Neena	Punjab School of Economics, Guru Nanak Dev University, Amritsar.
Nayak, Narayana Chandra	Associate Professor in Economics, Indian Institute of Technology (IIT), Kharagpur
Panda, Prasant Kumar	P.G. Department of Economics, Dr. SRK Government Arts College, Yanam.
Patra, Rabi N.	P.G. Department of Economics, Ravenshaw University, College Square, Cuttack.
Radha Krishna, S.	Department of Economics, University P.G. College, (Kakatiya University) Khammam, Andhra Pradesh.

Rajesh Raj S.N.	Department of Humanities and Social Sciences, Indian Institute of Technology (IIT) Madras, Chennai.
Rout, Himanshu Sekhar	P.G. Department of Economics, Dr. SRK Government Arts College, Yanam.
Rout, Sarit Kumar	Fellow, Health and Population Innovation, Population Council, New Delhi.
Sahu, Nirmal Chandra	Reader and Coordinator, Department of Economics, Berhampur University, Berhampur.
Sankaraiyah, K.	Lecturer, Department of Zoology, Dr. SRK Government Arts College, Yanam.
Sengupta, Keya	Professor, Department of Economics, Assam University, Silchar.
Singh, Yoginder	Lecturer, P.G. Department of Commerce, Dr. SRK Government Arts College, Yanam.
Sugirtharani, A.	Lecturer, Department of Economics, Periyar University, Salem.
Shweta	Punjab School of Economics, Guru Nanak Dev University, Amritsar.
Upadhyay, Shweta	Department of Economics, University of Allahabad, Allahabad.

Contents

1

Introduction and Overview

Himanshu Sekhar Rout and
Prasant Kumar Panda

A. Introduction

Health and Development: Economic growth and development affect the health of the people by increasing their level of income, and hence in the consumption – increasing goods and services. It means, there is a positive relationship between health and stages of economic growth and development but it is not always true (see ninth article of this book: Sahu and Bali). In this connection it is useful to note two important consequences of the improvement of health: *demographic transition and epidemiological transition.*

As population become healthier, they also live long which is known as demographic transition. It occurs due to two reasons. Firstly, when health status of the individual improves, they live longer. Assuming given birth rate, the net addition to the population each year increases, increasing the share of older people in the total population (see sixth article of this book: Balasubramanian). Secondly, the fertility rate (the average number of children born to a representative woman in her life) may tend to decline (which may not be always true) due to better health and greater economic security. Of course, this has more indirect effect of the change in health status.

Secondly, as development proceeds, the pattern of diseases change which is known as epidemiological transition. This has also two effects. Firstly, when some diseases and ill-health are controlled or eliminated, the relative importance of other diseases increases as a matter of arithmetic. Secondly, as individuals live longer, diseases that only affect older individuals increase in absolute term. Similarly, reduction in maternal mortality leads to larger number of older women and to a greater prevalence of post-menopausal health problems.

Determinants of Health: The fact that the health status of a person is largely determined by chance, that health is perishable and lacks tradability, does not rule out considering health being result of a production process. Health of a individual is complicated and multi-dimensional; and influenced by plethora of factors such as income of the person; pattern of educational attainment (schooling); population growth; density of population and age structure; abundance of natural resources; personal and government saving (investment rate); physical capital stock; economic policy, for example liberalization, globalization and privatization; the quality of public institutions; the geography, for example the location and climate of a country; food; housing; basic sanitation; social practices; measures to control environmental hazards; and communicable diseases positively or negatively.

Per capita income is highly correlated with indicators such as life expectancy and infant mortality (as health outcomes), not only in between but also within countries, which is known as income-health linkage. This is because of two reasons. First, as income increases, it has become easier, or cheaper, to attain and maintain a given level of health over time. Second, individuals' preferences have been changed over time, and that, for a given level of income, individuals have become more concerned about health. The close linkages between the two (income and health outcome) have not been fully appreciated (Mishra, Chatterjee and Rao, 2003).

Good health is not only an outcome of increase in income, but is also a determinant of the latter. Apart from governing the core of human well-being, health itself promotes development via increase in productivity and hence income, which is known as health-income linkages. The improvement in the health status of people is essential to sustain economic and social development. It is not difficult to imagine that healthier people tend to be more fit, strong, and energetic than unhealthy individuals and they can add more value within the same time. The two-way linkages between health and development have been well-documented.

Features of India's Health Sector

After independence in 1947, India decided to expand and improve the health services of the country as one of a comprehensive package programme to raise the standard of living of the people. She adopted the western model of health services, as it was ideally suited for her. The basic emphasis in this model was on the adoption of the latest medical technology developed in the west and to make it available to her people through the expansion of the bureaucratic machinery of the medical and public health departments; the expansion of the institutions of medical education to train the agents required for the delivery of health care (such as doctors and nurses); the creation of necessary infrastructure needed for the primary health centers and dispensaries in rural areas; and the indigenous production of the essential drugs and chemical required.

The Indian Constitution does not list health as a fundamental right. The recommendatory Directive Principles of State Policy enjoin the state to raise nutrition level and improve public health (Article 47). But many court rulings have interpreted the fundamental right of protection of right of life and liberty (Article 21) as inclusive of the right to health, implying state obligation to protect citizens from medical negligence. The state is required to concentrate on the development of health infrastructure because of its welfare oriented goals, market failures, to promote rural health facilities and the recommendations of Bhore Committee. [1] The constitution places 'public health and sanitation, hospitals, and dispensaries' in the state list. But some related activities – medical education, drugs, family planning, the control of the spread of communicable diseases from one state to another, mental health, and the medical professions – are in the concurrent list. The only area of exclusive central jurisdiction (the Union list), are institutions of national importance in medical education, and research. But the centre has played a dominant role in all aspects of health, mainly because of its financial clout in centrally planned economy.

There is no doubt that India has achieved a good deal during the last 60 years. She has a huge Ministry of Health and Family Welfare at the centre and also in states. Government of India's (GOI) initiatives in the pubic health sector has recorded some noteworthy successes over time. Smallpox and Guinea Worm Disease have been eradicated from the country; Polio is on the verge of being eradicated; Leprosy, Kala Azar, and Filariasis can be expected to be eliminated in the foreseeable future. There has been a substantial drop in the Total Fertility Rate and Infant Mortality Rate. The successes of the initiatives taken in the public health field are reflected in the progressive improvement of many demographic/epidemiological/infrastructural indicators over time (Table 1.1). Life expectancy has gone up from 36.7 years in 1951 to 64.6 years in 2000 (GOI, 2002b). Infant mortality rate is down from 146 in 1951 to 71 in 2001 (GOI, 2002a). Crude birth rate has been reduced from 40.8 in 1951 to 25.8 in 2000 and crude death rate from 25.1 to 8.5 in the same period (GOI, 2002a).

These achievements are very impressive and we have every right to be proud of them but it is also realized that our failures are even more glaring. Before independence, we made a number of solemn pledges to the people of India in whose name we fought the war for political independence, viz., that we shall abolish poverty, ignorance, and ill health and raise substantially the standard of living of the masses but we adopt hidden and implied goals of pursuing our own class interest. This is understandable (but not excusable) because a ruling class rules for its own benefit and only incidentally for that of others (Naik, 1977). In a spirit of optimistic empathy for the health needs of the people, particularly the poor and under-privileged, had hoped to provide 'Health for All by the year 2000 AD', through the universal provision of comprehensive primary health care services. In retrospect, it is observed that the financial resources and public health administrative capacity which it was possible to marshal, was far

Table 1.1: Achievements through the Years: 1951-2000

Indicator		1951	1981	2000
Demographic Changes	Life Expectancy	36.7	54	64.6
	Crude Birth Rate	40.8	33.9	26.1*
	Crude Death Rate	25	12.5	8.7*
	IMR	146	110	70*
Epidemiological Shifts	Malaria (cases in million)	75	2.7	2.2
	Leprosy cases per 10,000 Population	38.1	57.3	3.74
	Small Pox (no of cases)	>44,887	Eradicated	
	Guinea worm (no. of cases)		>39,792	Eradicated
	Polio		29,709	265
Infrastructure	SC/PHC/CHC	725	57,363	1,63,181*
	Dispensaries and Hospitals (all)	9209	23,555	43,322**
	Beds (Private and Public)	117,198	569,495	8,70,161**
	Doctors (Allopathy)	61,800	2,68,700	5,03,900***
	Nursing Personnel	18,054	1,43,887	7,37,000***

* In 1999, ** In 1995-96, *** In 1998-99

Source: GOI, 2002b

short of that necessary to achieve such an ambitious and holistic goal.

Secondly, in India, the present health care system provides health care services mostly to the urban. In the period when centralized planning was accepted as a key instrument of development in the country, the attainment of an equitable regional distribution was considered one of its major objectives. Despite this conscious focus in the development process, the statistics given in Table 1.2 clearly indicate that the attainment of health indices has been very uneven across the rural – urban divide.

A micro study conducted in Orissa showed that in an average, a person in rural area spends forty six per cent of what a person in urban area spends on health expenditure from his own pocket as his/her income is only around forty one per cent of his/her urban counterparts. But a person in rural area spends around nine per cent of his/her income on health care from his own pocket which is more than a person in urban area who spends only around eight per cent of his/her income. This is because (i) government spending on health care is more in urban than rural area which reduces people's expenditure on it from their own pocket; (ii) in urban area, government and people take more preventive measures than rural area which reduces people's expenditure on their curative care; (iii) urban people take more precautionary measures for health care due to their higher education than rural people; and (iv) a person in rural area spends more on transport cost, which is one of the main component of the health expenditure, to avail the medical facility, than a person in urban area, as it is available far away from his/her residence (Rout, 2005).

Also, the statistics bring out the wide differences between the attainments of health goals in the better- performing States as compared to the low-performing States. It is clear that national averages of health indices hide wide disparities in public health facilities and health standards in different parts of the country. Given a situation in which national averages in respect of most

Table 1.2: Differentials in Health Status among States

Sector	Population BPL (%)	IMR/Per 1000 Live Births (1999-SRS)	<5 Mortality per 1000 (NFHS II)	Weight For Age-% of Children Under 3 years (<-2SD)	MMR/ Lakh (Annual Report 2000)	Leprosy cases per 10000 population	Malaria Positive Cases in year 2000 (in thousands)
India	26.1	70	94.9	47	408	3.7	2200
Rural	27.09	75	103.7	49.6	---	---	---
Urban	23.62	44	63.1	38.4	---	---	---
Better Performing States							
Kerala	12.72	14	18.8	27	87	0.9	5.1
Maharashtra	25.02	48	58.1	50	135	3.1	138
Tami Nadu	21.12	52	63.3	37	79	4.1	56
Low Performing States							
Orissa	47.17	97	104.4	54	498	7.05	483
Bihar	42.60	63	105.1	54	707	11.83	132
Rajasthan	15.28	81	114.9	51	607	0.8	53
U.P	1.15	84	122.5	52	707	4.3	99
M.P.	37.43	90	137.6	55	498	3.83	528

Source: GOI, 2002b

indices are themselves at unacceptably low levels, the wide Inter-State disparity implies that, for vulnerable sections of society in several States, access to public health services is nominal and health standards are grossly inadequate.

Thirdly, the health care system is still over-weighted in favour of curative programmes in spite of the clear conviction that, in our present situation, it is the preventive, socioeconomic, and educational aspects of the health care systems that are most significant. It is widely accepted that school and college students are the most impressionable targets for imparting information relating to the basic principles of preventive health care. After 55 years, only in the National Health Policy 2002 envisages giving priority to school health programmes which aim at preventive-health education, providing regular health check-ups, and promotion of health seeking behaviour among children. The school health programmes can gainfully adopt specially designed modules in order to disseminate information relating to 'health' and 'family life'. This is expected to be the most cost-effective intervention as it improves the level of awareness, not only of the extended family, but the future generation as well.

Fourthly, access to, and benefits from, the public health system have been very uneven between the better-endowed and the more vulnerable sections of society. This is particularly true for women, children and the socially disadvantaged sections of society. The statistics given in Table 4 highlight the handicap suffered in the health sector on account of socio-economic inequity.

Fifthly, in India, the present day doctors are commercial physicians, motivated by profits. They are no more social physicians or peasant physicians who generally attract the people and guide them for healthier and happier life. Their main aim is to how to get maximum profit. It is more a business than human service. The concept of *daridra narayan seva* is no more valid.

Sixthly, the multiple systems of health care services in India– allopathy, *ayurveda*, homoeopathy, *unani*, *sidha*; various types of ownership patterns – public (central and state governments, municipal and *panchayat* local government), private (for-profit and not-for-profit); and different kinds of delivery structures– teaching hospitals, secondary level hospitals, first level referral hospitals (CHCs or rural hospitals), dispensaries, PHCs, sub centers, health posts, occupational groups such as, ESIS, defence, CGHS, posts and telegraphs, railways, and mines; have resulted a complex plurality that makes the development of an organized system difficult.

Seventhly, inappropriate policies, poor governance structure and inadequate financial arrangement in the supply side and high incidence of poverty, ignorance and traditional practices and cultural factors operating at the demand side influence the health outcomes of India. Public spending on health care in India is one of the lowest and as per the national health accounts 2001-02 spending by the health departments of both centre and state accounts for 0.9 per cent of GDP. Fiscal pressure has resulted in the compression of state expenditure and steady decline in social expenditure. The combined expenditure of the states in the 1990s on health, water supply sanitation and family welfare programme declined from 8.4 per cent of total expenditure in 1990s to 7.2 per cent in 2001-02 (GOI, 2005).

Eighthly, as per the United Nations Development Programme's (UNDP) Human development Reports, the value of the Human Development Index (HDI) – composite indicator based on income, education and health – has increased consistently over the years. However, India's relative global ranking on this index has remained at a low of 127 among 177 countries for three years in a row. The unsatisfactory relative progress, in spite of rapid growth in income, continued to underscore the need for accelerated improvements in education and health.

Health Service Delivery in India

Though data on public health care facilities in India are available, data about their uses are not available in a systemic manner. Data inadequacy, inaccuracy and underestimation on health care services and their uses are the main drawbacks in the health research. Again conflicting conclusions and wide discrepancies exist on the available data. State performance budgets do provide some relevant utilization data, but neither are these documents easily available nor do the health statistics authorities compile data from them (Duggal, 2006).

However, in recent years, national surveys such as the National Sample Survey Organization (NSSO) utilization surveys in 1987 and 1996, the National Council for Applied Economic Research (NCAER) surveys in 1990 and 1993, National Family Health Surveys (NFHS) in 1993 and 1999 and the rapid household survey (RCH) in 1999 apart from small studies, have provided reasonably good estimates of utilization of public facilities and programmes (Table 1.3) (Duggal, 2006).

India's social services were used relatively little by the poor. The health and education of the poor has improved but not as much for the population as a whole. Physical access to education and health services has improved but inequalities exist because of biases in locating facilities. The access of the poor to housing, social security, and social welfare services has been limited because these services were inadequate relative to needs and services leak to the *non-poor*. Social service policies are not comprehensive enough and the quality of service is low. The bureaucracy is inadequate to reach the poor. Existing capacity and resources are inadequate, particularly for education and health (Murthy, Hirway, Panchmukhi, and Satia, 1990).

Too often, services fail poor people – in access, in quality, and in affordability. Freedom from illness and freedom from illiteracy are two of the most important ways people can escape from poverty. To achieve these goals, economic growth and financial resources are of course necessary, but they are not enough. It needs a framework where citizens, governments and donors can take action and accelerate progress towards the common objectives of poverty reduction, as specified in the Millennium Development Goals (MDGs) (World Bank, 2003).

Table 1.3: Differentials in Health Status among Socio-Economic Groups

Indicator	Infant Mortality/ 1000	Under 5 Mortality/ 1000	% Children Underweight
India	70	94.9	47
Social Inequity			
Scheduled Tribes	84.2	126.6	55.9
Other Disadvantaged	76.0	103.1	47.3
Others	61.8	082.6	41.1

Source: GOI, 2002b

Note

1. The recommendations of the Bhore Committee 1946 are (i) no individual should lack access to medical care because of inability to pay for it; (ii) special emphasis should be placed on preventive methods and on communicable diseases; (iii) health services should be as "close to the people as possible in order to ensure the maximum benefit to the community to be served"; (iv) all facilities for diagnosis and treatment should be available in the health services when it is fully developed; (v) one primary health unit per 10-20,000 populations with 75 beds and six doctors and six public health nurses; (vi) one bed per 175 populations, one doctor per 1,600 and one nurse per 600 populations; (vii) one 650 bed hospital at taluka (three lakh population) level and one district hospital of 2,500 beds; (viii) no patents in pharmaceutical products; and (ix) fifteen per cent of the government expenditure on health care.

References

Duggal, Ravi (2006): Utilization of Health Care Services in India, In Sujata Prasad and C. Sathyamala (Eds.) *Securing Health for All: Dimensions and Challenges*, Institute for Human Development, New Delhi, pp. 31-32.

GOI (2002a): *Economic Survey 2002-2003*, Economic Division, Ministry of Finance and Company Affairs, New Delhi, p. 230 and S-113.

GOI (2002b): *National Health Policy 2002*, Ministry of Health and

Family Welfare, New Delhi.

GOI (2005): *Report of the National commission on Macro Economics and Health*, Ministry of Health and family Welfare.

Mishra, Rajiv, Rachel Chatterjee and Sujatha Rao (2003): *India Health Report*, Oxford University Press, New Delhi.

Murthy, Nirmal, Indira Hirway, P. Panchmukhi, and J. Satia (1990): How well do India's Social Service Programs serve the Poor? *World Bank Policy Research Working Paper WPS 491*, World Bank, New Delhi.

Naik, J. P. (1977): *An Alternative System of Health Care Services in India: Some Proposals* Allied Publishers Private Limited, New Delhi.

Nandraj, Sunil et. al. (1999): *Accreditation of Hospitals*, CEHAT, Mumbai.

NSSO (1998): *Morbidity and Treatment of Ailments*, Report No. 441, 52nd Round, New Delhi.

Rout, H. S. (2005): *Health Expenditure in Orissa: A Micro Analysis*, Unpublished Ph.D Thesis submitted to Utkal University, Bhubaneswar, Orissa, India.

World Bank (1981): *World Development Report 1981*, Oxford University Press, New York.

World Bank (2003): *World Development Report 2004*, A Copublication of World Bank and Oxford University Press, Washington D.C.

2

Health and Health Economics: A Conceptual Framework

Himanshu Sekhar Rout and Narayana Chandra Nayak

I. Concept of Health

Health is a multifaceted concept and thus it defies any precise definition. The narrow definition of health posits it as the absence of disease. The broad definition of health, however, does not rest merely on the absence of disease but the fulfillment of a whole range of personal, physiological, mental, social and even moral goals. World Health Organization's (WHO) constitution defines health as "*a state of complete physical, mental and social well being and not merely the absence of disease or infirmity*" (WHO, 1992). Although, this definition is a fine and inspiring concept and its pursuit guarantees health professionals unlimited opportunities for carry out work in future, it may not be of much practical relevance (Doll, 1992) and also it seems to work against its effective functioning (Saracci, 1997). Such a definition is too wide and not amenable for any meaningful economic analysis or for any resource allocation.

Necessarily, health has to be defined from a practical point of view and, therefore, it has been defined according to life expectancy, infant mortality, and crude death rate, etc (Reddy, 1992). In fact, it is studied as a function of medical care, income, education, age, sex, race, marital status, environmental pollution, and also certain personal behaviour like smoking habits, exercise, and the like. It is also used as an independent variable to explain labour force participation rates particularly at old age. Not only do retired persons frequently cite poor health as the reason for retirement, but also current workers, who report health limitations, are more likely to withdraw from work in future. Health status is often used to explain wages, productivity, school performance, fertility and the demand for medical care. The results are quite sensitive to the particular measures of health that are used but the direction of the effect generally confirms *a priori* preconditions (Fuchs, 1987).

Problems with the WHO Definition: The WHO definition of health is subjected to serious problems at the conceptual level that impair its guiding role in the wake of the conflict between health needs and resources, both nationally and internationally. In fact, a state of complete physical, mental and social well-being corresponds more closely to happiness than to health. The latter two terms designate distinct life experiences. Sigmund Freud experienced the same clearly after stopping smoking on health reasons. He confessed, "I learned that health was to be had at a certain cost ... Thus, I am now better than I was, but not happier" (Saracci, 1997).

Not only health and happiness are distinct but also their relationship is neither fixed nor constant. Having suffered from a serious disease is likely to make one less happy, but not having the same does not necessarily amount to happiness. Common existential problems – involving emotions, passions, personal values, and questions on the meaning of life – can make one less happy or even overtly uncomfortable, but they may not be leading to health problems.

The distinction between health and happiness is relevant in terms of rights, in particular 'positive rights or entitlements', that may seek societal actions to ensure that rights materialize completely and effectively. Whereas it can be argued that health is a positive and universal right, at the same length, it may be difficult to construct an argument that happiness (though not its material and social preconditions) is a positive right as happiness cannot be delivered or imposed on a person by any societal action. Happiness is strictly subjective both as an achievement and as an appreciation (Saracci, 1997).

Consequences of the Definition: Failing to distinguish health from happiness has four major consequences (Saracci, 1997).

Firstly, any disturbance to happiness may come to be seen as a health problem. This may make the purpose self-defeating as one brings in subjectivity, while the other is seen from certain objective criteria.

Secondly, because the quest for happiness is essentially boundless, the quest for health also becomes boundless. This legitimizes an unlimited demand for health services. Of course, some people may legitimately decide that they want to pursue happiness as well as health by medical means, as other people may do through music, religion, or love. For example, some people may wish to have their features surgically redesigned to suit some aesthetic ideals. But this preference represents a personal way to happiness rather than a universal right to health.

Thirdly, annexing happiness to health as a universal positive right introduces an underlying prescriptive view of happiness in society. This undervalues personal autonomy and could be established only in totalitarian regimes.

Finally, and more significantly, trying to guarantee the unattainable -happiness for every citizen - may inevitably subtract resources and jeopardize the chances of guaranteeing the attainable - justice and equity in health. The necessary and formidable task of reducing inequalities and achieving equity in health, an emerging issue in the reformulation of the WHO's programmes of action, becomes meaningless if it is not even clear what needs to be equitably distributed.

Towards a Solution: With a view to remove the fundamental ambiguity that surrounds happiness and health, health may be construed as a condition of well being free of disease or infirmity and basic human rights. This description does not necessarily contradict the definition of health as per the WHO's constitution, rather it provides an intermediate concept linking the WHO's ideas to the health and disease as measurable by appropriate indicators like mortality, morbidity, and quality of life. By removing the ambiguity between health and happiness and emphasizing health as a basic human right, it provides a reference criterion against which one can gauge how far health programmes incorporate and meet the requirements of health equity (Saracci, 1997).

II. Why does Health Matter?

For an individual, health has a double function. On the one hand, perfect health represents a value of its own, a target that needs to be reached as closely as possible. On the other hand, there are other aims in life as well e.g. good health gives good income in labour market (Zweifel and Breyer, 1997). World Development Report, 1993 explained good health as a crucial part of well-being. It further asserted that spending on health can also be justified on purely economic grounds. Improved health contributes to economic growth in four ways: it reduces production losses caused by worker illness; it permits the use of natural resources that had been totally or nearly inaccessible because of disease; it increases the enrollment of children in schools and makes them better able to learn; and it makes alternative uses of resources that would otherwise have to be spent on treatment (World Bank, 1993). A further elaboration may make the understanding better.

Gains in Worker Productivity: The most obvious sources of gain from healthier workers are savings of workdays, increased productivity, greater better-paying job opportunities, and longer working lives. A study on lepers in urban Tamilnadu estimated that the elimination of deformity with them would enhance the expected annual earnings of those with job by more than three times. The prevention of deformity in all of India's 645,000 lepers would have added an estimated $130 million to the country's GNP in 1985. This amount would be equivalent to 10 per cent of all the official development assistance received by India in 1985. Yet, leprosy accounted for only a small proportion of the country's disease burden, less than 1 per cent in 1990 (World Bank, 1993).

Improved Utilisation of Natural Resources: Some health investments raise the productivity of land. In Sri Lanka the near-eradication of malaria during 1947-77 is estimated to have raised national income by 9 per cent in 1977. Over the period of three decades, the cumulative cost of such an initiative was $52 million as compared to the cumulative gain in national income of $7.6 billion, implying a spectacular benefit-cost ratio. Areas previously blighted by mosquitoes became attractive for settlement. Migrants moved in and output increased (World Bank, 1993).

Benefits to the next Generation through Education: Poor health and nutrition reduces the benefits of schooling primarily in three areas: enrollment, ability to learn, and participation by girls. Children who enjoy better health and nutrition during early childhood are better prepared for school and more likely to enroll. A study in Nepal has found that the probability of attending school is only 5 per cent for nutritionally stunted children as compared to 27 per cent for those at the norm (World Bank, 1993).

'Further, there is no denying the fact that schooling pays off in terms of higher incomes. Four years of primary education boosts farmers' annual productivity by 9 per cent, on an average, and workers who do better at school earn more. Studies in Ghana, Kenya, Pakistan, and Tanzania indicated that the workers who scored 10 per cent above the sample mean in various cognitive tests had a wage advantage ranging from 13 to 22 per cent. In Nepal, farmers with better mathematical skills were more likely to adopt new crops which were more profitable (World Bank, 1993).

Reduced Costs of Medical Care: The spending that reduces the incidence of disease can result in big savings in treatment costs. For some diseases, the expenditure pays for itself even when all the indirect benefits – such as higher labour productivity and reduced pain and suffering – are ignored. Polio is one such example. Estimation for the Americans made prior to the eradication of polio in the region showed that investing US$ 220 million over 15 years to eliminate the disease would prevent 22,000 cases and save between US$ 320 million and US$ 1.3 billion (depending on the number of people treated) in annual treatment costs. The programme's net return, after discounting at even as much as 12 per cent a year, was estimated to be between

US$ 18 million and $480 million (World Bank, 1993).

III. Economics and Health Economics

Economics is the study of how people and society end up choosing, with or without the use of money, to employ scarce productive resources that could have alternative uses, to produce various commodities and distribute them for consumption, now or in the future, among various persons and groups in the society. It analyses the costs and benefits of improving patterns of allocation of resources (Samuelson, 1976). In the context of health as a commodity/service, such a definition treats economics as the study of scarcity and choice; of how to choose the best combination of resources to deliver in-patient care, for instance, or how best to allocate a given quantity of resources between alternative ways of improving health. The definition does not restrict economics to any one kind of human activity. Economics applies to all activities where scarcity and choice exist (Lee and Mills, 1983a). Health is no exception to that.

Over the last about three decades, treating health economics as an independent scientific discipline and providing specific treatment to the topics related to the economics of the health care sector have become more and more common. Currently, the field is so well established that it has appeared in the ordinary curriculum of most universities, and even if health economists are mainly to be found in the medical departments, the connections to economics proper are being strengthened, and the methodologies applied are getting refined.

Health economics is the study of how scarce resources are allocated among alternative uses for the care of sickness and the promotion, maintenance and improvement of health, including the study of how health care and health-related services, their costs and benefits, and health itself are distributed among individuals and groups in society. It can, broadly, be defined as 'the application of the theories, concepts and techniques of economics to the health sector' (Lee and Mills, 1983a). It is, thus, concerned with such matters as the allocation of resources between various health promoting activities, the quantity of resources used in health services delivery; the organization and funding of health service institutions, the efficiency with which resources are allocated and used for health purposes, and the effects of preventive, curative and rehabilitative health services on individuals and society (Lee and Mills, 1979).

As such, health economics has become a distinctive field of study, emphasizing in particular the application of economic theory to the practical problems of improving the use of resources to achieve the supply of effective and efficient health services (Shanmugasundaram, 1994). Economic aspects of relationship between health status and productivity, financial aspects of health care services, economic decision making in health and medical care institutions, planning of health development and such other related aspects are the major areas covered under health economics. Some salient features of health economics are health and medical care as economic goods, health as a private or a public good, measurement of health, stock of health, investment aspects of health, loss due to ill health, resource costs of different diseases, effects of health and medical care provision, planning of health and medical care, choice of technology in health care system, etc.

There are both positive and normative ways of looking at the problem in health economics. The normative issues relate to what should be, for example, what should be the appropriate budget allocation for HIV/AIDS control. The positive branch of health economics applies all modern micro economic theory in health care/medical care. Demand for health care that depends on the income of the individual, his/her taste, public and private supply of health care, etc is a subject matter in positive health economics.

The connection between the health status of the individual (or the population as a whole) and consumption of medical services builds the link between "economics of health" and "economics of health care". Health care refers to any type of services provided by professionals or paraprofessionals with an impact on health status. Health care system is a formal structure for a defined population, whose finance, management, scope and content is defined by laws and regulations. It provides for services to be delivered to people to contribute to their health...delivered in defined settings such as homes, educational institutions, workplaces, public places, communities, hospitals, clinics, et cetera.

IV Justification of Health Economics

In order to understand the role of economics in relation to health care, we have to return to the basic structure of economic science and its functions. Economics is concerned with describing the interrelationship between different individuals and organizations related to production and consumption of goods and services. The main point of the study of these interrelationships is to explain how the institutional framework and the rules of behavior specified for the individuals and organizations influence the final outcome. Classical economic disciplines like price theory and welfare theory investigate the market mechanism. Industrial organization focuses at the consequences of imperfect competition for prices, welfare, and incomes. The theory of international trade investigates the workings of different rules for international commodity exchanges, gains from trade and the like.

At this level, it should come as no surprise that health economics may be viewed as the economic discipline which deals with the institutional frameworks for health care (consumption, provision, financing) and the interconnections between rules and institutions on the one side and the resulting health condition in the population on the other. There still remains a somewhat loose description of the field, and it seems difficult to get closer in a few words. It may be emphasized here that health economists do necessarily deal with cost-effectiveness analyses or benefit-cost ratio analysis of health management. However, that is not the only task of a health economist. Rather, cost-effectiveness is perhaps treated as the least important aspect of what a health economist can contribute.

In principle, economists are concerned with better choices and in particular making best use of existing resources and growth in the availability of resources. As economists started to work on problems in the health sector, the new discipline of health economics emerged. Economists in all sectors are concerned with the allocation of resources between competing demands (Samuelson and Nordhaus, 2000). Demands are assumed to be unlimited – there is no end to consumption needs. Resources (labour, raw materials, production equipments, land, etc), in contrast, are always scarce in supply. The scarcity of resources (not in the sense of 'rarity' but in the sense of resource availability *relative* to demand) becomes the fundamental problem to which economists attempt to address (McPake et al, 2002). Economists concerned with health also try to address the same specifically in the context of scarce health resources and the competing ends.

There are two ways in which society can make choices about the allocation of resources to production in the health sector and the distribution of services that are produced among those who want that. A society can leave these decisions to the *market* – letting demand and supply and prices determine resource allocation – or it can *plan*, usually by giving its government the task of collecting resources from the population, allocating those to define production activities and distributing the produced services among the population. The *plan-market dichotomy* has prevailed as a matter of concern in academics and otherwise throughout the last century. Health economics also falls under its ambit.

Health economics is becoming a subject of increasing significance particularly in the developing countries primarily because of (i) an economic climate where resources are extremely scare and decisions on priorities are crucial but difficult; (ii) a growing appreciation among health professionals and policy-makers that health economics and economists can help them formulate policies and make decisions; (iii) the increasing maturity of the sub-disciplines of health economics; and (iv) the growing of interest among economists and others in applying their economic skills to health issues (Lee and Mills, 1983a).

Currently, the task before economists is to elicit the valuations which may be useful to formulate health services policy. First, it might be in the form of demand studies, or by trying to discover what policy makers' preferences are. Second, there is a need to establish the true costs of delivering health care or to estimate all real costs like the use of patients' time, loss of output elsewhere in the system etc. Third, it is necessary to evaluate the relative costs and benefits of particular policy options. Fourth, the effects of certain economic variables like user charges, time and distance costs of accessibility, etc on the utilization of health services may be estimated. Fifth, planning and budgeting systems and possible changes therein in health care delivery system are to be made (Shanmugasundaram, 1994). Table 2.1 presents an overview of relevant health issues and consequent tasks of economists to address them.

The economics of health is by no means trivial but has a wider scope. The health care sector is not just another sector as agriculture, industry or financial services. Its output is somewhat elusive but it certainly goes beyond what can reasonably be measured in terms of money. It is primarily due to the fact that here the final output is individual health, or to be more specific, improvements in individual health conditions, the quantities which are not readily comparable between individuals and not measurable in terms of money. This special nature of the sector gives rise to many fundamental problems, which by themselves represent challenges to economic theory. There are several other peculiar difficulties that may arise in the application of economic concepts in the field of health. There is perhaps no satisfactory measure of health outputs or benefits to the society from health services expenditure and consequently, no criteria for assessing productivity or determining allocation of resources according to the principle of equality.

The task before a health economist is thus quite challenging and manifold. While aligning the basic principles of economics

Table 2.1: Relevance of Economics to the Health Sector

Some Health Policy Issues	Some Prior Questions	Relevant Corpus of Economics
I. *Health and Economic Development* (health and health care as determinant and consequence of socioeconomic development)	1. What constitutes health and health improvement? 2. What are the determinants of health improvement? 3. How do health and health services affect production and the economy?	Identification and Measurement issues on health and illness/diseases; Basic needs measures; Macroeconomic models of economic development; Determinants of growth; Human capital theory; Investment and consumption elements of health expenditure; Household production functions for health; Ill-health and the productivity of labour
II. *Organization and delivery systems* (structure of health care and health related activities)	1. What are the economic characteristics of health care and health related activities? 2. What is the relevance of these characteristics for the pursuit of health through market and non-market mechanisms? 3. How do different health care systems handle their organization and distribution of decisions?	Welfare theory and market failure: rationality, consumer sovereignty, income and wealth issues, indivisibilities, externalities, public goods and merit goods

Contd...

III. *Finance of the health sector* (income aspects of health care and health related activities)	1. What are the sources of health care financing? 2. What type and quantity of resources are being utilized to finance the health sector? 3. What do alternative financing methods achieve both in terms of yield and of incidence (burden)?	Social accounting systems and public finance: revenue generation and tax incidence; Self financing, insurance and pre-payment mechanism; Ability and willingness-to-pay concepts
IV. *Demand analysis* (the demand and the need for health and health services)	1. What determines the demand (or absence of demand) for specific health services, and for traditional healers, herbalists and practitioners? 2. What factors determine the provider response to an individual's demands for health care, including factors such as the availability of referral facilities? 3. How do health payment systems (e.g. charges, pre-payment methods) affect the demand for and utilization of health services?	Theories of household, individual and supplier induced behaviour: generation and interpretation of demand schedules, determinants of demand, price, income, and cross elasticities; Time costs

Contd...

V. *Supply analysis* (Physical Resources and Costs)	1. What determines the cost behaviour of Organizations and health agencies? 2. How and why will costs vary with changes in the scale, location and type of medical and health services and facilities provided? 3. What mix of resources will produce specific services?	Production function and substitutability between inputs; Estimation of short run and long run cost curves, average and marginal costs, private and social costs; Determinants of hospital and health centres cost variation (case-mix quality factors); Economies of scale
VI. *Health manpower* (Human Resources: their availability, motivation and remuneration)	1. What determines the supply and distribution of each type of human resources? 2. How do forms of remuneration and other determinants of behaviour affect manpower recruitment, absenteeism, retention and geographical distribution? 3. What are the productivities of various types of health workers in relation to their training costs and rates of pay?	Labour markets and the demand for and supply of health workers; Marginal Productivity theory; Factors influencing supply elasticities: impact of income levels and financial incentives, leisure preferences, private practice, the brain drain.

Contd...

VII. *Financial Management* (cost containment and cost efficiency)	1. How is the budget divided, who controls the budget, and how is that control exercised? 2. Can economics be affected in the procurement and distribution of resources? 3. What is an 'appropriate' technology?	Budgeting system and accountability (cost centres, cost units); Inventory management; Determinant of supply behaviour (local, national and multi-national); Shadow pricing and social opportunity costs
VIII. *Organizational behaviour* (individual and corporate objectives and motives underpinning behaviour of health agencies.	1. Who does make the resource allocation decisions to and within the health sector, and what are their objectives? 2. What is the feasibility of reconciling the conflicting goals, values and interests of the various groups and individuals involved in the health sector? 3. What types of controls or incentives (monetary or otherwise) can be introduced to encourage efficient behaviour?	Managerial and behaviourial theories of government, not-for-profit, profit and voluntary organizations; Notion of efficiency and the role of inducements (rewards and penalties)

Contd...

IX. *Project evaluation* (desirability and implications of reducing, expanding, or redeploying existing services or introducing new activities	1. Does the service do any good or have any discernible effect on health? For whom? 2. What are the relative efficiencies (merits and demerits) of alternative health activities? 3. What are the distributional consequences of health activities (who incurs the costs and who receives the benefits?)	Managerial and behaviourial theories of and cost-effectiveness analyses; Notions of 'effectiveness' and the 'margin'; Size and incidence of costs and benefits
X. *Health policy, equity, and social justice* (providing the right services in the right places to the right people at the right time)	1. How best can resources be matched to the people's needs, mortality and morbidity patterns, demands and utilization? 2. What impact do different health care systems have upon eligibility, access, take-up and benefits received by target groups in the population? 3. What are the barriers, if any, to the provision of an equitable (fair) health services?	Optimum welfare criteria and the concept of the social welfare function; Inequalities in health care; Definition and measurement issues; Effects of socioeconomic variables and physical access to utilization pattern

Source: lee and mills, 1983b, pp.215-217.

with health economics may bring in certain pertinent solutions to the problems that the sector is faced with, the subjectivity attached to the health services may demand alternative mechanisms. In any case, health economics may continue to gain its importance as health remains the single most significant requirement of human beings.

References

Doll, R. (1992): Health and the environment in the 1990s, *American Journal of Public Health*, Vol. 82, pp. 933-41.

Fuchs, Victor R. (1987): Health Economics in Palgrave's Dictionary of Economics, *Health Economics*, Vol. 2, p.614.

Lee, Kenneth and A. J. Mills (1979): The Role of Economists and Economics in Health Service Planning: A General Overview, In K. Lee (Ed.), *Economics and Health Planning*, Croom Helm, London.

Lee, Kenneth and Anne Mills (1983a): Developing Countries, Health, and Health Economics, In Kenneth Lee and Anne Mills (Eds.), *The Economics of Health in Developing Countries*, Oxford University Press, Oxford.

Lee, Kenneth and Anne Mills (1983b): The Economics of Health in Developing Countries: a Critical Review, In Kenneth Lee and Anne Mills (Eds.), *The Economics of Health in Developing Countries*, Oxford University Press, Oxford

McPake, Barbara, Lilani Kumaranayake and Charles Normand (2002): *Health Economics: An International Perspective*, Routledge, London.

Reddy K N (1992): Health Expenditure in India, *Working Paper No. 14*, NIPFP, New Delhi

Samuelson, P.A. (1976): *Economics*, McGraw-Hill, New York.

Samuelson, P.A. and W. D. Nordhaus (2000): *Economics*, McGraw-Hill, New York.

Saracci, Rodolfo (1997): The World Health Organization Needs to Reconsider its Definition of Health, *British Medical Journal*, Vol. 314, pp.1409-10

Shanmugasundaram, Yasodha (1994): *Theory and Practice of Health Economics in India*, Institute of Advanced Studies and Research, Chennai.

World Health Organization (1992): *Basic Document*, 39th Edition, Geneva.

Zweifel, Peter and Friedrich Breyer (1997): *Health Economics*, Oxford

University Press, New York, pp. 1-15.
World Bank (1993): *World Development Report: Investing in Health*, Oxford University Press, New York.

3

Health Scenario in India: Progress and Challenges

Mihir K. Mahapatra and Rajesh Raj S.N.

I. The Backdrop

The economic reforms introduced in 1991 focused on Structural Adjustment Programme and the Stabilization Policy so as to ensure economic growth with justice. [1] It stressed on compression of public expenditure and improvement in efficiency with competitiveness. But there is apprehension about adverse effect of expenditure on growth of social sector. The failure to sustain growth of expenditure for basic needs especially health and education can nullify the slogan 'reforms with a human face'. This can also rule out substantial improvement in Human Development.

In the backdrop of unprecedented upsurge in current consumption followed by quantum leap in fiscal deficit and mounting debt service burden, skepticism has arisen about sustaining high growth of social sector expenditure in the major states, especially the underdeveloped economy. Added to this, the provision of private participation in health care services can have a bearing on access and utilization of health services by the deprived sections of the society. For instance, the impact of reforms on pharmaceutical industry can be reflected by improvement in the supply of essential drugs especially to the backward region. But there can be rise in price of drugs especially the life saving one. Further, tertiary care is likely to be favoured, Medicare is supposed to be costlier and Medicare process is likely to be more elongated with tests-orientation. Against this backdrop, the present paper makes an attempt to analyze the health scenario in India during the pre-reforms and reforms period. Again, to examine the performance of health sector in different socio-economic environments, 15 major states have been selected for the study. To assess the performance of health indicators, attempt has been made to examine the growth of expenditure on medical and public health across major states in India.

The paper is structured as follows. Section I introduces the paper. Section II is devoted to analyze the progress of health sector in Indian economy over the years and its status in comparison to selected few other countries. In section III, an attempt has been made to examine health scenario across 15 major states in India during the reforms period. In order to identify the progress of Health sector an attempt has been made to analyze growth of social sector expenditure with focus on Medical Health and Family Welfare (MHFW). This follows summary and concluding observations.

II. Health Scenario in India: An Overview

The population of India grew by one and a half times in the first half of the twentieth century while in the latter half; it recorded almost a phenomenal three-fold increase. The latter period can be further subdivided into period of rapid high growth (1951-1981) and high growth with definite signs of slowing down (1981-2001). In other words, the demographic transition in India is now widely believed to have entered the fifth phase, usually characterized as rapidly declining fertility (Census of India, 2001). From Table 3.1, it is evident that there has been almost a consistent decline in growth of population during the last two decades. The natural growth rate (NGR) of population defined as the difference between crude birth rate (CBR) and crude death rate (CDR) has declined from about 21 per 1,000 to around 16 per 1,000 between 1980 and 2005. The extent of decline is relatively more during the 1990s and onwards as compared to the 1980s. For instance, average annual growth of population based on NGR was –0.27 per cent per annum during the 1980s while it is as high as –1.33 per cent per annum during the 1990s (Table 3.3).

Table 3.1: Health Performance Indicators in India

Year	CBR	CDR	NGR	IMR	LE
1971	36.9	14.9	22	129	-
1975	35.2	15.9	19.3	140	-
1980	33.7	12.6	21.1	114	52.84
1981	33.9	12.5	21.4	110	50.4
1985	32.9	11.8	21.1	97	56.22
1990	30.2	9.7	20.5	80	58.7
1991	29.5	9.8	19.7	80	59.4
1992	29.2	10.1	19.1	79	60.8
1995	28.3	9	19.3	74	62.97
1999	26.1	8.7	17.4	70	65.67
2000	25.8	8.5	17.3	68	66.34
2001	25.7	8.7	17	68	62
2002	25	8.1	16.9	63	62.5
2003	24.8	8	16	60	62.5
2004	24.1	7.5	16.6	58	-
2005	23.8	7.6	16.3	58	-

Not available.*: For the period 1998-2002. **Provisional, Life Expectancy at Birth of Male and Female in India during 2001-06 is 59.7 and 66.9 respectively.

Sources: 1. Government of India (GOI) (2000): Department of Family and Welfare, Ministry of Health and Family Welfare, Government of India, New Delhi and earlier issues. 2. Registrar General of India, Sample Registration System Bulletin, Government of India (various issues). 3. IAMR (2002): India Year Book 2002, Man Power Profile, Institute of Applied Manpower Research, New Delhi. 4. GOI (2006): India Economic Survey 2005-06

A disaggregation of fall in growth of population reflects acceleration in decline in birth rate as compared to death rate. As evident from Table 3.1, birth rate in India declined by about 3.5 points and 4 points respectively during 1980s and 1990s with further decline in the subsequent years to arrive at 23.8 per 1000 live births in 2005. There has been relatively more decline in annual average growth of crude birth rate during the reforms period (Table 3.2). Nevertheless, as compared to some other developing countries, the performance of India is not very satisfactory. During the late 1990s, CBR in Chile, China and Sri Lanka was 18, 16 and 18 respectively (Kadekodi et.al., 2004).

As regards CBR, it declined from 12.6 per 1000 to 7.6 per 1000 during 1980-2005. The extent of decline during the 1980s is much higher than that is noticed in the subsequent one and a half decades (1990-2005), implying relatively sharp falls in the pre-reforms period (Table 3.1). Slow decline in growth of CDR is also evident from Table 3.2. This can be due to changing age structure of the population with rise in median age. There has been decline in fertility in all states and improvement in life expectancy at birth. However, the persistence of high death rate is partly because the economy failed to check the top ten killer diseases including Asthma and Bronchitis, Heart Attack, Pneumonia, T.B. of Lungs, Prematurity, Cancer, Anemia, Paralysis, Vehicular Accident and Suicide.

In terms of CDR, performance of Indian economy is relatively better during the 90s as compared to Chile, China and Sri Lanka. Chile showed a decline in CDR by –0.36 per cent during 1991-98 while China witnessed a positive growth of 0.97 per cent and Sri Lanka observed a declining trend of –0.14 per cent (Kadekodi et al. 2004). The CDR in Chile, China and Sri Lanka is 5, 8 and 6 respectively during the late 1990s.

Table 3.2: Annual Average Growth of Health Indicators in India (per cent)

Indicators	1980-81 to 1989-90	1991-92 to 1999-2000	1991-92 to 2004-05
CBR	-1.08	-1.55	-1.43
CDR	-2.51	-1.26	-1.82
NGR	-0.27	-1.66	-1.33
IMR	-3.41	-1.58	-2.71
LE	1.10	1.24	0.56*

* The period is 1991-92 to 2001-02

Source: Estimated based on Registrar General's SRS figures.

In death rate, the performance of the Indian economy is not quite promising in infant mortality rate (IMR) (Table 3.2). In absolute number the extent of decline is much higher during the 1980s (fall by 34 points) as compared to the 1990s (12 points). It is during the last five years when sharp decline in IMR has been noticed (a fall by 10 points during 2001-05). No doubt, there has been a noted decline in IMR over the years yet there is enough scope for further reduction. For instance, IMR in Sri Lanka is about one-fourth of India in 2003 (Table 3.3). The IMR figures for Chile and China hover around 10 and 31 respectively during the closing years of the 1990s. Similarly in child mortality rate (CMR), there has been considerable decline during the reforms period (a fall by 36 points during 1990 to 2003) but still the economy has to go a long way to be on par with Sri Lanka and China (Table 3.3).

The proximate determinants of IMR can be classified into exogenous and endogenous factors (Bourgeois-Pichat, 1964). [2] The exogenous factors are infections and parasitic in nature while the endogenous is mainly congenital malformations and usually difficult to control or prevent. The decline in IMR is more often associated with control of exogenous factors. The death of children during the first month (neo-natal) or first week (early neo-natal) of their birth is primarily determined by the endogenous factors (Visaria, 1985). In the early 1970s around 54 per cent of infant deaths in India are accounted for neo-natal death while the remaining 46 per cent of it was due to the post-natal death. But during the last few years, there has been lot of changes in share of neo-natal and post-natal in IMR.

The prevalence of high IMR in the 1990s can be partly explained by the decline in combine public expenditure (of Centre and states) on social sector as percentage of gross domestic product (Dev et.al., 2002). In other words, the extent of expenditure on education, health and family welfare, sanitation and water supply, and poverty alleviation programme can determine the trend of child and infant mortality. However, a comparative analysis of the 42nd and 52nd round of NSS surveys

Table 3.3: India's Global Position in Terms of Socio-Demographic Parameters

	Life Expectancy at Birth	Under-five Mortality Rate (per 1,000 live births)		Infant Mortality Rate (per 1,000 live births)		Maternal Mortality Ratio (per 1 lakh live births)
Country	2000-05	1990	2003	1990	2003	2005
China	71	49	37	38	30	56
India	63	123	87	80	63	540
Nepal	61	145	82	100	61	740
Pakistan	63	128	103	96	81	500
Sri Lanka	74	23	15	19	13	92
Bangladesh	63	144	69	96	46	380
South Asia	63	126	91	84	66	NA

Source: GOI (2006): India Economic Survey.

also reflects worsening of access to health services during the 1990s (Sen et. al., 2002).

Broadly, the persistence of high IMR can be explained by considering some of the important factors such as the level of education of mother, standard of living of the households, pre-natal and post natal care provided, age of mother at the time of child birth, health care facilities available during pregnancy and at child birth, birth order and birth interval. [3] Therefore, it implies that a substantial decline in infant mortality and child mortality necessitates 100 per cent immunization, supply of clean drinking water and provision of sanitation facilities (to prevent infections), professional attention during child birth and nutritional supplements for pregnant women. A large number of infant and child deaths are due to infections and water related diseases. The polluted rivers in the rural areas and lack of access to drinking water in the urban areas are primarily held responsible for it (Parikh, 2002).

The equity in access to health services can be assessed by achievement of the economy in maternal death. The persistence of wide disparity in health infrastructure across the states especially the low income states leads to high maternal death. The Sample Registration System (SRS) estimate reveals that during 1997-2003, there are 4,484 maternal deaths of female in the age group of 15-49 while the number of live births reported to be 1,321, 378 in about 11 lakh homes. This indicates about 330 maternal deaths per 1 lakh live births. Over the years there has been a decline in maternal mortality rate (MMR) from around 400 noticed in 1997-98 to around 300 in 2001-03 but there is enough scope for further absolute decline and smoothening of disparity.

For instance, around two-third of total maternal deaths was noticed in empowered action group (EAG) states and Assam during 1997-2003. [4] The Millennium Development Goals (MDG) specified the target of achieving 200 maternal deaths per lakh live births by 2007 and it needs to come down to 109 by 2015.The Maternal Mortality Ratio in India is still much higher than that of China, Sri Lanka, Bangladesh and Pakistan (Table

3.3). In this context, it needs to specify that some of the major factors accountable for maternal deaths include Haemorrahage, Sepsis, Abortion, Obstructed labour, Hypertensive Disorders. Among the said factors, Haemorrhage alone accounts for 38 per cent of total maternal death followed by Sepsis (11 per cent), Abortion (8 per cent) while Hypertensive Disorders and Obstructed Labour accounts for 5 per cent each and the remaining 34 per cent is on account of other conditions (RG, 2006).

The life expectancy at birth indicates the longevity of the people in a country. It depends on various factors, namely, per capita income, extent of poverty and access and utilization of health care facilities. In this context, few issue deserve attention include decline in level of fertility and development of health awareness among the people. On account of decline in fertility, the proportion of middle age (15-59) and older people (60 and above) can go up while the share of population below 15 years can come down. Therefore, the economy has witnessed a sustained improvement life expectancy over the years especially during the reforms period. But the country is still lagging behind China and Sri Lanka (Table 3.3). The life expectancy at birth in China and Sri Lanka is 71 and 75 respectively during 2000-05 while it is 63 in India in 2003.

III. Key Health Indicators of Major States

The broad picture of health status in the country may not necessarily reflect inter-state disparities in the quality of health care services and need for specific health care needs. In this section an attempt is made to assess performance of health indicators across different categories of major states.

No doubt, performance of certain health indicators reflect improvement during the last one and a half decades (1991-2005) as evident from decline in mean value of various parameters but there is enough scope for further improvement (Table 3.4). In spite of the success, one of the major issues that deserve urgent attention is persistence of high level in MMR and IMR with wide disparity across 15 major states (Tables 3.5 and 3.6). In the above

Table 3.4: Health Indicator of Major States in India

No.	States	IMR		CBR		CDR		NGR		MMR	Life Expectancy at Birth	Total Fertility Rate
		1991	2005	1991	2005	1991	2005	1991	2005	1997-2003	1998-2002	1999-2001
1.	A.P	73	57	26	19.1	9.7	7.3	16.3	11.8	204	63.5	2.3
2.	Assam	81	68	30.9	25	11.5	8.7	19.4	16.3	484	57.9	3.1
3.	Bihar	69	61	30.7	30.4	9.8	8.1	20.9	22.3	436	60.8	4.3
4.	Gujarat	69	54	27.5	23.7	8.5	7.1	19	16.6	137	63.4	2.9
5.	Haryana	68	60	33.1	24.3	8.2	6.7	24.9	17.6	159	65.2	3.2
6.	Karnataka	77	50	26.9	20.6	9	7.1	17.9	13.5	247	64.5	2.4
7.	Kerala	16	14	18.3	15	6	6.4	12.3	8.6	136	73.5	1.8
8.	M.P	117	76	35.8	29.4	13.8	9	22	20.4	411	56.9	4.0
9.	Maharashtra	60	36	26.2	19	8.2	6.7	18	12.3	161	66.2	2.5
10.	Orissa	124	75	28.8	22.3	12.8	9.5	16	12.8	377	58.5	2.7
11.	Punjab	53	44	27.7	18.1	7.8	6.7	19.9	11.4	214	68.5	2.4
12.	Rajasthan	79	68	35	28.6	10.1	7	24.9	21.6	484	61.1	4.1
13.	Tamil Nadu	57	37	20.8	16.5	8.8	7.4	12	9.1	144	65.2	2.0
14.	Uttar Pradesh	86	73	36.1	30.4	12.7	8.7	23.4	21.7	553	59.1	4.7
15.	West Bengal	56	38	24.5	18.8	8.3	6.4	16.2	12.4	238	63.9	2.4

Contd...

	India	80	58	29.5	23.8	9.8	7.6	19.7	16.3	339	62.5	3.2
	Maxi mum	124	76	36.1	30.4	13.8	9.5	24.9	22.3	553	73.5	4.7
	Minimum	16	14	18.3	15	6	6.4	12	8.6	136	56.9	1.8
	Max/Min	8	5	2	2	2	1	2	3	4	1	2.6
	Mean	72	54	29	23	10	8	19	15	292	63	3
	C.V. (%)	34	32	18	22	22	13	20	29	49	7	28.9

Sources: (i) http:// www.censusindia.net; (ii) Registrar General's SRS Bulletin, various issues

Table 3.5: Rank of Selected Health Indicators of Major States in India

Sl No.	States	IMR		Improvement/ Deterioration	NGR		Improvement/ Deterioration	MMR	Life Expectancy
		1991	2005	(1991-2005)	1991	2005*	(1991-2005)	1997-2003	1998-2002
	High Income States								
1.	Gujarat	7	7	0	8	10	-2	2	9
2.	Haryana	6	9	-3	14	11	3	4	4
3.	Maharashtra	5	2	3	7	5	2	5	3
4.	Punjab	2	5	-3	10	3	7	7	2
	Middle Income States								
5.	A.P	9	8	1	5	4	1	6	8
6.	Karnataka	10	6	4	6	8	-2	9	6
7.	Kerala	1	1	0	2	1	1	1	1
8.	Tamil Nadu	4	3	1	1	2	-1	3	4
9.	West Bengal	3	4	-1	4	6	-2	8	7

Contd...

Low Income States									
10.	Assam	12	11	1	9	9	0	13	14
11.	Bihar	7	10	-3	11	15	-4	12	11
12.	M.P.	14	15	-1	12	12	0	11	15
13.	Orissa	15	14	1	3	7	-4	10	13
14.	Rajasthan	11	11	0	14	13	1	14	10
15.	Uttar Pradesh	13	13	0	13	14	-1	15	12

Notes: (i) Ranking is in the ascending order (lowest values is assigned 1st rank) for all indicators except Life Expectancy which is in the descending order. (ii) Negative sign indicates deterioration in 2005 over 1991 and vice-versa.

aspects, there is wide gap between average value of 15 major states and India, implying performance of other states are not quite promising. There has been about 1.5 points decline in IMR per year in India during 1991-2005 though it is much higher in Orissa and very low in Kerala partly due to enough scope for further decline in the former (Orissa) and limited scope for decline in the latter (Kerala).

Table 3.6: Composition of Revenue Expenditure for all States

	All States		
Year	Developmental Expenditure as % of Revenue Expenditure	Exp on Social Services as % Revenue Expenditure	Exp on Med. Pubic Health & Family Welfare as % Revenue Expenditure
1980-81	71.0	40.2	9.4
1984-85	70.5	40.1	9.8
1990-91	68.1	39.0	6.4
1991-92	67.9	36.1	5.9
1995-96	61.6	37.0	5.8
1999-00	58.0	36.8	5.5
2001-02	55.1	34.8	5.1
2002-03	54.3	33.5	5.1
2003-04	54.1	31.7	4.5
2004-05	52.9	32.3	4.5
2005-06RE	55.7	34.7	4.9
2006-07BE	54.6	34.5	4.9

Source: Annual Report of State Finances, Reserve Bank of India, RBI (various issues)

The state-level analysis reveals that extent of disparity in certain health indicators has gone up during the reforms period among the 15 major states and therefore, this is the cause for serious concern. A comparative analysis of various categories of states reflects encouraging outcome of some of the middle income states. In contrast, some of the BIMARU states have to go a long way to meet the achievement level of better performing states especially Kerala (Table 3.5). On an average around 340 women in 15-49 age groups die per 1 lakh live births in India though it is the highest in Uttar Pradesh (553) and lowest in Kerala (136). This reflects wide disparity in access to health care services. Similarly, around 54 infants (per 1,000 live births) die before completing one year in India though it is as high as 76 for Madhya Pradesh and the lowest in Kerala (14).

In IMR, the gap among the selected three states from different levels of development has come down to some extent during the last 20 years (1985-2005) though there is wide difference between Maharashtra and Orissa. In this aspect, the performance of Karnataka is not quite outstanding in the recent years as compared to mid-1990s.

The persistence of low level of female literacy especially in the rural areas also contributes to rise in risk of maternal death to a large extent. Overall, it necessitates substantial improvement in female literacy rate and improvement in institutional delivery especially in low income BIMARU states through development of health infrastructure.

The overall improvement in quality of life gets reflected by fertility rate and life expectancy at birth. The fertility rate has come down over the years but there is wide disparity. The fertility rate is the lowest (1.8) in Kerala while it is close to 5 in Uttar Pradesh. The life expectancy in India hovers around 63 during 1998-2002 but it is much higher in Kerala (73.5) and very low in Madhya Pradesh (57). A consistent decline in fertility, very low mortality rate and improvement in life expectancy can change composition of population, i.e., proportion of people in different age groups. There can be improvement in proportion of older people in the total population. It is projected that every sixth individual in Kerala can be a senior citizen by 2026 (Census of India, 2001).

IV. Expenditure on MHFW

The outcome of health scenario can be determined by the growth of expenditure on health by the state government, Union government and private organization. From Table 3.6, it is evident that there has been decline in share of developmental expenditure in total revenue expenditure of all states together. Developmental revenue expenditure was around 71 per cent of total revenue expenditure during the first half of the 1980s, dropped marginally in the early 1990s with further substantial decline in the second half of the 1990s and reached the lowest 53 per cent in 2004-05. In other words, it declined marginally by about three percent points during the 1980s to about 13 percent points during the 1990s with further decline in recent years.

An unprecedented growth in certain committed expenditure including salary payment, pension outgo and interest payment necessitated a quantum leap in non-developmental revenue expenditure during the reforms period and thereby left limited fiscal space for developmental expenditure. In other words, the growth of non-developmental current consumption was at the cost of developmental outgo especially the social sector as the latter suffered a setback during the said period. The percentage share of Social Service expenditure in total revenue expenditure was around 40 per cent in the early 1980s while it remained between 30-35 per cent during the last few years. Again, the percentage share of MHFW in revenue expenditure also witnessed a declining trend - a fall from about 10 per cent during the 1980s to 5-6 per cent in the 1990s with further decline in the subsequent period.

In order to examine the extent of disparity in social sector expenditure across different categories of states, three selected states have been chosen from different levels of development (Table 3.7). Almost similar trend of decline in share of developmental expenditure is noticed in different categories of states though the extent of fall is quite pronounced in Orissa.

A substantial fall (from about 45 per cent in early 1980s to 38 per cent in first half of the 1990s with further decline to 32 per

Table 3.7: Composition of Revenue Expenditure across Maharashtra, Karnataka and Orissa

Year	Maharashtra			Karnataka			Orissa		
	Dev. Exp as % of Rev. Exp	Exp. on Soc.Serv as % Rev.Exp.	Exp on Med. PH & FW as % Rev.Exp.	Dev. Exp as % of Rev. Exp	Exp on Soc.Serv as % Rev.Exp.	Exp on Med. PH & F.W. as % Rev.Exp.	Dev. Exp as % of Rev. Exp	Exp on Soc.Serv as % Rev.Exp.	Exp on Med. PH & F.W. as % Rev.Exp.
1980-81	66.7	34.1	8.4	67.7	36.2	7.9	74.2	44.6	10.2
1984-85	65.0	33.4	9.5	64.9	32.6	7.6	70.7	42.9	11.0
1990-91	70.0	35.4	5.5	67.9	38.8	6.1	68.0	38.4	6.2
1991-92	67.9	35.8	5.2	68.9	38.2	6.0	66.0	39.5	5.9
1995-96	67.2	38.3	5.2	67.2	38.3	5.9	65.6	39.1	5.4
1999-00	55.7	37.9	4.6	62.3	36.0	5.7	65.6	47.2	5.0
2001-02	52.3	36.9	4.6	63.6	34.6	5.3	48.5	33.0	4.2
2002-03	51.9	36.7	4.3	60.4	32.0	5.3	51.6	35.9	5.1
2003-04	51.2	37.4	4.1	54.5	32.7	4.5	50.4	34.1	4.2
2004-05	54.7	34.3	3.7	57.0	30.9	4.1	46.3	32.1	5.0
2005-06RE	56.1	38.3	4.2	57.6	31.9	4.0	50.9	35.5	4.8
2006-07BE	51.6	35.1	3.9	57.7	32.7	3.9	49.5	32.5	4.3

Note: RE = revised estimate; BE = Budget estimate; PH = Public Health; FW = Family Welfare.

Source: Annual Report of State Finances, Reserve Bank of India, RBI (various issues).

cent in the recent years) in share of social services expenditure in revenue expenditure is noticed in Orissa. In contrast, the share of social services in revenue expenditure went up in a developed state Maharashtra during the last few years.

Per Capita Health Expenditure

The per capita revenue expenditure on MHFW across 15 major states reflects wide disparity (Table 3.8). Of late, per capita health expenditure hovers around Rs. 185 though it is the maximum of Rs. 275 in Kerala and lowest in Bihar (Rs. 97).

The state level per capita health expenditure reveals that Middle income states relatively spend more than that of High Income states. At the other end, in health outcome parameters some of the middle income states (Kerala, Tamil Nadu & West Bengal) occupy the top 5 positions among the 15 major states, indicating a positive relationship between health expenditure and health outcomes.

Ironically, the annual average growth of per capita revenue expenditure on MHFW is lower during the reforms period as compared to the pre-reforms period. Of the 15 major states, 11 noticed relatively slow growth in the reforms period as compared to the prc-reforms period (Table 3.9).

One of the major issues that need to be addressed urgently is the persistence of wide disparity across the states in health outcome. During the reforms period (1991-2007) the level of disparity across the major states has gone up as evident from rise in coefficient of variation to 24.6 per cent from 23 per cent noticed during the 1980s. Again, the minimum per capita expenditure was close to 50 per cent of the average of the major states during the 1980s while it is less than 20 per cent in the reforms period.

The household expenditure on health based on NSSO data shows that people in economically developed states like Maharshtra and Karnataka spend more on health care than the people in Orissa.

Table 3.8: State Per Capita Revenue Expenditure on MHFW

(Average amount in Rupees)

State	1981-90	1991-2000	2001-07	1991-07
High Income				
Gujarat	45	105	172	133
Harayana	52	88	172	123
Maharastra	54	96	189	134
Punjab	56	133	271	190
Middle Income				
A.P.	40	87	195	131
Karanataka	40	101	194	140
Kerala	42	110	275	178
TamilNadu	46	117	210	187
W.B.	38	89	176	125
Low Income				
Assam	35	78	184	122
Bihar	19	53	97	71
M.P.	39	65	133	93
Orissa	37	71	146	102
Rajasthan	43	99	175	130
U.P.	27	61	171	106
Major States				
Mean	40.7	90.1	184.1	131.0
Min/Max (%)	33.3	39.6	35.2	37.4
C.V. (%)	23.1	23.6	23.9	24.6
Min/Mean (%)	46.1	26.2	13.0	18.8

Sources: (i) RBI (2006): Annual Report on State Finances: 2005-06, Reserve Bank of India; (ii) www.censusindia.net.

V. Summary and Concluding Observations

To sum up, there has been considerable improvement in the health sector during the last few decades in India but there is a long way to go to meet the target stipulated in the Millennium Development Goals and to be on par with some of the Asian Countries. A comparative analysis of health status during pre-reforms and reforms period reveals that performance is not encouraging during the latter period. It can be partly on account of erosion in growth of social sector expenditure especially MHFW. With the substantial rise in current consumption primarily on account of implementation of the fifth Pay Commission recommendations, persistence of high interest payment and improvement in life expectancy at birth; the major states in India failed to sustain high growth of social sector expenditure. Again, there has been widening of disparity in revenue expenditure on public health during the 1990s and onwards.

Table 3.9: Annual Average Growth of per Capita MHFW in Major States (Revenue Account)

State	1981-90	1991-2007BE
High Income		
Gujarat	12.9	9
Harayana	7.4	11
Maharastra	11.1	9
Punjab	13.5	10
Middle Income		
A.P.	9.7	11
Karanataka	13.2	10
Kerala	12.1	12
TamilNadu	13.1	9
W.B.	8.2	8
Low Income		
Assam	16.3	15.0
Bihar	13.0	11.4
M.P.	8.1	10.1
Orissa	8.9	10.2
Rajasthan	9.8	8.9
U.P.	14.2	10.6

To ensure improvement in Human Development Index (HDI), social sector need to be prioritized and adequate investment to be made so as to improve equity in access to health care. On account of resource constraint, there is a need to explore avenues for public-private partnership so as to develop Health infrastructure, attract and retain skilled manpower. This necessitates introduction of user fee.

Notes

1. The economic reform was in the backdrop of double digit inflation, high fiscal deficit, adverse Balance of Payments and low foreign exchange reserves.

2. Bourgeois-Pichat J (1964): Evaluation Recents de la Mortalite Infantile, 436-437. Cited in United Nations, Department of Economic and Social Affairs, 1973. "The Determinants and Consequences of Population Trends", Vol. 1, United Nations, New York.

3. "Pre-natal care service include regular medical check up and monitoring of pregnant women, medical intervention as is necessary in individual cases and professional advice regarding health, hygiene, nutrition and other related areas regarding pregnancy and child bearing. Vaccination against tetanus and control of anaemia by supply of iron and Folic Acid tablets constitute an integral part of the pre-natal care (National Family Health Survey -2, 1998-99, IIPS, Mumbai)".

4. EAG states include Bihar, Jharkhand, Orissa, Madhya Pradesh, Chattisgarh, Rajasthan, Uttar Pradesh and Uttaranchal. These states are considered as low income states.

References

Kadekodi, Gopal and Keerti Kulkarni (2004): Status of Health and Medical Care in India: A Micro Perspective, in P. R. Panchmukhi (Ed.): *Economic Reforms and the Health Status in India: Action and Empirical Perspectives*, Project Report CMDR, Dharwad.

Dev, Mahendra and Jos Mooji (2002): Social Sector Expenditure in the 1990s: Analysis of Central and State Budgets, *Economic and Political Weekly*, Vol. XXXVII, No.9.

IIPS (2000): *National Family Health Survey, India (NFHS-2): 1998-99*, International Institute for Population Sciences, Mumabi.

Parikh, Kirit (2002): Social Infrastructure, in K S Parikh and S Radhakrishna (ed.) *India Development Report*, Oxford University Press, New Delhi.

Registrar General of India (2006): *Maternal Mortality in India: 1997-2003*, Sample Registration System, New Delhi.

Registrar General of India (2001): Provisional Population Totals, Census of India, Paper-1 of 2001, Census of India, 2001.

Sen Gita, Aditi Iyer, Asha George (2002): Structural Reforms and Health Equity: A comparison of NSS Surveys, 1986-87 and 1995-96, *Economic and Political Weekly*, Vol.. XXXVII, No.14.

Visaria, Leela (1985): Infant Mortality in India: Levels, Trends Determinants, *Economic and Political Weekly,* Vol. XX, No.32.

4

Fiscal Reforms and Health Care Spending: An Inter-State Analysis

Sarit Kumar Rout

I. Introduction

An increase in the aggregate national income and in per capita income tends to increase the welfare of the society. But if the improvement in the wealth of the society gets concentrated in the hands of a few, then the national income is not an accurate indicator of economic welfare. There is increasing evidence that wealth created does not trickle down to all sectors of the society. In India in spite of having eight per cent growth rate, malnutrition, hunger and deprivation persist among large sections of the society. An increasing disparity is noticed among the Indian states so far as achievement in social indicators is concerned. Thus the planers, policy makers and development thinkers have been putting emphasis on education, health and other social sector activities to improve the welfare of the masses. This has been popularized by United Nations Development Programme (UNDP) with introduction of Human Development Index (HDI) in the 1990s.

Good health is considered as an integral element of development. It is a well known fact that poor health status forbids economic opportunity worsening the financial position of an individual further. It reinforces poverty and ill health disproportionately affects the poor and leading to higher morbidity and mortality.

In this context the provision of basic health facilities lies with the state and the state should take appropriative measure to improve the health status of its citizens. In India health is a state subject and the constitution lays down guidelines for provisions of health care facilities. The Art 38(2) and 41 stresses the need to provide equitable access and assistance to the sick and undeserved. Similarly the Art-47 emphasises on improving the nutrition status, standard of living and public health situation of the general citizens. For achieving these goals Indian government has framed policies for increasing access to health care, reducing disease burden and finally improving the quality of life of the people. After independence, it was for the first time in 1983 India adopted a formal or National Health policy. Prior to the adoption of this policy, health activities were formulated through five-year plans. So health for all by increasing access to health services has become the primary focus of national government and accordingly it has designed strategies to improve the delivery of services.

Though India has progressed well in many of the health indicators, its achievement is worse when compared to countries like China and Republic of Korea. Within the country there are interstate and intrastate variations in health indicators. The life expectancy at birth of Kerala was 73.5 years (1995-99) as against 56.4 years in case of Madhya Pradesh, a difference of 18.1 years. During 2002 the IMR of Orissa stands at 87 per 1,000 live births as against 10 for Kerala. There are also inequalities among the economically and socially deprived groups. Many studies in India have proved that Scheduled Castes (SCs), Scheduled Tribes (STs) and women in poorer states face serious health problems and have a greater share of the burden of diseases.

A large number of factors account for these failures. Inappropriate policies, poor governance structure and inadequate financial arrangement in the supply side and high incidence of poverty, ignorance and traditional practices and cultural factors operating at the demand side influence these outcomes. It is beyond the scope of this paper to look in to all the factors influencing health outcomes. Financing health care being an important element, the present paper seeks to examine the pattern of public financing of health care in 14 major non special category states of India. There are four sections in this paper. Section I introduces the paper. Section II discusses the financial crises of the major states in India. Section III examines the trend of public spending on health care among 14 major states of the country during 1990-91 to 2005-06. It makes a comparative analysis of health care spending in pre fiscal crisis (1990-91 to 1997-98) and the crisis period (1998-99 to 2005-06). The two time periods are defined taking in to consideration the financial crisis faced by most of the states after the implementation of fifth pay commission recommendations during 1997-98 onwards. It also presents some theoretical understanding of health care spending and its components. Section IV concludes the paper.

II. Fiscal Crisis and Reform Initiatives by States

In the second half of the nineties there has been a significant deterioration both in the center and state fiscal position. The combined fiscal deficit of the center and state had increased to around nine per cent of Gross Domestic Product (GDP) in 2000-01. The most striking point is that the states deficit increased significantly at the end of the nineties that contribute to the rise in the combined deficit. Among various factors that are responsible for the rise in the deficit among the Indian states, the first and foremost culprit is the implementation of the fifth pay commission recommendations. The salary bill in most of the states increased causing a sharp rise in revenue deficit. The revenue deficit of all the major states of the country went up during 1998-99 to 2005-06. It increased by 17 per cent of total expenditure on an average during 1998-99 to 2005-06 in comparison to 1990-91 to 1997-98 for West Bengal, which is the highest among the 14 major states of the country. On the other hand this increase is two per cent for Bihar which is lowest. For the states like Kerala, Gujarat and Rajasthan the deficit went up by 13.55, 11.89 and 11.39 per cent respectively (Table 4.1).

Along with this there has been a secular decline in the state government finances over last twenty years and this has been further aggravated by the decline in central support to the states. So the decline in revenue and the sharp rise in expenditure in latter half of the nineties led to increase in borrowing by most of the states. The poor states like Orissa, Bihar, Uttar Pradesh, Madhya Pradesh and Rajasthan suffered a lot and the debt to Gross State Domestic Product (GSDP) ratio of these poor states was 39 per cent as against 28 per cent in case of other states during 2001-02 (World Bank, 2005).

Table 4.1: Revenue Deficit of the States (per cent)

State	Average 1991-92 to 1997-98	Average 1998-99 to 2005-06	Difference
A	B	C	C-B
Andhra Pradesh	5.14	7.72	2.58
Bihar+	8.04	9.82	1.78
Gujarat	3.11	15	11.89
Haryana	4.14	8.02	3.88
Karnataka	1.94	6.79	4.85
Kerala	8.02	21.57	13.55
Madhya Pradesh+	3.27	10.07	6.8
Maharashtra	3.63	13.36	9.73
Orissa	9.27	16.52	7.25
Punjab	12.76	18.44	5.68
Rajasthan	4.13	15.52	11.39
Tamil Nadu	9.07	11.3	2.23
Uttar Pradesh+	10.11	17.28	7.17
West Bengal	11.83	29.02	17.19

+ indicates undivided states.

Source: Compiled from Handbook of Statistics on State Government Finances, 2004/05, State Finances: A study of Budgets of 2005/06, RBI,

The state wise position of debt GSDP ratio has been presented in Table 4.2. The average Debt-GSDP ratio for Orissa stands at 63.7 per cent during the period 2000-03 rising from 36.21 per cent in 1993-96. The deterioration during the period 1993-96 to 2000-03 was most marked in the case of Orissa at 27.5 per cent points followed by West Bengal, Gujarat and Rajasthan among the general category states.

Table 4.2: Outstanding Debt Relative to GSDP: State-wise Position (per cent)

No	Name of the States	1993-96 (A)	2000-03 (B)	Col (B-A)
1.	Andhra Pradesh	21.86	29.93	8.07
2.	Bihar	36.80	44.35	7.55
3.	Goa	41.64	33.54	-8.10
4.	Gujarat	21.07	37.92	16.85
5.	Haryana	19.85	28.02	8.17
6.	Karnataka	19.62	27.27	7.65
7.	Kerala	27.27	37.58	10.32
8.	Madhya Pradesh	19.95	30.42	10.47
9.	Maharashtra	15.63	27.11	11.48
10.	Orissa	36.21	63.68	27.47
11.	Punjab	34.55	46.66	12.10
12.	Rajasthan	28.28	44.88	16.60
13.	Tamil Nadu	18.87	26.16	7.29
14.	Uttar Pradesh	33.94	46.94	13.00
15.	West Bengal	23.26	42.73	19.47
	Total GCS	24.12	36.06	11.94
	All States	24.86	36.65	11.79

Source: Report of the Twelfth Finance Commission (2005-10), November 2004, Government of India.

Consequently most of the states adopted fiscal reform programmes which aimed at enhancing revenue and controlling expenditure to restore fiscal balance. For augmenting revenue the states introduced Value Added Tax (VAT) and users charges in case of essential services. On the expenditure side there is a widespread agreement on a three point agenda. The first is to control aggregate expenditure; the second is the need to restructure the expenditure away from salary to non salary and developmental expenditure. And the third is effective management and increase the efficiency of public expenditure. The states like Karnataka, Uttar Pradesh and Orissa etc also published the Medium Term Fiscal Plan indicating the fiscal objectives achievable within a time limit. In August 2002 Karnataka passed the first Fiscal Responsibility Act and since then other states such as Punjab and Tamil Nadu have also passed the fiscal responsibility legislation. Along with this the states took steps to restructure the state electricity boards as poor performance of State Electricity Boards (SEBs) has aggravated the state finances. Twenty one states have constituted state electricity commissions for determining the power tariff structure. Some states like Andhra Pradesh, Karnataka started governance reform programmes in order to improve the service delivery.

III. Health Care Financing: Inter-State Comparison

Defining Health Care Spending: There has been no standard definition of health care expenditure. It is a well known fact that the health status of the people is influenced by a large number of factors and is a function of medical care, income, education, sex, martial status, and environmental pollution et cetera. Given too many factors influencing health it becomes difficult to define what items constitute health care spending and what truly reflects health care expenditure. However, expert on health economics have explicitly mentioned that all that activities that primarily and significantly contribute for improving health status of the people should be included and others should be judged on their merit. (*Berman Peter, 1994*)

Health being a state subject majority of the funding is made by the state government. The central government supports the states for implementing central sponsored programmes aimed at achieving the national health goals. The primary sources of public financing are the general tax and non tax revenue which include grants in aid available from the central government. In addition to that some of the states have introduced user fees which are also used for financing health care. Another important source of financing health care is the resources available from external agencies. The most important project is the introduction of World Bank initiated Health Systems Project, which is operational in Andhra Pradesh, Punjab, Utter Pradesh, Karnataka, Orissa, Maharashtra and West Bengal. Expenditure under this project is outside the state budget and hence could not be included in the analysis.

In India the state and central governments have adopted certain functional heads to represent budgetary allocations based upon the coding pattern developed by Comptroller and Auditor General of India. These functional heads are shown in different ministries or departments as items of expenditure. For instance 2210 is a major head which shows the expenditure for medical and public health. Other heads related to health expenditure are 2211 (family welfare), 4210 –capital expenditure on medical and public health, 4211- capital expenditure on family welfare. These heads are not presented in the Health department budget only. It is shown in the budget of other departments such as Works Department, Rural Development, Labour and Employment. But it is important to mention here that a major share of health budget is routed through the health department or ministry. There are certain other programmes for instance water and sanitation and nutrition which contribute for promoting health, but these are not reflected in the budget of health department. The nutrition and water sanitation heads are shown in the department of Women and Child development, Housing and Urban Development and Rural development budget in case of Orissa. This arrangement varies from state to state.

In this section the allocation towards medical and public health and family welfare programme under revenue and capital heads has been examined. The expenditure on water sanitation and nutrition programmes have not been taken in to account as they are broadly considered as health related expenditure. The data has been pulled from various issues of 'State Finances: A Study of Budgets' published by Reserve Bank of India.

Inter State Analysis of Health Care Spending

The health care sending of 14 major states in the county has been examined here. It is also important to mention here that public spending in India is one of the lowest and as per the national health accounts 2001-02 spending by the health departments of both centre and state accounts for 0.9 per cent of GDP. Fiscal pressure has resulted in the compression of state expenditure and steady decline in social expenditure. The combined expenditure of the states in the 1990s on health, water supply sanitation and family welfare programme declined from 8.4 per cent of total expenditure in 1990s to 7.2 per cent in 2001-02 (GOI, 2005).

The real per capita health expenditure (1993-94 prices) and its share from the state expenditure have been presented in this section. As observed from the Table 4.3 Punjab with Rs. 132.5 has the highest real per capita spending during 1991-92 to 2005-06 where as Bihar spends the least. The poor states like Orissa, Madhya Pradesh and Uttar Pradesh stand at 11th, 12th and 13th respectively. Kerala with better HDI occupies second position among 14 major states of the country. But as a share of state expenditure, West Bengal makes highest budgetary spending towards health sector. The average share is 5.68 per cent during 1990-91 to 2005-06 against 3.08 per cent for Haryana which is the lowest in the country. The high income states like Punjab, Haryana and Gujarata allocate relatively lower share of state expenditure towards the health sector in comparison to poor states like Bihar, Orissa and Uttar Pradesh (Table 4.3). In spite of a lower share of the state budget the per capita health care spending of these states is found to be more in comparison to the poor states. In case of Kerala which performs significantly better in most of the health indicators the rank in the share of state expenditure and per capita health spending is same during the period.

It is also important to look in to whether the state governments have maintained the same level of expenditure as earlier or reduced the share towards health sector due to the financial crisis. As observed from the Table 4.4, except Haryana, all the states have reduced the share towards health after the onset of financial crisis during 1998-99 onwards.

Table 4.3: Real Per Capita Health Spending and its Share in State Expenditure

State	Average Real Per capita Health Spending	Rank	Average Share in State Expenditure (1990-91 to 2005-06)	Rank
Andhra Pradesh	92.32	8	4.47	8
Bihar+	53.38	14	5.17	3
Gujarat	96.01	6	3.81	13
Haryana	86.43	10	3.08	14
Karnataka	102.35	4	4.74	6
Kerala	130.08	2	5.46	2
Madhya Pradesh+	67.38	12	4.42	9
Maharashtra	95.59	7	3.96	12
Orissa	72.02	11	4.25	10
Punjab	132.5	1	4.03	11
Rajasthan	96.97	5	5.16	4
Tamil Nadu	113.6	3	5.02	5
Uttar Pradesh+	61.75	13	4.58	7
West Bengal	89.67	9	5.68	1

+ indicates undivided states.

Source: Compiled from Handbook of Statistics on State Government Finances, 2004/05, State Finances: A Study of Budgets of 2005/06, RBI.

The highest decline is observed in case of undivided Bihar followed by Uttar Pradesh and West Bengal. In case of Bihar the decline is 1.52 per cent, for Uttar Pradesh it is 1.44 and it is 1.19 per cent for West Bengal (Table 4.4). This indicates the poor states have reduced their share towards the health sector after the onset of the financial crisis. Another important revelation is that Gujarat is the only state among the high income states which has declined its share by 1.01 per cent in the post crisis period.

Table 4.4: Inter-State Comparison of Health Sector Expenditure

States	Share of health Expenditure to Total expenditure (1991-92 to 1997-98)	Share of health Expenditure to Total expenditure (1998-99 to 2005-06)	% Change over the period
1	2	3	4 = 3 - 2
Andhra Pradesh	4.67	4.04	-0.63
Bihar+	5.78	4.27	-1.52
Gujarat	4.23	3.22	-1.01
Haryana	2.83	2.94	0.12
Karnataka	5.05	4.22	-0.83
Kerala	5.68	5.01	-0.67
Madhya Pradesh+	4.57	3.85	-0.72
Maharashtra	4.21	3.51	-0.70
Orissa	4.59	3.82	-0.77
Punjab	4.02	3.70	-0.32
Rajasthan	5.54	4.67	-0.87
Tamil Nadu	5.33	4.51	-0.82
Uttar Pradesh+	5.25	3.81	-1.44
West Bengal	6.02	4.83	-1.19

+ indicates the undivided states

Source: Compiled from Handbook of Statistics on State Government Finances, 2004/05, State Finances: A Study of Budgets of 2005/06, RBI.

The extent of disparity among various category of states and the improvement in real per capita expenditure on medical and public health and family welfare during 1991-92 to 2005-06 has been presented in the Table 4.5. It is found that during 1991-92 Punjab's per capita health spending was highest and that of Madhya Pradesh was the lowest. In this period the disparity between the highest spending and lowest spending state was 1:2.05. The situation of Madhya Pradesh improved during 1996-97 and stood 12th position and the per capita health spending of Bihar was lowest while Kerala occupied the first position during the same period.

During this period the disparity between highest and lowest spending state increased and reached to 1:2.92. In 2001-02 again Punjab spent highest in per capita terms and Uttar Pradesh had lowest spending. But in 2005-06 Kerala and Bihar were the highest and lowest spending states respectively. So the point to mention here is that the per capita health spending of poor states like Bihar or Uttar Pradesh is found to be lowest in last 15 years. The highest increase in per capita spending is for Kerala in 2005-06 against 1991-92 followed by Andhra Pradesh and West Bengal. In case of Kerala, the rise is 91.11 per cent and for Andhra Pradesh it is 67.74 per cent. The lowest increase in per capita health care spending is for Gujarat. The regional inequality measured in terms of co-efficient of variation among different states is widening over the years. The co-efficient of variation, which was 21.60 in 1991-92, has increased to 29.92 in 2001-02. During 2005-06 it was 26.12. During the process of reforms the gap between the poor and rich states is rising indicating the poor states are not in a position to allocate more and more resources towards health sector.

With the rise in national income a higher proportion of income is spent towards health sector. It has been proved in earlier studies that, the ratio of health expenditure to GDP increased as the countries developed economically and socially [Abel-Smith (1963, 1967) as quoted by Bhat and Jain (2006)]. Again another study found a positive linear relationship between the percentage of health care expenditure to GDP and GDP [Newhouse (1977) as quoted by Bhat and Jain (2006)]. In case of eight states in India the share of health in GSDP is less than one

Table 4.5: Real Per Capita Health Expenditure

States	1991-92	Rank	1996-97	Rank	2001-02	Rank	2005-06	Rank	% increase in 2005-06 over 1991-92
A.P.	66.77	10	83.87	8	109.75	6	111.99	5	67.74
Bihar+	56.84	13	39.7	14	61.23	13	70.68	14	24.36
Gujarat	80.62	5	88.06	6	87.36	10	94.55	11	17.28
Haryana	73.3	8	79.04	9	92.06	9	99.93	9	36.33
Karnataka	78.4	7	84.96	7	125.34	3	116.11	4	48.11
Kerala	94.1	2	116.05	1	145.89	2	179.9	1	91.19
M.P+	55.69	14	60.86	12	69.74	12	83.82	13	50.51
Maharashtra	80.75	4	90.38	5	115.03	5	104.31	8	29.18
Orissa	63.7	11	64.37	11	74.6	11	94.86	10	48.91
Punjab	113.95	1	110.18	2	154.51	1	146.55	2	28.62
Rajasthan	79.34	6	100.64	4	106.69	8	106.4	7	34.1
Tamil Nadu	92.55	3	104.63	3	119.83	4	142.36	3	53.82
UP+	57.24	12	60.11	13	52.83	14	85.04	12	48.58
West Bengal	70.76	9	75.88	10	107.5	7	107.35	6	51,71

+ indicates the undivided states

Source: Compiled from Handbook of Statistics on State Government Finances, 2004/05, State Finances: A study of Budgets of 2005/06, RBI.

per cent. And for other states it is marginally higher than one per cent varying from 1.08 to 1.15 per cent. It is also observed that in the post crisis period the health expenditure as proportion to GSDP has declined in almost all the states except Andhra Pradesh, Orissa and Punjab. But the rise in these three states is marginal. This reveals that the share of GSDP has not increased in the states. Comparing the health care expenditure to GSDP and GSDP in 14 major states it is found that the correlation is found to be negative for all the states in the country. So increasing GSDP doesn't contribute the rise in health care expenditure (Table 4.6).

Table 4.6: Share of Health Expenditure in GSDP

States	Pre Crisis	Post Crisis	Correlation between % of health care expenditure to GSDP
Andhra Pradesh	0.86	0.87	-0.434
Bihar+	2.03	1.53	-0.757
Gujarat	0.7	0.67	-0.583
Haryana	0.58	0.55	-0.117
Karnataka	0.92	0.88	-0.500
Kerala	1.08	1.03	-0.820
Madhya Pradesh+	1.08	0.92	-0.805
Maharashtra	0.62	0.6	-0.661
Orissa	1.05	1.08	-0.606
Punjab	0.77	0.87	-0.148
Rajasthan	1.15	1.1	-0.759
Tamil Nadu	0.96	0.86	-0.928
Uttar Pradesh+	1.06	0.89	-0.566
West Bengal	0.89	0.89	-0.618

+ indicates undivided states.

Source: Compiled from Handbook of Statistics on State Government Finances, 2004/05, State Finances: A study of Budgets of 2005/06, RBI.

IV. Conclusion

The reform process initiated by the sates has definitely affected the health care spending among the states. It is observed that out of 14 states, 13 states have reduced the share of budgetary allocations to health sector during the post crisis period. The poor states particularly Bihar, Uttar Pradesh which have a significantly lower HDI in comparison to Kerala and Gujarata have reduced the health expenditure more. The regional inequality measured in terms of co-efficient of variation among different states is widening over the years. During the process of reforms the gap between the poor and rich states is rising indicating the poor states are not in a position to allocate more and more resources towards health sector. Another issue was whether the share of health expenditure increased with the rise in state income measured in terms of GDP. There exists a negative correlation between ratio of health care expenditure to GSDP and GSDP for 14 major states of the country during the period of analysis. So increasing GSDP doesn't contribute to the rise in health care expenditure in case of Indian states.

One of the objectives of the fiscal reform programme was to control unproductive expenditure and bring fiscal balance. In the name of fiscal balance most sates have reduced expenditure on health sector which is an important item of social services expenditure. The important challenge is for the poor stats like Orissa, Bihar and Uttar Pradesh which have a low HDI as compared to advanced states like Kerala and Gujarata. There is an urgent need to step up social sector spending as it has profound influence in the HDI of the state. Higher allocations and prioritization of specific areas like health sector should be the focus areas in the coming years. The experts in the National Commission on Macro Economics and Health have made a detailed estimate of expenditure requirement for health sector and pointed out that Rs. 74,000 crore would be required for provisioning of health facilities. A detailed sectoral analysis has been made in the health sector indicating the resources for different physical components, Community Health Centers

(CHCs) and Primary Health Centers (PHCs). Based upon such criteria the states like Bihar, Uttar Pradesh, Madhya Pradesh, Orissa and West Bengal require highest increase in the expenditure. These states have also lowest per capita spending on health as revealed from the analysis presented in the section II. So such states should find out modalities to step up investment in health in future.

It is not the allocation alone rather the service delivery mechanism should be improved to translate the outlays to outcomes. The long route of accountability that exists in the service delivery chain should be broken. The service providers should be accountable to the citizens rather than the policy makers, where the accountability route is found to be long (World Bank, 2004). In order to improve the quality of delivery of services, the states are making efforts to transfer power to the Panchayati Raj Institutions (PRIs). The PRIs will monitor the day-to-day functioning of these institutions so as to improve the delivery of services. Such efforts should be streamlined and state level legislations should be introduced. The states are required to design policies to increase efficiency of public expenditure and maximize the benefits of every rupee spent for public purpose. This needs well integrated policies and political commitments.

References

Bhat Ramesh and J. Jain (2006): Analysis of Public and Private Healthcare Expenditures, *Economic and Political Weekly*, Vol. XLI, No. 1.

Devaranjan, Shantayanan and Shekhar Shah (2004): Making services work for India's poor, *Economic and Political Weekly*, Vol. XXXIX, No. 9.

GOI (2005): *Report of the National commission on Macro Economics and Health*, Ministry of Health and family Welfare.

Howes, Stephen, Ashok K. Lahiri and Nicholas Stern (Eds.) (2003): *State Level Reforms India towards more Effective Governance*, Macmillan, New Delhi.

Joshi, Seema (2006): Impact of Economic Reforms on Social Sector Expenditure in India, *Economic and Political Weekly*, Vol. XLI, No.4.

K. Seeta Prabhu and Somanath Chatterjee (1993): Social Sector Expenditures and Human Development: A Study of Indian States, *Development Research Group Series 6*, Reserve Bank of India.

Panchamukhi P.R. (2004): Social Impact of Economic Reforms in India A Critical Appraisal *Economic and Political Weekly*, March 4.

Paul Samuel (2006): Public Spending, Outcomes and Accountability: Citizens Report Card as a Catalyst for Public Action, *Economic and Political Weekly*, Vol. XLI, No. 4.

Reddy, M. Gopinath, K Jayalakshmi and Anne Marie Goetz (2006): Politics of Pro-poor Reform in the Health Sector: Primary Health care in Tribal Areas of Visakhapatnam, *Economic and Political Weekly*, Vol. XLI, No. 5.

Reddy K.N. and V. Selvaraju (1994): *Health Care Expenditure by Governments In India: 1974-75 to 1990-91*, National Institute of Public Finance and Policy, New Delhi.

Reserve Bank of India (2004): *Handbooks of Statistics on State Government Finances*, Bombay.

Reserve Bank of India (2004): *State Finances A Study of Budgets*, 2000-04 to 2006-07, Bombay.

World Bank (2004): *World Development Report 2004: Making Services Work for the Poor*, Oxford University Press, Washington D.C.

World Bank (2005): The state level fiscal reforms in India; Progress and prospects, New Delhi.

5

Health Status of Tribals in India: Evidence from Andhra Pradesh

Prasant Kumar Panda, Atulya Bhoi, Yoginder Singh and K. Sankaraiyah

I. Introduction

Health is an important aspect of human resource development. Good health care facilities and services are essential for creating healthy citizen and society that can effectively contribute to social and economic development. With increased urbanization, industrialization, changing environment and ecosystem, deterioration of health resistance and the changing nature of health problems has become a great concern for world today. Therefore, three of the eight Millennium Development Goals [1] emphasize on health. They are to reduce child mortality, improve maternal health, combat HIV/AIDS, Malaria and other diseases. The capability theory of living standard (Sen, 1987) holds that "income, commodities, and wealth" do not ensure a decent living standard to their owners. It is the aggregate of certain capabilities like (1) capability to live long, (2) capability to avoid illiteracy, (3) capability to be free from hunger and undernourishment and (4) capability to enjoy personal liberty and freedom provides a decent standard of living. Health is one of the important aspects that help to develop capabilities and sustainability to work long and to contribute to economic growth.

Health is required for all irrespective of cast and community. Though tribals are mainly living in forest and hills, very close to nature, they are not free from the health related problems and complicacies. They are vulnerable to endemics like malaria, deficiency diseases, tuberculosis and venereal diseases including AIDS. Malnutrition and under nutrition are common among the tribals. The poor nutritional status of tribal women directly influences their reproductive performance and their infants' survival, growth and development. Their illiteracy, poverty, alienation from the society and their apathy to modern form practices and practitioners are adding much to the poor status of tribal health. There is a general agreement that the health status of tribal population is very poor in India. Different studies (Basu et al.1986 and 1990; Roy, 1986; Sen, 1986; Rizvi, 1986; Mukherjee and Nandy, 1986; Huq, 1990) have tried to establish this with the help of morbidity, mortality and health statistics.

The health aspects of tribals are much influenced by their living styles, habits, their beliefs, customs and values. The two basic but important characteristics of tribal life according to Margaret Mead (1954) are their-(a) Physical isolation and (b) self-reliance based on ecological adjustment to their environment. Over the years knowingly or unknowingly, though these aspects have shown a slow change, but the tribals, particularly the primitive groups are still bound to the geographical area as well as their culture. They have their own system of medicines and beliefs for different diseases. They believe in supernatural, magic powers, folk healers and their hard bound social codes. They depend on nature and ethno medicines for treating their illness. Inspite of the few commonalities and traits, the tribal groups in the country also show heterogeneity. There are 67.8 million Scheduled Tribe people, constituting 8.08 per cent of India's population. There are 698 Scheduled Tribes spread all over the country(barring few states) [2] out of which 75 are identified as Primitive tribal groups considering them as more backward and live in pre-agricultural stage of the economy. Each clan has its specific culture and practices. This makes again difficult for government to adopt for a common approach to develop the health status of tribals. In this scenario a study on tribals' health will be useful to find out an appropriate approach to the health service provisions in the tribal areas.

Andhra Pradesh (AP) is one of the states having hilly and forest areas and sizable tribal population. Though health status of tribal population in AP is little better than that of all India average but it is not satisfactory if it is compared with the non tribal population of AP .The health status of tribals is marked by all the negative features that one can find in terms of persistent morbidity and high mortality, lack of personal hygiene and environmental sanitation, absence of proper health education and awareness. The maternal and child health is grossly neglected. Malnutrition and undernourishment, lack of prenatal and post-natal care, low coverage of preventive measures and vaccination are main factors for high maternal and infant mortality. This rate is further higher among the tribal groups like Savaras, Gadabas and Jatapus (Rao, 1998). "Andhra Pradesh also faces tremendous logistical problem in reaching its most disadvantaged citizens: tribal groups living in remote and inaccessible area. In these areas the public infrastructure is barely present. Such rural health facilities as do exist are characterized by phenomenal level of doctors and nurse absenteeism, and absence of drugs and equipment in primary health centers (PHCs), a weak referral system and absence of an orientation in rural health system to preventive care instead of curative care. As a consequence, health indicators for tribal population in AP are considerable worse than those for the rest of the population" (Gopinathreddy et al., 2006).

In this perspective the paper is a modest attempt to critically evaluate the health status of tribal women and children in Andhra Pradesh on the basis of different determinants and health indicators like provision of sanitary and drinking water facilities, mortality and morbidity among tribals, fertility and family planning, diet and nutritional status of tribal women and children and their access to different forms of health care services and their relative rationality.

The paper starts with an introduction to tribal health in general and tribal women and children health in particular, their back-log, and the tribal health scenario in AP in section-I, the methodology of the study is explained in section-II, the section-III explains various health indicators and status of tribal health in Andhra Pradesh, the section-IV deals with various health care practices among tribals in AP and their relative determining factors, and the paper concludes with few suggestions for development of health of these marginalized section of the people in the society.

II. Methodology

Both primary and secondary data are collected for the present study. Secondary data are collected from National family health survey1 and 2, South Indian human development report, Census of India, Statistical abstract of Andhra Pradesh for the present paper. Primary data are collected by multistage sampling from 150 tribal (Savara and Jatapu) respondents covering five Mandals (Bhanini, Kothur, Seethampeta, palkonda and Hiramandalam) of Srikakulam District of Andhra Pradesh. This district lies on the northern part of Andhra Pradesh along the coast of Coromandel. It is located with the geographical cardinals of $18^{0}50'$-$19^{0}12'$ of northern latitude and $83^{0}32$-$84^{0}47'$ eastern longitude with an altitude range of 50-1120m.The district is bounded by Orissa state on the north, Bay of Bengal in the east and south east and Vizianagaram district in the west and south west. It is covered by both costal plain as well as hilly forests. This district is inhabited by major tribal communities like Savara, Jatapu, Kuttiya, Gadaba, yerukula and Kondadora. Simple per cent ratio method is used to substantiate the objectives.

III. Health Indicators and Status of Tribal Women and Children in AP

Andhra Pradesh is one of the states having hilly and forest areas and sizable tribal population. As per 2001 census the tribal population in state is 50.24 lakh which constitutes 6.31 per cent of the total population of the state. In 1981 the tribal population constituted 5.91 per cent of the total population of the state. The total tribal population consists of 33 tribes, out of which 30 tribes live in hilly and forest areas of AP while the other three clans are dispersed through out the state. The tribal sub plan area is spreaded over nine districts and consists of 33 tribes and 22 lakh of the total 42 lakh (1991 Census) Scheduled tribe (ST) population in the state. The health status of tribal population in AP is better than that of all India average but it is not satisfactory if it is compared with the non tribal population of AP. The expectation of life in AP among STs is 60.9 years as against 58.6 years at the all India level. Maternal and child health care is an important aspect of health seeking behavior, which is largely neglected among tribal groups in Andhra Pradesh.

In this section the health status of tribals particularly women and children in Andhra Pradesh is evaluated on the basis of various determinants like morbidity and mortality, reproductive health and family planning, and malnutrition.

Morbidity and Mortality: "One of the major issues in the health status measurement is the health seeking behavior of a community which governs the morbidity and mortality pattern" (Basu et al., 1994). Though the morbidity is lower, infant and under five mortality rate are much higher among STs as compared to the general population in AP. The Infant Mortality Rate (IMR) is 85.4 among STs as against 68 in others. Similarly the IMR under five is 134 for ST as against of 89.1 for others. So infant mortality is 26 per cent higher than the general population. Maternal mortality is 8 per one thousand (going up to 25 among some tribal groups) as against four per 1000 for the state. The wide gap between tribal and non tribal areas is mainly due to uneven provision and utilization of heath care services. "The poverty is the prime cause for ill health, persistent morbidity and early death. Lack of access to right food: iron, protein, and micronutrients such as iodine and vitamins, causes a very high incidence of nutritional deficiency diseases, anemia, diarrhea, night blindness, goitry, etc.

These factors combined with lack of access to basic health care services is the main reason for the marked gap in health indicators between tribals areas and the more developed parts of the state" (Rao,1998). Lower morbidity among tribals does not necessarily indicate better health because the former is determined by many factors like socioeconomic developments, poverty, availability of health care services and facilities and their willingness to acknowledge their ill health. "It has generally been observed that the morbidity rates are positively associated with socio-economic status and level of development. In other words the better-off segment or the area is likely to report higher level of morbidity than the not so well-off" (Sinha, 2006). This could be an outcome of a reporting bias against the poor who may not be able or willing to acknowledge their own ill health (Sen et al., 2002).Poor maternal health has direct impact on child health and developments. From the inception of pregnancy to its termination, no specific nutritious diet nor required vitamins-iron and calcium are given to the women. In the post delivery period mother is also not consuming proper diets. Besides breast feeding, no supplementary food is given to the child before one year. Vaccination and immunization of infants and children among the tribal groups are not proper. As a result infant mortality and maternal mortality are high among the tribals.

Reproductive Health and Family Planning: The fertility rate among rural ST women in AP was 3.74 as against 2.5 among rural non-STs (NFHS-1).Though there is decline in the fertility rate, it is much lower in STs as compared to non-STs. As per NFHS-2, it is 2.75 among STs and 2.25 among non-STs. The first Pregnancy occurs at an early age among STs (17 years , mean age) as compared to non- STs (18.7Yrs). The low age of marriage, early delivery and lower acceptance to contraceptives increase the fertility. Girls in tribal societies are given in marriage generally after puberty (Basu, 1994). From the study at Srikakulam it is observed 2 per cent of women respondents delivered their first child at age of 14. 15.25 per cent at age of 15, 30.8 per cent at age of 17 and 12 per cent at 18 and 11 per cent at age of 19. However, there are cases that women had their first child at age of 40 also. Sterilization among STs is not popular as it is in general population. It is evident from the study 60 per cent women are not willing to do family planning operations and 10 per cent people are having doubts on family planning operations. Maximum delivery takes place at home (92 per cent) and only 8 per cent delivery is undertaken at PHCs. This clearly indicates that the tribal people do not have trust on modern health care services nor do they have social and economic viability to utilize these services.

Malnutrition: The tribal group mainly subsists on agriculture and income from forest produce, they do not have special provision of diet for pregnant and lactating mothers and as a result every tribal passes through the vicious cycle of malnutrition-infection complex. Diarrhea is the leading causes of child mortality in tribal areas claiming an estimated 5 million child death each year (Chakravarti, 1994). According to surveys conducted by the National Institute of nutrition (1971), Gopalan (1971) and the planning commission of India during the sixth five year plan, Pingle (1975) the nutritional status of the tribal population which together with their economic status determines their health status is not satisfactory. Tribals of Andhra Pradesh also suffer from malnutrition and undernourishment. (1) Nutritional deficiency is high among the tribals in AP. Chronic energy deficiency is usually indicated by a Body mass index (BMI) of less than 18.5. In AP, 44.2 per cent ST Women (below 30 years of age) have a BMI below the minimum requirement of 18.5. (2) Ever-married ST women in AP are having iron deficiency Anemia is 48.6 per cent (some degree), 34.2 per cent mild anemia, 11.8 per cent moderate anemia and 2.6 per cent severe anemia. This results in premature delivery and low birth weight of child. (3) There is deficiency in the use of iodized salt among the ST women in AP, which cause brain disorders, sub-optimum mental development of their children. 37.7 per cent of ST population use non-iodized salt, 44.2 per cent use inadequately iodized and 18.2 per cent use non iodized salt (NHFS-2).

Poverty, Malnutrition, lack of safe drinking water; poor hygiene and environmental sanitation, ineffective coverage of national health and nutritional services, are the factors responsible for dismal health conditions revealed among these tribal populations.

IV. Health Care Practices among Tribals

Health care practices among tribals are mainly traditional and much influenced by their customs, beliefs, traditions and religious taboos. Inspite of the development of modern form of medicines and treatment, and extension of PHCs services to tribal areas, a large section of tribal people rely on indigenous health practices. Tribal population in Srikakulam District mainly depends on Ethno- medicine practices by the folk healer. From the total population under study, 58.87 per cent population relies on this.23.3 per cent depends on private doctors or private run small clinics or voluntary health centers.17.83 per cent of population depends on Primary Health centers (PHC). This is because there are no adequate PHCs in these areas and 2ndly 70 per cent of tribals do not know about free medical treatment at the PHCs and the rest won't believe on PHC treatment. Absenteeism of doctors, lack of adequate facilities, distance from their location and moreover the approach of the doctors and medical staff discourage them to reap the services of PHCs. Lack of accommodation, poor infrastructure, large scale absenteeism and vacancies, poorly trained and unmotivated manpower, are thus reasons for the near absence of healthcare services in the tribal areas (Rao,1998).

Ethno medicines practices among the tribals are as old as their humanity is. These practices have been derived from centuries of experience in the use of various herbs and other substances to cure a variety of illness. Many studies like Jain, 1966; Mittal, 1979; Sinha, 1979 highlight the importance traditional practices by use of plants and herbs and the importance to document them. According to Herbal Folklore Research centre surveys in India there are 500 medicinal plants (out of 7,500 species in India) are used for treatment of various diseases in AP. In Srikakulam district hill tribes like Savara and Jatapu have faith in nature and they use product of plants and animals for healing their diseases. The possible reasons why tribals prefer ethno medicine- health care practices are:

- Tribals have strong faith in tradition and socio-cultural

aspects. They more believe the traditional medicine practitioner than the registered doctors.

- Their closeness to nature helps them to easily access to Ethno-medicines
- Cost saving and no side effects of these medicines.
- Poverty and non- affordability to modern medicines
- Lack of sufficient modern health care facilities in tribal areas.
- Their apathy to the language and approach of registered doctors
- Their alienation to civic society and lack of education and awareness

V. Suggestions

Although tribal people live usually close to nature, a majority of them need health care on account of malnutrition, lack of safe drinking water, poor hygiene and environmental sanitation and above all poverty. Lack of awareness and apathy to utilise the available health services also affect their health status. In wake of the opening of tribal areas with highways industrialization, and communication facilities, diseases have spread to tribal areas. Endemics like malaria, deficiency diseases, and venereal diseases including AIDS are not uncommon among tribal populations. However, lack of safe drinking water and malnutrition are well-recognized major health hazards for tribals. The reproductive and child health of tribals is also poor on account of mothers' malnutrition and their hesitation to use available maternal health care facilities at PHCs.

The study shows that the health status of tribal population in AP is better than that of all India average of tribals but it is not satisfactory if it is compared with the non tribal population of AP. Infant mortality and child mortality are very high among the tribals. The declining in fertility is much lower in STs as compared to non-STs. This is due to early marriage, lower acceptance to contraceptives, and low rate of sterilization among STs. Wide prevalent of malnutrition among the tribal women also supplement to the poor reproductive and child health among them.

Tribals also mainly depend on ethno medicines and traditional practices for healing their diseases. They prefer more to the traditional form of medicines and practices than the health care facilities available in private run clinics and PHCs. The possible reasons may be the lack of awareness, illiteracy, and tribals' apathy to modern form of practices and the approach of the practitioners. Moreover distance of PHCs from their location, inadequate of PHCs and facilities, frequent absenteeism of doctors and staff and their approach to service delivery are also equally accounted for poor health status of tribals.

A multipronged approach with the active participation of Government, NGOs and public is essential to promote tribals' health. Three questions are pertinent to be asked while formulating policies for tribal health. – (1) how could we create awareness and make the tribals believe about the various kinds of diseases which they face and the availability of modern medicines and cure for those, (2) how can the health infrastructure and facilities be made available adequately in tribal areas mostly in the interior tribal villages in forests, and (3) how can the services be truly reached the poor tribals and utilized to full extent?

These questions emphasizes that only formulation of policies or provision of services is not enough, implementation and utilization are also equally important. Both availability and acceptability are important for determining the utilization of services. For attracting the tribals to use modern health care services, it is important to win their psychology, create trust among them and show respect for their culture and language, which the present system lacks. So Up-scaling and extending the health care facilities into tribal areas including non-revenue tribal villages, proper mechanism to deliver the services and more importantly dedicated service attitude by the doctors and officers posted in the tribal areas will help to promote health services in tribal areas. When the tribal people find it difficult to access market for health care services, mainly due to their poverty, and ignorance, it is duty of the government to provide a package of health care services and to find ways and means to make services available and use by the tribals. Failure of Government sector in this regard means the exclusion of tribals from obtaining health services. Following few points are suggested in general for the development of the status of tribals' health in India.

Integration of both indigenous and modern form of medicines- Scientific evaluation and documentation of indigenous medicine practices are essential.

Provision of adequate health care facilities, PHCs and free medicines in tribal areas as well as in the non-revenue tribal villages can help to bring a transition in the status of tribal health.

- Massive health care awareness and education among tribal women, provision of safe drinking water, sanitation, Universal immunization and vaccination programme needs to be promoted at faster rate in tribal areas.
- Joint participation of Government, NGOs, and public is essential to promote health services to tribal areas
- Formation of SHGs among tribal women and sufficient awareness and training to them are necessary for promoting maternal and child health in their village. Massive appointment of community health workers will help to promote health education and awareness among the tribal women.
- Involvement of tribal educated youths and traditional medicine practitioners in promoting modern health care facilities, awareness for vulnerable diseases like malaria, AIDS etc will help to create trust among the tribals and promote their health. They can better communicate these by their own tribal dialect.
- A well co-coordinated health policy for tribals should be implemented.

Notes

1. Millennium development goals (MDGs) were signed at the global level; they were agreed upon at the Millennium Summit in September 2000 and again confirmed at the International Conference on Financing for Development in March 2002.There are eight goals including the important one, eradication of poverty and hunger. For details see Human

Development Report 2003.

2. Chandigarh, Delhi, Haryana, Pondicherry and Punjab

References

Basu, S (1994): The State of the Art: Tribal Health In India, in Salil Basu (Ed) "*Tribal Health in India*", Manak Publications (P) LTD, Delhi

Basu, Salil, A Jindal and G Kshatriya (1994): "Perception of Health and pattern of health Seeking behaviour among the selected tribal population groups of Madya Pradesh and Orissa" in Salil Basu (Ed) " *Tribal Health in India*", Manak Publications (P) LTD, Delhi

Basu, S.K (1986): Genetics, Socio-cultural and Health care among Tribal Groups of Jagdalpur and Konta Tehsils of Bastar Districts, M.P. in A.K. Kala and K.S. Singh (Eds.), *Anthropology development and nation building*. Concept Publishing company, New Delhi, pp.87-105.

Basu, S.K and A.Jindal (1990); Genetic and Socio cultural Determinants of tribal health: A Primitive Kutya Kondhs-a tribal group of Phulbani district of Orissa, ICMR Final report, NIHFW, New Delhi..

Chakravarti M.R. (1994) Health Profile Among Mother Child Groups, In Salil Basu. (Ed)," in Salil Basu (Ed) "*Tribal Health in India*", Manak Publications (P) LTD, Delhi Pp. 225-240.

Gopalan, C (1971): Nutritional Atlas of India, ICMR, New Delhi

Gopinathreddy M, K Jayalakshmi and Anne-Marie Goetz (2006): "Politics of Pro-poor Reform in the Health Sector: Primary Healthcare in Tribal areas of Visakhapatnam", *Economic and Political Weekly*, February 4, Pp. 419-426

Huq, M.(1990):Height, Weight and Nutrition among six Tribes of India in B.Chaudhary(Ed),*Cultural and environmental dimensions on health*, Inter-India Publication, New Delhi, pp. 192-206

Jain, S.K. (1966): *Medicinal Plants*, National Book trust, New Delhi.

Mead, Margaret (1954): *Cultural patterns and technical change*, UNESCO.

Mittal (1979): Primitive Medicines Versus Modern Medicine among the Santhal, *Jr.Sr.Res*, Vol.22, No.1, pp. 49-54.

MukherjeeD.P, S.K.Nandy (1986): Anthropology of Tribal health: the case of Asur in Netarhat plateau in B.Chaudhary(Ed), *Cultural and environmental dimensions on health*, Inter-India Publication, New Delhi, pp. 247-258.

National Institute of nutrition (1971): Annual report, Hyderabad.

Pingle, U (1975): Some studies in two tribal groups of central India, Plant food for man, 1:195.

Rao, K Sujata (1998): "Health Care Services in Tribal Areas of Andhra Pradesh: A Public policy perspective", *Economic and Political Weekly*, Vol 33, No 9, Pp. 481-48.

Rizvi, S N H (1986): Health Practices of Jaunsaris: A Social Cultural Analysis in Chaudhary, B(Ed), *Tribal health: Socio-cultural dimensions,* Inter India publication, New Delhi, pp. 223-246

Roy, B.K (1986): Morbidity and Nutritional status of the scheduled tribes of India in Chaudhary, B(Ed), *Tribal health: Socio-cultural dimensions,* Inter India publication, New Delhi, pp. 223-246

Sen, A K (1987): *Commodities and Capabilities*, North Holland, Amsterdam.

Sen, D.K. (1986): Some Notes on the Fertility of Jaunsari Women, Eastern Anthropolist, Vol. 10, No.1, pp. 60-67.

Sen, Gita et al. (2002), "Structural reforms and Health Equity; a Comparison of NSS Surveys, 1986-87 and 1995-96, *Economic and Political Weekly*, Vol 37, No 14, Pp. 1342-1352.

Sinha, R.K (1979): Disease and Disease spirits among the Pandu Tribe, Jr.Soc.Research, vol.22, no.1, Pp. 89-96.

Sinha, Sachidanand (2006): "Health Status and Health Care among Tribals: The Case of Jharkhand", in Sujata Prasad and C.Sathyamala (Eds), *Securing Health for All: Dimensions and Challenges*".Instiute for human Development, New Delhi.

6

Health Status of the Elderly in India

A. Balasubramanian

I. Introduction

The riddle of the sphinx aptly summarizes the adaptation of human behaviour to physiological changes over the entire life course. This piece of writing studies behaviour in the last stage of the life course, old age, and addresses the last part of the famous riddle: a stage in life when human functionality is reduced by the onset of chronic health conditions, and by the use of human capital and other resources to compensate for impaired health conditions in old age.

Old age is a natural part of human life. It has been seen as an opportunity for intellectual development, as the elderly [1] persons constitutes the storehouse of knowledge of both past and present and have the ability to predict the future. They play an important role through volunteer work, transmitting experience and knowledge and helping the families with caring responsibilities. Their experience and accumulated wisdom are essential assets in child-rearing and for other adults in the family. Older people are a resource for their families and for the society at large. The efficient use of this (elderly people) capital would benefit the family and the society as a whole, even after their regular employment has been ceased. Hence, care should be taken for maintaining and monitoring the health status of the older peoples, and to recognise that the elderly are not a burden but as an asset and assist them to get ride of their health problem by improving or maintaining their health capital.

Healthy individuals are able to function well in order to perform social roles; ill health reduces their ability to do so. It is widely held belief that advancing age is always associated with poor health, illness and disability. Health is a major concern in later life because it is the most important factor in predicting life satisfaction and well-being of the aged people. Problems related to health are higher for elderly people than for other age groups. Hence, it becomes an important issue as the population of older persons in India is rising significantly.

As longevity of men and women increases, their function of the bodily system deteriorates as age advances. The physiological changes also have negative effect on the function of the brain, leads to progressive loss of functional capacity after a point of maturity. Therefore, it is necessary to assess the covariates of health difficulty in this population group in order to effectively model interventions that will delay the onset of their functional limitations.

II. Background and Literature

Ageing in economics term is described as depreciation of the individual's health capital. The rate at which an individual's health stock depreciates generally varies over his or her life-cycle. It may decline during some periods of life, but eventually, as the individual ages, the depreciation rate increases. Thus, the health capital of older people is likely to deteriorate faster than the health capital of younger people, at least after some years. This depreciation in health capital can be totally or partly offset by gross investments in health. The higher the depreciation rate, however, larger the costs of health investments. Thus, an individual will generally increase his or her gross investment in health as he or she ages, while at the same time his or her health capital declines (Zöllner, et al., 2003).

Population ageing is a universal phenomenon. Of course, it varies from one country to another depends on fertility, mortality rates and migration trends. Ageing of the population, until recently is a concern of the developed countries of the world, has now become an important issue for developing countries, including India. The ageing of the population in India has been steady increasing from 5.6 to 7.9 per cent during 1960-2005 and the growth rate among different cohorts of elderly such as 60 plus, 70 plus and 80 plus during the decade 1961-2005 was much higher of 3 per cent than the general population growth rate of 2 per cent per annum during the period (Rajan, 2006). This has serious implications in terms of how the future elderly - more particularly, the elderly poor will survive and, therefore, is a subject of serious concern with huge policy implications. The multiple problems faced by elderly persons were studied in different disciplines like economics, demography, sociology, psychology, epidemiology, and gerontology.

Recent evidence from India suggests a growing prevalence of morbidity and poor health status along with significant increases in longevity in the elderly population (Alam, 2000). Old people in India, like those in other countries, suffer from a range of problems. However, 'of all the problems associated with an aging population, health care demands top priority' (Ory and Bond 1989).

There have been some excellent studies of the various dimensions of the elderly phenomenon in India carried out over different periods of time e.g., Chanana *et al.*, (1987) dealt with the growth rate of the aged population in India, the dependent population in the non-productive age groups, the old age dependency ratio, sex ratio, marital status, literacy among males and females, and working and nonworking aged. The health status of the aged was also analysed; James (1994) argued about the Indian Elderly is an Asset or Liability for the nation; Reddy (1996) examined the health of the aged in India; Kumar (1999) for the health situation of elderly women, there have been fewer multivariate analyses of the determinants of health status.

Much research work on the population growth and health of the elderly in India was carried out by Rajan *et al.*, (1995, 1996, 2000, 2006) provides recent review of the elderly situation in India. Gupta *et al.*, (2001) analysed the health-seeking behaviour of the elderly and concluded that income and education played key roles in determining who sought care; Mahal (2001) analysed health policy challenges in India; Indrani *et al.*, (2003) have studied the health status of the elderly in India using multivariate analysis on the basis of the data collection in the 52nd round of the NSS in 1995-96.

Sengupta *et al.*, (2003) have studied the gender, health, marriage and mobility difficulty among older adults in India using the data from NSS 42nd round data in 1986-87; Sarmistha (2004) analysed the living arrangements of elderly population by means of children act as old age security in rural India using NSS 52nd round data.; health seeking behaviour of aged population of a rural block in West Bengal studied by Satyajit (2005).

These studies have focused on the different dimensions of the elderly problems and factors affecting health states of the elderly in India consists of statistical correlations, often in the form of empirical nature and of multiple regressions. In such cases, the analysts concerned can do little but simply record the result; since they commonly have no detailed analytical or theoretical framework. These studies have analysed the health status of the elderly in India empirically without any economic theoretical foundation. Advantage of applying a theoretical foundation is well understood by its predicting power and interpretational usage.

The gaps in research also include the lack of information on income and wealth of the elderly in developing countries, the interaction between the wealth of the elderly and their social dependency and the relationship of the elderly living arrangements to health and housing for young people. There are also gaps in knowledge about the effects of socioeconomic conditions on the health of the elderly, changes in risk factors and morbidity, and the needs of the elderly. The present study attempts to fill the gap by studying the health-seeking behaviour of the old age people in India using National Sample Survey 52nd round (1995-96) health care data applying human capital theoretical frame to find out the major factors influencing the health status of the elderly.

III. Conceptual Framework

In the early sixties the classic article of Arrow (1963)

announced the entry of health economics as a new discipline in economics. Some years later, in a study that tried to figure out the importance of the health care sector in the economy, Fuchs (1966) wrote "Good health is one of man's most precious assets". In line with the original economic perspective which recognizes human capital as a determinant of investment and growth, several studies began to consider health not only as a good that individuals consume to enhance their personal satisfaction, but also as a capital stock that allows to increase the number of healthy days useful to work, to earn money and to consume other commodities to enjoy life, and have more opportunity to experience happiness. Health is considered to be both a consumption commodity and an outcome of a production process, which involves medical care and depends on individual behaviour and choices (Balia, 2005).

To study the health related behaviour of households or individuals a well established literature is available at present from the new household economics. In his theory of the allocation of time, Becker (1965) outlined a model where households are seen as producers of "commodities" instead of solely consumers of goods and services. Households are assumed to derive utility from the basic commodities they produce by combining their own time with market goods.

Health commodities are not physical goods like car or computers that are readily manufactured, packaged, and sold in markets or stores. They fall into a category that economists call "household commodities". The study of household commodities, sometimes called "the new home economics", was pioneered by Gary S. Becker in the 1960s. Since then it has greatly expanded the boundaries of economics, enabling economists to analyze behaviour traditionally deemed beyond their reach: health, fertility, education, marriage and divorce, discrimination, and even crime.

In Becker's theory of the allocation of time, households consume and produce commodities, using goods and time as inputs. Investments in human capital and knowledge should be measured in terms of market goods and of the opportunity cost of time lost for competing and alternative uses. The concepts of household production and human capital prove their value by generating testable predictions. Some of these predictions provide theoretical explanations for facts that are already well known but not well understood. Others suggest new lines of empirical research (Iannaccone, 1990).

Economists consider health as human capital for a long time, e.g. Mushkin (1962), Becker (1964) and Fuchs (1966). Following this idea, extension of the conceptual framework of Becker in the context of health was first given by Michael Grossman (1972) in his model of the "demand for health". In that he views "health" both as a pure consumption good, that increases utility, and a pure investment good and states that the demand for health care is derived from the demand for health. His model defines health broadly as longevity and illness-free days in a given year is both demanded and produced by consumers. Health is a choice variable because it is a source of utility (satisfaction) and it determines income or wealth levels. That is, health is demanded by consumers for two reasons. As a consumption commodity, it directly enters their preference functions, or, put differently, sick days are a source of disutility. As an investment commodity, it determines the total amount of time available for market and non-market activities. The derived demand for these inputs depends on a vector of variables such as income, prices, preferences, efficiency in production and health endowments.

Building on the human capital theory, Grossman (1972) provides a formal model to analyze health capital. According to the approach of Grossman, the main distinction between health and education is that health increases income through adding healthy working days while education through improving productivity. Following the standard model of Grossman (1972, 2000) for health, it is assume that the utility function of an elderly person is as follows:

$$U = U(\phi_t H_t, Z_t), \quad t = 0,1,......,n \qquad \textbf{(1)}$$

where H_t is the stock of health capital at time t, ϕ_t is benefit produced by one unit of health capital, $h_t = \phi_t H_t$, with $\phi_t > 0$, is the health consumed at time t, and Z_t is consumption for other goods at time t.

The initial stock of health capital H_0 is exogenous. H_t at other time and the length of life n are endogenous. The following equation describes the change of health capital.

$$H_{t+1} - H_t = I_t - \delta_t H_t \quad \textbf{(2)}$$

where I_t is the investment in health and δ_t is the rate of depreciation of health capital at time t. δ_t is changing with age. Consumers make gross investments in health and the other commodities in the utility function according to a set of household production function: I_t and Z_t are produced by the following equations:

$$I_t = I_t(M_t, TH_t; E) \quad \textbf{(3)}$$

$$Z_t = Z_t(X_t, T_t; E) \quad \textbf{(4)}$$

where M_t are market goods that contribute to the person investments in health at time t (e.g., doctor visits, pharmaceuticals, non traditional medicine, et cetera). TH_t is the time allocated to improve health. E is other exogenous component of human capital besides health, such as education. Equation (4) is home production function for other consumption items Z_t. They are produced by market goods X_t, time T_t and other human capital E (education).

From the point of view of the individual, both market goods and own times are scarce resources. The goods budget constraint equates the present value of outlays on goods to the present value of earnings income over the life cycle plus initial assets. Hence, the consumer faces the following budget constraint:

$$\sum_{t=0}^{n} \frac{P_t M_t + Q_t X_t}{(1+r)^t} = \sum_{t=0}^{n} \frac{W_t TW_t}{(1+r)^t} + A_0 \quad \textbf{(5)}$$

where P_t and Q_t are prices, W_t is wage rate, TW_t is hours of work, r is the discount rate and A_0 is initial wealth.

Beside budget constraint, the consumer also needs to meet the 'Ω' time constraint. Ω must be used up at each period as following:

$$TW_t + T_t + TL_t + TH_t = \Omega \quad (6)$$

where the time constraint implies that total time available is allocated across working time (TW_t), leisure time (T_t), illness time (TL_t) and time investment in the production of health (TH_t).

If we assume that $\partial TL_t / \partial H_t < 0$ (i.e., sick time and stock of health H are inversely related), that the unit of observation is days per year (i.e., $\Omega = 365$), and if ϕ_t is the flow of healthy time per unit of health stock H_t, then h_t is the number of healthy days in a given year, and $TL_t = \Omega - h_t$. In order to obtain an expression of a full wealth constraint of an individual who could be economically active, leisure, or both, assume that the cost of the illness time as well as the time devoted to the production of health is distributed proportionally across leisure and working time

$$\phi_t = \frac{TW_t}{TW_t + T_t}(TL_t + TH_t), \quad (7)$$

where ϕ_t is the proportion at rate W_t and $(1-\phi_t)$ is the proportion at rate T_t. Using this assumption and by substituting for TW_t from Equation (6) into Equation (5), one obtains the single "full wealth" constraint:

$$\sum_{t=0}^{n} \frac{P_t M_t + Q_t X_t + W_t(TL_t + TH_t + T_t)}{(1+r)^t} = \sum_{t=0}^{n} \frac{W_t \Omega}{(1+r)^t} + A_0 \quad (8)$$

According to the Equation (8), full wealth equals initial assets plus the present value of the earnings an individual would obtain if he spent all of his time at work. Part of this wealth is spent on market goods, part of it is spent on non-market production time, and part of it is lost due to illness. The equilibrium quantities of H_t and Z_t can now be found by maximising the utility function given by Equation (1) subject to the constraints given by Equations (2), (3) and (8). Since the inherited stock of health and the rates of depreciation are given, the optimal quantities of gross investment determine the optimal quantities of health capital.

The individual therefore chooses the stock of health H_t and the demand for market goods Z_t that maximizes the utility function (1), subject to the change of health capital equation (2), the health production function (3) and the full wealth constraint (8). Hence, Equations (1) to (8) constitute the Grossman model and they jointly determine the demand for health

Based on the conceptual framework, the demand for health can be studied through two approaches: Pure Investment Model and Pure Consumption Model. Grossman (2000) have stressed "the estimation of the investment model rather than the consumption model because the former model generates powerful predictions from simple analysis and less innocuous assumptions." This paper is based on pure invest model. The first order derivative is:

$$\frac{\pi_{t-1}}{(1+r)^{t-1}} = \frac{W_t G_t}{(1+r)^t} + \frac{(1-\delta_t)W_{t+1}G_{t+1}}{(1+r)^{t+1}} + \ldots + \frac{(1-\delta_t)\ldots(1-\delta_{n-}1)W_n G_n}{(1+r)^n} +$$

$$\frac{Uh_t}{\lambda} G_t + \ldots(1-\delta_t)\ldots(1-\delta_{n-1})\frac{Uh_n}{\lambda} G_n \tag{9}$$

where $G_t = \partial h_t / \partial H_t = -(\partial TL_t / \partial H_t)$ Marginal Product of Health capital; W_t = Hourly wage rate; λ is marginal utility of wealth; π_{t-1} is marginal cost of gross investment in health. The optimal condition of the model is:

$$\frac{G_t W_t}{\pi_{t-1}} + \frac{G_t\left[\left(\frac{U_{ht}}{m}\right)(1+r)^t\right]}{\pi_{t-1}} = r + \delta_t \tag{10}$$

where $G_t = \partial TL_t / \partial H_t$ is the marginal product of health capital, $U_{ht} = \partial U_t / \partial H_t$ is marginal utility directly produced by health, m is marginal utility produced by monetary income, and π_{t-1} is the shadow price of health, which is determined by the cost of health care services, wage rate, et cetera.

Condition (**10**) is similar to other optimal conditions in economics. Namely, it means that marginal benefit equals marginal cost. The benefit of health includes two aspects: one is monetary benefit, i.e. $G_t W_t / \pi_{t-1}$ and the other is utility gain from health, i.e. $(G_t[(U_{ht}/m)(1+r)^t]/\pi_{t-1})$ Cost is the same as cost incurred on other standard investment, including interest and depreciation.

Grossman model provides an analytical framework to understand the relationship between health and its factors. It also allows having a better understanding on how changes in the determinants of health affect the levels of health among individuals and why, according to, the relationship between health with age, education and income, (as a proxy of the wage rate), from the model. This facilitates prediction of differences in the desired health states for different individuals and for one individual over time. It can also be used to analyse the use of medical care, when this is seen as derived demand from the more fundamental demand for health itself. [2]

It is important to note that one of the fundamental implications of Grossman model is that what really matters is stock. Current inputs to health production function and contemporary change of behaviour and life style will have an incremental effect on the stock of health capital, which is determined by the entire history of past, but unlikely will change the stock of health significantly.

Though Grossman model is formulated based on working adults, it is a powerful tool to understand and to analyze health of other age groups as well. Nonetheless, the model has different implication for younger population and older population. For the elderly population being studied here, depreciation factor dominates investment factor. Their health statuses are mainly dictated by the stock of health capital and the rate of depreciation. Factors on health investment will likely have smaller impact than factors on health stock and factors on health depreciation do. Current factors, such as current income, changing of risky behaviour very recently, are unlikely to have big influence, but historical factors, such as life style in the past, permanent income, education level, et cetera, will exhibits larger effect.

IV. Empirical Framework of the Study

The model has been tested in a number of empirical works carried out on the demand for health model (Grossman 1972; Cropper 1981; Wagstaff 1986, 1993; Van Doorslaer, 1987; Leu and Gerfin, 1992; Erbsland et al., 1995; Pohlmeier & Ulrich 1995; Nocera and Zweifel, 1998). The work that has been done has yielded conflicting results, with many that have been inconsistent with the predictions of the model. Measures of health status have been constructed based on various health indicators, e.g. various health problems and symptoms. This has led to problem in interpreting the resulting health measures. There is thus a need for further empirical work on the demand for health model. Unobservable factors might exist, leading to biased estimates and to spurious relationships with the dependent variable 'health'.

To overcome these problems Gerdtham, et al., (1999) recently carried out an analysis with some direct measures of overall health status from a data set from Uppsala Country in Sweden. A categorical measure of overall health status was used that divided health status into three categories: Poor health, fair health, and good health. This type of categorical health measure has been shown to capture important information about the individual's health and to be an important predictor of mortality and morbidity

Self-assessed health status (SAHS) is an increasingly common measure of health in empirical research (e.g. Smith, 1999; Kennedy et al., 1998; Deaton and Paxson, 1998; Schofield, 1996; Ettner, 1996; Saunders, 1996). This is supported by a literature that shows that SAHS predicts mortality and morbidity (e.g. Idler and Kasl, 1995; McCallum et al., 1994; Connelly et al., 1989; Okun et al., 1984). Furthermore, Gerdtham et al. (1999) have demonstrated that a continuous health status measure constructed from a categorical response by the method of Wagstaff and van Doorslair (1994) is highly correlated with other continuous measures of health. In this paper health is measured by Self-assessed health status measure with four categories in an increasing order from poor to excellent health status.

V. Econometric Specification of the Model

The empirical estimation is based on Grossman's basic model, but considering the data availability slight modifications are made. Maximization of the utility function subject to the health production function (**3**) and full wealth constraint (**8**) yields the following demand for health function at time t, the reduced form demand function for health as a linear model (**11**) that relates health with its determinants, The purpose of the reduced form is to solve out for the endogenous variables in the system by expressing health as a function of all the exogenous variables, according to the availability of data, is expressed as follows:

$$H_t = f(H_{t-1}, A_t, E_t, Y_t, WR_t, DV_t, HP_t, HB_{t-1}, \varepsilon_t) \qquad \textbf{(11)}$$

where the stock of health capital in the demand for health model for the elderly depends on the past health status which is included in five scale points as relative health status from better to worse with a reference period of one year. H_{t-1} is the previous year health status reported by the individual himself as a relative status of current level. In order to accommodate the nonlinearity of age, we adopt two approaches. One is using age or age squared and the other is using age group dummies, A_t is the rate of depreciation of health capital, age is used.

The human capital variable is E_t, indicates the level of education, in the Grossman model it is assumed to increase the productivity of producing health. Y_t is the income variable, due to the non availability of the income data a better proxy variable of household monthly consumption expenditure was used (Deaton, (1997), Blundell (1995) and Dachs (2002)) it reflects more accurately the consumption on daily life issues among individuals in the households such as, food, health, education and housing. For wage rate a proxy variable of past employment status was used due to data inadequacy. Other demographic and social variables like gender, marital status, region, social group, household size and number of children's are included and health problems like any chronic ailment, physical immobile and functional disability and past habits like Alcohol drinking, smoking et cetera, are used, ε_t stands for non-observable attributes. The price variable is not included in the empirical analysis due to the non availability of the data.

The reduced form health demand function (**11**) to be estimated is specified as:

$$H_t = \beta_1 H_{t-1} + \beta_2 A_t + \beta_3 E_t + \beta_4 HMCE_t + \beta_5 EMP_{t-1} + \beta_6 G_t + \beta_7 R_t + \beta_8 SG_t + \beta_9 NS_t + \beta_{10} ND_t$$
$$+ \beta_{11} MS_t + \beta_{12} HHSZ_t + \beta_{13} HP_t + \beta_{14} PIM_t + \beta_{15} HB_{t-1} + \varepsilon_t \qquad \textbf{(12)}$$

where Equation (12) cannot be estimated directly because the health status H_t, at period t, is not observable. So a latent variable model is used for estimation. β_1 - β_{15} are coefficients to be estimated and ε_t is an error term with zero mean and constant variance.

VI. Estimation Method

The statistical model for health demand should take account of a special feature of the health data – health status, is recorded as a categorical variable with 4 response categories which represents the excellent, very good, fair and poor health status. An appropriate specification for similarly recoded responses where the categories represent choices is the multinomial probit or logit model. However, the application of such models here would fail to account for the ordinal nature of the dependent variable. According to Greene (2000), ordinary regression analysis would err in the opposite direction, however. That is, linear regression would treat the difference between two adjacent response codes as the same, irrespective of where they lie in the distribution of responses, whereas in the fact they are only a ranking.

The most common way to deal with ordered response data is to use an ordered qualitative response model, usually either the ordered probit model or the ordered logit model. The key feature of ordered qualitative response models is that all the choices depend on a single index function. Ordered probit model is designed to model a discrete dependent variable that takes ordered multinomial outcomes. For example, h = 0,1,2,3... it should be stressed that h is measured on an ordinal scale and the numerical values of h are arbitrary, except that they must be in ascending order.

A linear dependence between health and the regressor variables is assumed between latent health variable h_i* and x_i, β, and e_i:

$$h_i^* = \beta' x_i + e_i,\ e_i \sim N(0, \sigma^2)$$

The health variable h_i* defines variable h_i, which is related to the self-reported health has four health categories: poor, fair/good, very good and excellent is used, many investigations has also used this measures.

The health variable h_i and h_i* are related in the following way (where 0, 1, 2, 3 are unobservable thresholds θ_i):

$$h_i = 0 \quad if\ h_i^* \le \theta_0$$

$$h_i = 1 \quad if\ \theta_0 < h_i^* \le \theta_1$$

$$h_i = 2 \quad if\ \theta_1 < h_i^* \le \theta_2$$

$$h_i = 3 \quad if\ \theta_2 < h_i^*$$

For the estimations an ordered probit method is used (Maddala, 1983; Agresti, 1996; Johnston and DiNardo, 1997; Gerdtham and Johannesson, 1999; Greene, 2000).

Probability of observing health status h_i can be expressed as

$$\Pr ob(health = 1) = \Pr ob(\mu_{i-1} < \beta' x + e_j < \mu_i)$$

The model estimates the parameter vector β' along with the three cut points (μ_i).When normally distributed, the probabilities are:

$$\Pr ob(h = 0) = \phi(\mu_0 - \beta' x),$$

$$\Pr ob(h = 1) = \phi(\mu_1 - \beta' x) - \phi(\mu_0 - \beta' x),$$

$$\Pr ob(h = 2) = \phi(\mu_2 - \beta' x) - \phi(\mu_1 - \beta' x),$$

$$\Pr ob(h = 3) = 1 - \phi(\mu_2 - \beta' x)$$

where ϕ is the cumulative distribution function of ε. The threshold values μ are estimated along with the β coefficients by maximizing the log likelihood function:

$$l(\beta,\mu)=\sum_{i=1}^{N}\sum_{j=0}^{M}\log(\Pr ob(h_i=j|x_i,\beta,\mu))\cdot 1(h_i=j)$$

where $l(\cdot)$ is an indicator function which takes the value 1 if the argument is true, and 0 if the argument is false. Given four choices, without loss of generality Prob(h=3) can be set to 0 (as a reference), leaving only three thresholds to estimate: μ_i = 1,2,3 without a constant term.

With $\alpha = \beta/\sigma$ and $\mu_{j-1}/\sigma = \theta_j$, 0, 1, i.e., to note that only the ratios β/σ and μ_{j-1}/σ are estimable (Dustman 1996). If the regression contains a constant term, the full set of coefficients is not identified. A common normalization is to set $\mu_0 = 0$ which means that the estimated coefficients μ_i, i=1 represent the differences in the respective thresholds: $\mu_i = \mu_i - \mu_{i-1}$ (Greene 2000; Dustman 1996). Greene (1993) points out that the interpretation of the estimates is not straightforward. A positive estimate indicates that an increase in the respective variable shifts weight from category 0 (poor) into category 3 (excellent), which means that the probability of category 3 increases and the probability of category 0 decreases.

VII. Data and Variables

To carry out the analysis, National Sample Survey 52nd Round health care survey data for the year 1995-96 has been used. This round contains a sample size of 20949 for rural and 13032 for urban and a total of 33,981 households in the above 60 years age and which covers one forth of the total sample sizes. After a careful examination of the data omitting the missing case the employed sample stood at 33,490 households.

The 52nd round of the NSS provides data on the *morbidity patterns, use of medical facility, hospitalisation* and related details for the general population for 1995-96. This part of the survey has been used to extract data for the elderly. In addition, there is a special module on the elderly, which provides data on the various aspects of the elderly: these pertain to information on physical mobility, disability [3], current state of health [4], relative state of health [5], details regarding the withdrawal from economic activity, management of financial assets belonging to the aged et cetera. Both these modules have been used extensively in this analysis. Information on whether economically active, state of economic independence, amount of loans, living arrangements et cetera are also used for the analysis.

The definition and coding of endogenous and exogenous variables used in the analysis along with its expected sign from the theoretical model is presented in Table 6.1. The descriptive statistics for the data employed in the analysis is provided in Table 6.2. The frequency distribution statistics for the dependent and independent variables expressed in categorical forms, along with its marginal percentages are presented in Table 6.3. While estimating the reduced form demand function for health Equation (12), two models were used one with the past health status and another without the past health status.

VIII. Estimation Results

The statistical results are reported in this section. The ordered probit estimated effects of the covariates on the categorical health measure for the sample data are reported in the Table 6.4 containing two models. The goodness of fit values (pseudo R^2) [6] is at satisfactory level of 0.265 and 0.114. The explanatory power of equations (12) might seem low, but it is important to recall they are estimated from a large cross-section of over 30000 individuals, notes that 0.20 is a typical value of pseudo R^2 for various household behaviour functions estimated from a cross-section of above 3000 Kmenta (1971). Gerdtham and Johannesson (1999) in their paper they reported pseudo R^2 values are about 0.10 for the full sample and 0.07 for the employed sample. Medical demand models have generally had even lower values. Reviewing results where ordinary least squares had been used to estimate some form of a demand function for physician's care, Grossman's (1972) seminal study reports value of R^2 around 0.07, Newhouse and Phelps (1976) report values around 0.16, and Sindelar (1982) reports values of 0.11. Kenkel (1990) reports values of R^2 around 0.05 to 0.09 in his demand model.

With the ordered probit model the probability of each category is estimated a positive regression coefficient means that an increase in the respective variable decrease the probability of poor health and increase the probability of good health. The Ordered Probit coefficients [7] results are presented in the Tables 6.4.

The statistical results are reported in two models: one with the past health status (a lagged variable (one year)) and the model without that variable. Table 6.4 shows estimates for the four category measure of self-assessed health, it includes the coefficients, z – value and the probability or significance level. It also includes estimates of the threshold parameters μ_1, μ_2, and μ_3 (labelled as Cut point 1, cut point 2, and cut point3). These implies that a value of the latent variable less than 0.716 (model 1), –0.308 (model 2) corresponds to poor health, a value between 0.716 and 3.615 (model 1), –0.308 and 2.165 (model 2) corresponds to fair or good health, a value between 3.615 and 4.74 (model 1), 2.165 and 3.121 (model 2) corresponds to very good health and a value above 4.74 (model 1), 3.121(model 2) corresponds to excellent health.

Model 1 Estimations

As expected relative health status significantly influence the present health status at ($P<0.01$). As expected age square significantly decreases the demand for health, i.e. the estimated effects of AGESQR are negative and significant ($P<0.01$) but the age variable expressed in categorical term (AGE1, AGE2, AGE3) had no significant result. The estimated effects of household monthly consumption expenditure HMCE on the demand for health are clearly positive, i.e. the estimated effects of are significant ($P<0.01$). These effects tend to increase with increasing health status hence the proxy variable has resulted supportive evidence. Employment status as a proxy for wage rate worked out well it showed the expected positive result at highly significant level ($P<0.01$).

The human capital variable education has a negatively effect on health status if it is given in categorical form, indicates that individuals with higher education are not more efficient producers of health as the reference category is of higher level and above compared to that level all other levels resulted in negative sign at (P<0.01).

The estimated effect of the gender variables (MALE) and region variable (Rural) is negative and significant (P<0.01). Considering the social group it showed a positive and significant result as control for SC/ST other groups have better chance to be in good health. Finally, the additional variable included in the equation like number of children's, sons and daughters, in that Sons have positively significant result (P<.10), household size, health problems have negative and highly significant results (P<.01) except for the risk factor which produced positive and significant result.

Model 2 Estimations

As in the first model AGESQR had the same result for model 2 also. The estimated effects of education as continues scale is positive and significant (P<.01) as expected from the basic model. On the demand for health are clearly positive, i.e. the estimated effects of HMCE and EMPLY are significant (P<0.01) and positive. Gender (MALE) and Region (RURAL) had yielded significant (P<0.01) and negative results. Compared to female children's male ones take care the elderly was shown by the significant results of NSONS as positive and NDAUG as negative. Household size showed a negative and significant result. Health problems like acute disability and chronic health problems have showed the expected negative sign at highly significant level (P<0.01). Physical immobility expressed as the elderly is completely mobile in the higher order has resulted in the expected positive sign with highly significant level (P<0.01). Over all the results show that model 2 possess more clear results than model 1 after controlling for the lagged variable relative health status, but the explanatory power was higher for model 1 then the other one.

IX. Concluding Remarks

Applying Grossman model, the health determinants for elderly population in India is studied based on self-reported categorical health status. The econometric approach adopted here is reduced form cross-sectional analysis. Finally, it is important to note some limitations of the study. One limitation concerns the fact that there may be some omitted variables which affect the demand for health (e.g. the distance to health care services, affecting the effective price of medical care). This could lead to omitted variables bias. Another limitation concerns causality. For some variables there could be problems with reversed causality, e.g. that the health status affects income and education rather than the other way round. If this is the case, the estimated effects of income and education will be biased, along with the effects of all other correlated regressors. Unfortunately, the lack of instruments precludes any formal tests of endogeneity. In spite of these limitations I think that the results are interesting and provide some support for the demand for health model and provide an insight into the factors determining the health status of the elderly peoples in India.

I acknowledge my research guide Dr. P. Arumugam, Former Professor of Economics, Bharathiar University, Coimbatore for his continuous inspiration and valuable guidance, and my sincere thanks owes to Prof. Ulf-G. Gerdtham, Department of Economics, Stockholm School of Economics, Sweden for his valuable comments.

Table 6.1: Definition of the Variables Used in the Analysis

Variable	Definition	Expected Sign
	Dependent variable	
Categorical Health	Assessment of own health on a three-point scale (0=poor, 1=fair/ good, 2= very good and 3=excellent)	
	Independent variables	Expected Sign
RHS1	= 1,2,3,4,5 (Much Better to Much Worse)	(β' >0) +Ve
AGE1	= 1 if age is 60-69 years	(β' <0) – Ve
AGE2	= 1 if age is 70-79 years	(β' >0) – Ve
AGE3	= 1 if age is 80 < years	(β' >0) – Ve
AGESQR	= Age Square	(β' <0) – Ve
EDUC1	= 1 if Illiterate	(β' <0) – Ve
EDUC2	= 1 if Literate education	(β' >0) +Ve
EDUC3	= 1 If Middle and Secondary education	(β' >0) +Ve
EDUC4	= 1 if Higher and above education	(β' >0) +Ve

Contd...

HMCE	= Household Monthly Consumption Expenditure (Proxy for Income, applied in log form)	(β' >0) +Ve
EMPLY	= 1 if employed as Regular/salaried/waged in past; 2- Unemployed	(β' >0) +Ve
REGION	= 1 if the individual lives on Rural	(β' <0) – Ve
GENDER	= 1 if Male	(β' <0) – Ve
MS	= 1 if Separate/Divorce/Single	(β' <0) – Ve
SOCIAL GROUP	= 1 if SC/ST	(β' < 0) – Ve
HHSZ	is household size	(β' >0) + Ve
NSON	Number of Sons	(β' >0) + Ve
NDAUG	Number of Daughters	(β' >0) + Ve
HP	Number of health problem (any one or more acute disability and any one or more chronic health problem)	(β' <0) – Ve
PIM	= 1 if he/she is Physical completely mobile	(β' >0) + Ve
HB	Number of bad habit / risk behaviour	(β' <0) – Ve

Table 6.2: Sample Descriptive Statistics

Variable	Description	Mean	SD.	Min.	Max.	N.
Health	Categorical	.9274	.5672	0	3	33490
RHS	Categorical	3.1924	.6820	1	5	33490
AGE1	Dummy (60-69)	.6216	.4849	0	1	33490
AGE2	Dummy (70-79)	.2844	.4511	0	1	33490
AGE3	Dummy (80 and above)	.0939	.2917	0	1	33490
AGESQR	Square Age	4656.19	1022.37	3600	9801	33490
EDUC1	Dummy (Illiterate)	.6335	.4818	0	1	33490
EDUC2	Dummy (Literate)	.2196	.4139	0	1	33490
EDUC3	Dummy (Middle)	.1066	.3086	0	1	33490
EDUC4	Dummy (Higher above)	.0403	.1966	0	1	33490
EDUC	Categorical	.6665	.9503	0	3	33490
HMCE	Log MHHCE	7.647	.6774	4	10	33490
EMPLY	Dummy (Yes) Wage	.3257	.4686	0	1	33490

Contd...

GENDER	Dummy (Male)	.5074	.4998	0	1	33490
MS	Dummy (Separate)	.5927	.4913	0	1	33490
SG	Dummy (SC/ST)	.2321	.4221	0	1	33490
REGION	Dummy (Rural)	.6162	.4863	0	1	33490
NSONS	Continuous number	2.2535	1.462	0	10	33490
NDAUG	Continuous number	1.996	1.439	0	10	33490
HHSZ	Continuous number	6.0821	2.630	0	10	33490
HPACT	Dummy (Yes)	.6411	1.008	0	5	33490
HPCRN	Dummy (Yes)	.8283	.9501	0	8	33490
PIM	Categorical	2.866	.3952	1	3	33490
HB	Continuous number	.5123	.6778	0	5	33490

Note: SD: - Standard Deviation; Min: - Minimum; Max: - Maximum; N: - Sample Size.

Table 6.3: Frequency Distribution Statistics and Marginal Percentage of the Sample Dependent and Independent Variables

Dependent Variable	Frequency	Marginal %
Health		
0 Poor	6222	18.6
1 Fair/Good	23944	71.5
2 Very Good	2855	8.5
3 Excellent	469	1.4
Independent Variables	Relative Health Status	
1 Much better	587	1.8
2 Some what better	2117	6.3
3 Nearly the same	22359	66.8
4 Some what worse	7118	21.3
5 Much worse	1309	3.9
Region		
0 Urban	12853	38.4
1 Rural	20637	61.6
Gender		
0 Female	16339	49.1

Contd...

1 Male	16905	50.9
Age		
1 (60-69)	20819	62.2
2 (70-79)	9526	28.4
3 (80 and above)	3145	9.4
Education		
0 (Illiterate)	21030	63.3
1 (Literate; Primary, below)	3551	10.7
2 (Meddle, Secondary)	7318	22.0
3 (Higher and above)	1345	4.0
Social Group		
0 (Others)	25546	76.8
1 (SC/ST)	7698	23.2
Marital Status		
0 (Married)	13512	40.6
1 (Separate/Widow/Single)	19732	59.4
Health Problem		
0 (No)	13185	38.9
1 (Yes)	20305	61.1
Physical Immobile 0 (No) immobile bed, home	3775	11.4
1 (Yes) completely mobile	29469	88.6

Table 6.4: Ordered Probit Model: Maximum Likelihood Estimation Results Dependent Variable: Health (Sahs Categorical)

Exogenous variables	β'	z - value	Sig.	β'	z –value	Sig.
	Model 1			Model 2		
RHS(1)	4.034*	3.959	.000	--	--	--
RHS(2)	3.595*	3.531	.000	--	--	--
RHS(3)	2.564*	2.507	.000	--	--	--
RHS(4)	1.525*	1.466	.000	--	--	--
RHS(5)	Reference category			--	--	--
AGE1	0.074	0.017	.198	0.100***	1.873	.061
AGE2	0.019	-0.021	.634	0.046	1.262	.207
AGE3	Reference category					
AGESQR	–0.206*	-0.250	.000	–0.281*	-6.945	.000
EDUC	--	--	--	0.126*	12.511	.000
EDUC0	–0.323*	8.494	.000	--	--	--

Contd…

EDUC1	–0.117*	3.010	.003	--	--	--
EDUC2	–0.223*	5.868	.000	--	--	--
EDUC3	Reference category			--	--	--
HMCE (LN)	0.178*	0.161	.000	0.167*	10.837	.000
EMPLY (WAGE)	0.343*	0.324	.000	0.403*	23.307	.000
GENDER (M)	–0.044**	-0.063	.025	–0.070*	-3.893	.000
GENDER (F)	Reference category					
REGION (R)	–0.090*	-0.107	.000	–0.157*	-9.789	.000
MS (0)	–0.018	-0.035	.290	–0.010	-0.607	.544
MS (1)	Reference category					
SG (0)	0.039**	0.021	.030	0.026	1.548	.122
SG(1) (SC/ST)	Reference category					
NSONS	0.009***	0.003	.095	0.013*	2.598	.009
NDAUG	0.003	-0.002	.514	–0.009**	-1.973	.048
HSIZE	–0.015*	-0.019	.000	–0.017*	-4.521	.000
PIM	0.4974*	22.609	.000	0.6446*	33.325	.000

Contd...

ACUTE	–0.177*	-0.185	.000	–0.239*	-32.171	.000
CHRONIC – 1	–0.220*	-0.228	.000	–0.261*	-34.098	.000
RISK	0.024**	0.011	.055	0.027**	2.367	.027
$[\mu_1 - \mu_0]$cut point 1	0.716	1.7294	.084	–0.308	.9655	.335
$[\mu_2 - \mu_1]$cut point 2	3.615	8.7318	.000	2.165	6.786	.000
$[1 - \mu_2]$ cut point 3	4.740	11.421	.000	3.121	9.753	.000
Sample Size	33490			33490		
-2 Log likelihood	40493.76			48799.562		
Pseudo R2	.265			.114		

Significance Level: (*** 0.05<p<0.10 for 10 per cent level; ** 0.01<p<0.05 for 5 per cent level and * P<0.01 for 1 per cent level).

Notes

1. The elderly is defined in terms of those aged 60 and above in a population.

2. The empirical model of the present study differs from the original Grossman model (1972, 2000), hence, the original Grossman model is estimated using log-log specification but here a linear regression model was applied.

3. Morbidity prevalence rate and disability rate will be calculated for their objective assessment of health.

4. Respondents were asked to evaluate their current health status in four response categories, (1) excellent, (2) very good, (3) good/fair and (4) poor (i.e., subjective measurement of health). I have recoded it in ascending order as (0) poor, (1) fair/good, (2) very good and (3) excellent.

5. Respondents were asked to evaluate their health status as compared to previous year in five response categories, (1) much better, (2) somewhat better, (3) nearly the same, (4) somewhat worse and (5) worse (i.e., the subjective assessment of health).

6. The popular McFadden Pseudo R^2 is used (Pseudo R^2 = 1– exp ((– 2*(LU– LR/n)), where LU is the unrestricted log likelihood values and LR is the restricted log likelihood values (Magee, 1990)). The results presented in the Table shows the McFadden Pseudo R^2 values and the z values (similar to t – statistics).

7. In the case of ordered probit coefficients, the coefficient explains how much difference a unit change in the independent makes in terms of the cumulative normal probability of the dependent variable. This means the probit coefficient measures the effect of the independent on the z scores of the dependent. Note that the probability of the dependent is not a linear function of z, but rather is a cumulative normal function of z. the sample means of the independents into the probit regression equation to get the estimated z score, then one looks in a table of the standard normal distribution to find the corresponding probability level. Z score is computed using the formula $z = \beta' / s$, where β' is the estimated coefficient and s is the estimated standard error.

References

Alam, Moneer (2000): Ageing in India: A country profile, *Bold*, Vol. 10, No. 3, pp. 5-22.

Becker, G.S. (1964): *Human Capital*, Columbia University Press for the National Bureau of Economic Research, New York.

Becker, G.S. (1965): A theory of the allocation of time, *The Economic Journal*, Vol. No. 75, pp. 493–517.

Blundell, R. (1995): Income, expenditure and living standards of UK households, *Fiscal Studies*, Vol. 16, No.3, pp. 40-54.

Chanana, H.B. and P.P. Talwar (1987): Aging in India: its socio-economic and health implications, *Asia Pacific Population Journal*, Vol. 2, No.3, pp. 23-38.

Deaton, A. (1997): The Analysis of household surveys: A micro econometric approach to development policy, World Bank, Washington DC.

Dilip, T.R. (2002): Understanding levels of morbidity and hospitalization in Kerala, India, *Bulletin of the World Health Organization*, Vol. 80, No.9, pp. 746-751.

Ferraro, K.F. (1980): Self-ratings of health among the old and old–old, *Journal of Health and Social Behaviour*, Vol. 21, pp. 377–383.

Fuchs, R.V. (1966): The contribution of Health Services to the American Economy, NBER, New York.

Gerdtham, Ulf and M. Johannesson, (1999): New estimates of the demand for health: results based on a categorical health measures and Swedish micro data, *Social Science and Medicine*, Vol. 49, pp. 1325 -1332.

Greene, W.H. (1993): *Econometric Analysis*, Second Ed., Macmillan Publishing Company, New York.

... (2000): *Econometric Analysis*, Upper Saddle River, Prentice Hill, N.J.

Grossman, M. (1972): On the concept of health capital and the demand for health, *Journal of Political Economy*, Vol. 80, pp. 223–255.

... (2000): The human capital model, In Culyer, A.J. and J.P. Newhouse, (Eds.), *Handbook of Health Economics*, Vol. 1A, Elsevier, Amsterdam, pp. 347–408.

Government of India (1999): *National Policy on Older Persons*, Ministry of Social Justice and Empowerment, New Delhi.

Gupta, I., P. Dasgupta and M. Sawhney (2001: Health of the Elderly in India: Some Aspects of Vulnerability, Discussion Paper Series No 26, Institute of Economic Growth, University Enclave, Delhi.

Hatasa, Nobuhide (2001) Health and economic development: a cross-national empirical analysis, *Journal of National Institute of Public Health*, Vol. 50, No.3, pp. 168 -180.

Haveman, R.B. Wolfe, B. Kreider, F. M. Huang (1989): Disability status as an unobservable: estimates from a structural model, NBER

Working Paper No. 2831.

Indrani, Gupta, P. Dasgupta and M. Sawhney (2001): Health of the Elderly in India: Some Aspects of Vulnerability, Discussion Paper Series No 26, Institute of Economic Growth, University Enclave, Delhi.

Rajan, S. I. (2006): *Population Ageing and Health in India*, Centre for Enquiry into Health and Allied Themes, Survey No. 2804 and 2805, Mumbai.

..., U.S. Mishra, and P.S. Sarma (1999): *India's Elderly: Burden Or Challenge?* Sage Publications, Thousand Oaks.

..., U.S. Mishra and P. S. Sharma (1995): Living Arrangements among the Indian Elderly, *Hong Kong Journal of Gerontology*, Vol. 9, No. 2, pp. 20-28.

Kumar, P.V, 1999, "Elderly Women in Rural India: Need for Policy Intervention" *Help Age India*, 5 (3), pp. 27-30

LaRue, A., Bank, L., Jarvic, L., Hewtland, M., 1979. Health in old age: how physicians' ratings and self-ratings compare. *Journal of Gerontology* Vol. 34, 687–691.

Lairson, David Lorimor., Ronald Slater., 1984, Estimates of the Demand for Health: Males in Pre-retirement years, *Social Science and Medicine*, Vol. 19 (7): 741 -747.

Maddox, G., Douglas, E., 1973. Self-assessment of health: a longitudinal study of elderly subjects. *Journal of Health Social Behavior*, Vol. 14 (1), 87–93.

Magee, L., 1990, "R2 measures based on Wald and likelihood ratio joint significance tests", *The American Statistician* Vol. 44, pp: 250-253.

Mahal, A., 2001 "Health Policy Challenges in India: Some Lessons from the International Experience" NCAER.

Manisha Sengupta and Emily M. Agree., 2003. Gender, Health, Marriage and Mobility Difficulty among Older Adults in India, *Asia-Pacific Population Journal*, Vol. 18, No. 4: 53-65.

Martin, Linda G. 1990. The status of South Asia's growing elderly population. *Journal of Cross Cultural Gerontology* Vol. 5, (2) :93-117.

Mossey, J.M., Shapiro, E., 1982. Self-rated health: a predictor of mortality among the elderly *American Journal of Public Health*, Vol. 72, 800–808.

Nagi, S.Z., 1969. Congruency in medical and self-assessment of disability. *Indian Medicine*, Vol. 38, 74–83.

National Sample Survey Organization (NSSO). 52nd Round unit level data record of Survey on Health Care (52/25.0/1), Department of Statistics, Government of India, (June 1995- July 1996).

National Sample Survey Organization. The Aged in India A Socio-Economic Profile. NSSO Report Number 446 (52/25.0/3), Department of Statistics, Government of India, 1998.

Ory, Marcia G. and Kathleen Bond. 1989. Introduction: health care for an aging society. In *Aging and Health Care: Social Science and Policy Perspectives,* ed. Marcia G. Ory and Kathleen Bond. London: Routledge.

Prakash Jai Indira. Ageing in India. WHO, 1992 available from: http://www.who.int/hpr/ageing/ageinginindia .pdf

Reddy, P. H., 1996 "The health of the aged in India", *Health Transition Review,* Supplement to Volume 6, 1996, 233-244.

Sarmistha Pal., 2004. "Do Children Act as Old Age Security in Rural India? Evidence from an Analysis of Elderly Living Arrangements, *Working Paper 22* Cardiff Business School, UK.

Satyajit Chakraborty., 2005. "Health Seeking Behaviour of Aged Population of a Rural Block in West Bengal", *Working Paper* No. 8, Achutha Menon Centre For Health Science Studies, Thiruvananthapuram, Kerala.

Sisira K. Sarma., 2003. "Demand for Outpatient Health Care in Rural India: A Nested Multinomial Logit Approach", Department of Economics, The University of Manitoba, Winnipeg, MB.

Silvia Balia, 2005 "Health and Economic Behaviour: a Critical Survey of the Literature", *Working Paper* No. 2005/05, University of Cagliari and University of York.

Subrata Mukherjee 2003. "Socio-economic Inequalities in Health Care Utilisation in Indian States Evidence from NSS 52nd Round Data on Inpatient Care", Working Paper, Centre for Development Studies, Thiruvananthapuram.

Soumitra Ghosh., 2004. "Levels and Differentials of Morbidity in West Bengal", Seminar Paper for Master in Population Studies, IIPS, Mumbai.

Zöllner H., G. Stoddart and C. Selby Smith, 2003, "Chapter II Economics of health" *Learning to live with Health Economics*, ed. H. Zöllner, World Health Organization.

7

Referral Transport Scheme for Emergency Obstetric Care under RCH- Phase-I, Rajasthan

Manisha Chawla

I. Rationale of the study

India accounts for the highest estimated number of maternal deaths in the world (1,36,000) and has a very high maternal mortality ratio of 407 per 1, 00,000 live births, in the country. The maternal mortality ratio is a measure of the obstetric risk faced by a woman each time she becomes pregnant. Where women have many pregnancies, the risk of maternal death is magnified. The tragedy is that these women die not from any disease but during the normal, life-generating process of procreation. Most of these deaths cam be avoided if preventive measures are taken and adequate care is available during pregnancy and childbirth

Around eighty per cent of all maternal deaths are the direct result of complications arising during pregnancy, delivery, or the puerperium. The factors underlying the direct causes of maternal deaths operate at several levels. The low social status of women limits their ability to make decisions related to their health and nutrition. Women are denied access to care when it is needed either because of cultural practices of seclusion or because decision-making is the responsibility of other family members. Lack of access to and use of essential obstetric services is a crucial factor that contributes to high maternal mortality. Most of the states in the country face the problems of the tough geographical conditions, hilly and tribal areas, which have very weak communication infrastructure and the economic status of many families in villages, is also very low. In such a situation untrained birth attendants are forced to conduct home deliveries in spite of identification of complications.

Most of the obstetric complications cannot be predicted but can be detected and treated, underscoring the importance of early recognition of danger signs and proper referral at an appropriate health centre. Various studies have shown that most maternal deaths occur as a result of the "Three Delays", delay in deciding to seek medical care, delay in reaching medical facility with adequate care, and delay in receiving quality emergency obstetric care. To prevent the second delay i.e. delay in reaching the health facility at the time of emergency, the Government of India had initiated a scheme called "Referral Transport Scheme" under the first phase of the Reproductive and Child Health (RCH) Programme in 1999-2000, to promote access of women with obstetric emergencies to the first referral units.

Under the scheme, a sum of Rs. 70.8 lakh was allocated to Gram Panchayats for transportation of emergency cases to promote prompt access to services, in the first year, more money was to follow in the later years. Out of this first installment, a sum of Rs. 15.96 lakh (22.5 per cent) was spent to benefit 3,415 women till 31st January, 2005, in a period of 4-5 years. Initially, the Panchayats were entrusted with the disbursement of funds at the village level to ensure the ready access to money for referral transport. Fund was to be utilized for providing facility of a hired vehicle to bring pregnant woman to nearby referral health centre in case of obstetric emergency or for institutional delivery. The Panchayat Raj functionaries had a central role in this scheme, which with support of an ANM were to prepare the list of such pregnant women and would also make vehicle arrangements in advance. Due to poor utilization of funds and lack of active participation of the panchayats (reasons for this can be sought), later, referral funds were provided to ANMs of the sub-centers of a Gram Panchayat concerned to improve the implementation of the scheme.

Referral Transport Scheme being implemented through Gram Panchayats was a non- starter but gradually the scheme has picked up in a few districts. Keeping in view, low utilization (even non-utilization at some places) of the funds under the scheme, UNICEF, proposed to assess the referral transport scheme for emergency obstetric care under Phase-I of Reproductive and Child Health Programme. The present study was an effort to assess the utilization and factors facilitating and obstructing for the implementation of the scheme.

II. Objectives

The following are the specific objectives of the study:

- To assess perceptions of users and non-users about the scheme.
- To assess the utilization of funds under Referral Transport Scheme by the districts and beneficiaries.
- To identify the factors that affected the implementation and utilization of the scheme.
- To find out the reasons for the non-use of the Referral Transport Scheme for obstetric emergencies under the Programme.
- To find out the reasons facilitating or hindering the process of release of funds under the scheme at different levels.
- To elicit suggestions from the users, non-users and programme managers for increasing the access and utilization of the poor women.

III. Database and Methodology

Sample Selection: The Referral Transport Scheme was operational in more than half of the districts in this state. Based on the utilization of funds earmarked/released, these districts were further classified into three categories. The districts as per categorization were: **Better Performing Districts** (where fund utilization rate was more than 50 per cent of the released fund), **Under Performing Districts** (where fund utilization rate was less than 50 per cent of the released fund) and **Non Performing Districts** (where fund utilization was nil). For the purpose of the study, one district from each of the above mentioned categories was selected. Further, from each of these districts two blocks were selected and from each block 4-6 villages were covered to interview 25 respondents from each block and a minimum of four FGDs were conducted per block. The sampling of districts, blocks, and villages was based on the simple random method.

After the districts were finalized, some basic information was collected from these districts including block wise and village wise lists of beneficiaries along with the amount that was paid to them.

Besides the beneficiaries, the study team also interviewed health providers, Panchayat Samiti members, block officials, district officials and state officials, to assess their perception, and to find out the facilitating and hindering factors of the scheme.

The present study was both quantitative and qualitative in nature. The data collection methods included focus group discussions, in-depth interviews and case studies and mobility mapping besides the use of structured questionnaires to study the factors affecting the utilization of the scheme.

IV. Major Findings

Perception of Users and Non-users: The perception of the scheme among the users and non-users was assessed through a pre-designed questionnaire and focused group discussions. The data thus collected from the users and non-users was then compared, on various socio-demographic variables. The two groups (users and non-users) were almost similar in respect to age, caste, occupational status, economic status, age at marriage and emergency problems experienced. Therefore, it can be said that two samples were quite comparable.

The socio-demographic variables where users differed from the non-users were: literacy rate and birth preparedness. These are those variables with which use of the scheme can easily be associated.

Knowledge about the scheme was the only variable where a significant difference was seen comparing the users' and the non-users' profile. Among those who were listed in the records of

Reproductive Child Health Office (RCHO) as users, only 78 per cent had heard about the scheme and 22 per cent of the users had never even heard of the scheme (In one of the districts, the percentage of listed users who had never heard about the scheme was 40 per cent).

Among the non-users, only 5 per cent reported knowledge about the scheme. Can we say, 'how can those people use the scheme, who have never heard of it', and this is a large number, as it can be predicted by non-users' data.

Out of the 60 listed users, only 47 had heard about the scheme and 37 women reported to receive money for the transport used to reach the health facility for the delivery.

Even listed users who were supposed to receive money without any repercussion did not report to receive the allocated money from the distribution agents. Most of such users were found in District I (Churu), where only nine women out of 30 listed users reported to have received money for the transport. Among the ones who received, half of them got their payment in time while, in the rest, waiting period ranged within 2-4 months.

In District II (Baran), two-third (20 women) of the users got the payment on time, eight women got the payment with the average delay of one to two months and two women did not receive any fund.

Out of the women who knew about the scheme, more than half (66 per cent) got information from ANM/nurse/midwife/Lady Health Visitor (LHV) whereas the doctor was the source of information for 27 percent of the listed users. For others (7 per cent) Panchayat Raj Institution (PRI) members and other health care professional were the source of information.

In most of the FGDs, the study team found that there was no knowledge about the scheme at all in the entire village. In fact, people were surprised to hear about this scheme.

One of the male villagers responded during the FGD: ***"Yeh scheme agar itne din se chal rahi hai, aur paisa sarpanch ke pass hai to hamein to iska pata lagna chahiye."*** (if this scheme is running since such a long time, and money is with the sarpanch, then we should have known about it)

One of the female villagers reacted: ***"sari scheme sarpanch aur ANM ke milibhagat se chalti hai tabhi to sab ko pata na hoke kuch logo ko pata hai, jo ki unke karib ke log hai"*** (the scheme is run in the collaborationism of the sarpanch and ANM that is why only selected few know about it and not others)

Monitoring: According to the guidelines issued to all the districts at the initiation of the scheme: Reference: letter no.F.20 (26)/RCH/ FW/ 99/113; There was a provision for verifying at least 10 per cent cases in the field reported to have been referred to the health institutions. The report of such verifications was to be placed before Directorate of RCH (DRCH). Some activity regarding this was detected in District I, where according to the district officials this responsibility was assigned to a contracted male nurse but any such activity could not be confirmed at the peripheral level, whereas in District II and District III (Jodhpur), no such thing was reported.

Ownership of the Scheme: As mentioned earlier, some in-depth interviews were also done to assess the perception and clarity of the scheme, among the stakeholders, the findings from them are as follows: Although most of the officials involved in the implementation of the scheme were clear about the objectives of the scheme, their own role in the scheme and the process of disbursement of funds, but still the implementation was not found up to the mark. May be just giving them the knowledge about the scheme was not sufficient; as there was no feeling of ownership of this scheme. From the health provider's point of view, they could not own this scheme as the fund was in the hands of PRI members. On the other hand, the sarpanch did not know whom to target this scheme (he/she was not in constant touch of the information regarding the eligible women for the scheme, as it was not directly related to their work).

Clarity and Communication of the Guidelines among Managers: In spite of the same official letters being issued from the state to the various districts, the basic perception of this scheme in all the three districts was diverse but within a district it was uniform. Consequently, the criteria of eligibility of the potential beneficiary was also found to be diverse in the three districts e.g. in District-I, the eligibility of a woman depended upon her belonging to a poor or BPL family and (plus) having complicated or institutional delivery, whereas, in District III, a woman had to have a BPL card and complicated delivery to utilize the scheme. In District II, the potential beneficiary having a BPL card, and coming to the health institution from more than 7-8 km away, was given Rs. 500 flat up to two deliveries. The various letters issued from the district office to the facilitating agents could support this.

Mobility Mapping: In addition to the above information, efforts were also made to assess the mobility for availing the emergency obstetric care, from all the villages covered in the study. Institutional deliveries in districts were found to be in inverse proportion to the average distance needed to be covered to reach the health facility, time taken to reach there and cost needed to reach the health facility (District II > District I > District III), therefore, these factors can be labeled as hindering factors for use of health facilities, in time of need.

Distance and lack of transport: The scarcity of vehicles, telephone facilities and poor road conditions, especially in remote areas, can make it extremely difficult for women to reach even relatively nearby facilities. Walking is the primary mode of transportation, even for women in labour.

Qualitative analysis through FGDs also supported it and in one of the districts, also revealed that, the particular district had many Rajput families, who still followed the pardah system and, therefore, did not like to go for institutional deliveries.

Others: Some of the other factors hindering the process of the scheme were non-availability of the ANMs at the headquarters, lack of induction training of the medical officers, as most of them were contract based who kept on changing every 2 months and in one of the districts, funds were empty since last four years (year 2001), in most of the Panchayats.

V. Conclusions

Despite the development and existence of such cost-effective health interventions, they are not yet available to all women in need. Although there is an impressive establishment of health infrastructure in the State, their capacity to provide basic maternal health care, especially essential obstetric care, is often lacking. Even where such services are available, women in need cannot access them on time, mainly due to the lack of referral systems, their low socioeconomic status, cultural barriers and the distance of the facility. With deepening poverty among women, there is a compelling need for instituting alternative means and mechanisms for fair financing so that none in need, is barred from accessing the life-saving essential elements of obstetric care. The estimated cost for the entire package of transport for effective interventions in the state would be, not more than Rs 300 per person. This State has one of the highest maternal mortality ratios in the country, which is much more than the national average. To prevent the second delay in receiving quality emergency obstetric care i.e. delay in reaching the health facility at the time of emergency, the scheme "Referral Transport Scheme" was initiated in 1999-2000 under RCH- Phase-I. The present study was an effort to assess the utilization and factors facilitating and obstructing for the implementation of the scheme.

The basic model prepared was with the main objective of providing transport facilities (not only fund for transport) for the women in need and could have been a very good example of inter sectoral coordination, but Sarpanchs were not able to identify the eligibles (the active participation was lacking) and the ones who could identify them (health providers), could not own the scheme. And also, Sarpanchs belonging to the political field had a chance to get biased in giving benefit to the eligibles (by caste, his voters and supporters). Since the scheme was open it was prone to corruption.

Since, this scheme was a failure, therefore, it was withdrawn from RCH-II, but Government of India has recently announced Janani Suraksha Yojana **(JSY)** which is a safe motherhood intervention under the National Rural Health Mission (NRHM) being implemented with the objective of reducing maternal and neo-natal mortality by promoting institutional delivery among the poor pregnant women. JSY is a 100 per cent centrally sponsored scheme and it integrates cash assistance with delivery and post-delivery care. The success of the scheme would be determined by the increase in institutional delivery among the poor families which is to be monitored under the scheme.

The Yojana has identified ASHA, the accredited social health activist as an effective link between the Government and the poor pregnant women. ASHA is to be the first port of call for any health related demands of poor people, especially women and children. She is supposed to be an escort, motivator and guide for village community on health issues.

Although, the overall structure of JSY seems quite satisfying, the scheme can be further evaluated on the factors identified as bottlenecks in this study.

References

UNDP (1999): *Human Development Report, 1999*, Oxford University Press, New York, p.136.

World Health Organization (2001): Maternal Mortality in 1995: Estimates developed by WHO, UNICEF, UNFPA, *WHO/RHR/OL9*, Geneva.

Editorial (2001): Emergency Obstetric Care: the Keystone in Arch of Safe Motherhood, *International Journal of Gynaecology and Obstetrics*, Vol. 74, pp. 95-97.

Krasovac, K. (2004): Auxiliary Technologies Related to Transport and Communication for Obstetric Emergencies, *International Journal of Gynaecology and Obstetrics*, Vol. 85, Suppl. 1, pp. S14-S23.

Mavalankar, D.V. (2006): Policy and Management Constraints on Access to and Use of Life-Saving Emergency Obstetric Care in India, .

Table 7.1: Age and Caste Profile of the Users and Non-Users

Characteristics	Users				Non-users			
	Churu	Baran	Jodhpur	Total	Churu	Baran	Jodhpur	Total
Age group	n=30	n=30	n=0	n=60	N=20	n=20	n=20	n=60
10-14	0	0	NA	0	0	0	0	0
15-19	0	0	NA	0	15	0	0	5
20-24	33.3	63.3	NA	48.3	35	20	45	33.3
25-29	26.7	30	NA	28.3	15	55	45	38.3
30-34	30	6.7	NA	18.3	15	15	10	13.3
35-39	10	0	NA	5	20	10	0	10
Caste	n=30	n=30	n=0	n=60	N=20	n=20	n=20	n=60
SC	20	30	NA	25	30	0	5	11.7
ST	0	46.7	NA	23.3	0	90	0	30
OBC	26.7	20	NA	23.3	40	10	30	26.7
Others	53.3	3.3	NA	28.3	30	0	65	31.7

Source: Compiled from Primary data.

Table 7.2: Literacy Status of the Users and Non-Users

	Users				Non users			
Characteristics	Churu	Baran	Jodhpur	Total	Churu	Baran	Jodhpur	Total
Education(Women)	n=30	n=30	n=0	n=60	n=20	n=20	n=20	n=60
Illiterate	53.3	63.3	NA	58.3	55	75	65	65
Just Literate	10	23.3	NA	16.7	25	10	20	18.3
Primary	33.3	10	NA	21.7	20	10	15	15
Secondary	0	3.3	NA	1.7	0	0	0	0
Graduate& above	3.3	0	NA	1.7	0	5	0	1.7
Education(Husband)	n=30	n=30	n=0	n=60	n=20	n=20	n=20	n=60
Illiterate	13.3	20	NA	16.7	15	30	35	26.7
Just Literate	10	20	NA	15	10	20	10	13.3
Primary	46.7	36.7	NA	41.7	60	30	30	40
Secondary	23.3	20	NA	21.7	15	5	15	11.7
Graduate& above	6.7	3.3	NA	5	0	15	10	8.3

Source: Compiled from Primary data.

Table 7.3: Basic Obstetric Information of the Users and Non-Users

	Users				Non users			
Characteristics	Churu	Baran	Jodhpur	Total	Churu	Baran	Jodhpur	Total
Age at marriage	n=30	n=30	n=0	n=60	n=20	n=20	n=20	n=60
10-14	23.3	16.7	NA	20	10	10	15	11.7
15-19	73.3	76.7	NA	75	85	75	70	76.7
20-24	3.3	6.7	NA	5	5	15	15	11.7
Age at 1st pregnancy	n=30	n=30	n=0	n=60	n=20	n=20	n=20	n=60
10-14	0	0	NA	0	0	0	0	0
15-19	63.3	80	NA	71.7	85	75	55	71.7
20-24	33.3	16.7	NA	25	15	25	40	26.7
25-29	3.3	3.3	NA	3.3	0	0	5	1.7
No. of pregnancies	n=30	n=30			n=20	n=20	n=20	n=120
1	6.7	43.3	NA	25	30	25	10	21.7
2	16.7	46.7	NA	31.7	25	25	50	33.3
3	30	3.3	NA	16.7	15	25	15	18.3

Cont...

4	23.3	6.7	NA	15	15	25	15	18.3
>5	23.3	0	NA	11.7	15	0	10	8.3

Source: Compiled from Primary data

Table 7.4: Antenatal Profile among the Users and Non-Users

	Users				Non users			
Characteristics	Churu	Baran	Jodhpur	Total	Churu	Baran	Jodhpur	Total
Antenatal checkup	n =30	n =30	n =0	n =60	n =20	n =20	n =20	n =60
Yes	80	83.3	NA	81.7	80	90	65	78.3
No	20	16.7	NA	18.3	20	10	35	21.7
Women with problem during Pregnancy	n =30	n =30	n =0	n =60	n =20	n =20	n =20	n =60
Yes	66.7	60	NA	63.3	75	85	80	80
No	33.3	40	NA	36.7	25	15	20	20
Information about any danger sign	n =30	n =30	n =0	n =60	n =20	n =20	n =20	n =60
Yes	93.3	93.3	NA	93.3	95	100	95	96.7
No	6.7	6.7	NA	6.7	5	0	5	3.3

Source: Compiled from Primary data.

Table 7.5: Birth Preparedness among the Users and Non-Users

	Users				Non users			
Birth preparedness about	Churu	Baran	Jodhpur	Total	Churu	Baran	Jodhpur	Total
Responses*	n =30	n =30	n =0	n =60	n =20	n =20	n =20	n =60
Place of birth	46.7	40	NA	43.3	10	40	35	28.3
Mode of Transport to reach the facility	73.3	73.3	NA	73.3	65	80	40	61.7
Saved money	86.7	90	NA	88.3	90	75	85	83.3
No preparedness	6.7	3.3	NA	5	10	0	0	3.3

* Multiple responses

Source: Compiled from Primary data.

Table 7.6: Knowledge of the Scheme among the Users and Non-Users

	Users				Non users			
	Churu	Baran	Jodhpur	Total	Churu	Baran	Jodhpur	Total
Knowledge of the scheme	n =30	n =30	n =0	n =60	n =20	n =20	n =20	n =60
Heard about the scheme (%)	60	96.7	NA	78.3	5	5	5	5
Not heard about the scheme (%)	40	3.3	NA	21.7	95	95	95	95

Source: Compiled from Primary data.

8

Health and Development Inter-Links in India

Neena Malhotra and Shweta

I. Introduction

Good health is universally acknowledged to be of intrinsic value and therefore, constitutes an integral element of development. One can be rich but sick enough to, not to enjoy any opportunities that wealth opens up, and poor health may translate into worsening economic opportunities as well. Health is a multidimensional subject. The World Health Organization (WHO) highlights three specific dimensions of health – the physical, the mental and the social. Health is multifactorial as well. There are numerous factors that influence health like hereditary factors, environmental factors, life style, adequate housing, basic sanitation and socio-economic conditions including income, education, availability and quality of health infrastructure and per capita health expenditure (Park, 1994).

Income which is considered to be an important determinant of economic growth has a two way relation with health. Whereas level of income determines good health status, health status also contributes to increase in the level of income, as it is a critical factor for workforce to be productive. Healthy workers are considered to be more productive. (Nobuhide, 2005) Another major factor influencing health is per capita health expenditure. Available information shows that government is spending on health has stagnated around one per cent of gross domestic product (GDP) in India. The developed countries on the other hand spend 6 to 8 per cent of GDP on health, e.g., USA (7.2 per cent), Germany (8 per cent) and France (7.2 per cent) in the year 2000. China's public spending on health is 3.4 per cent of GDP in

2000 (GOI, 2005; Word Bank, 2004).

Apart from income and per capita health expenditure, level of literacy also influences health. The world map of illiteracy closely coincides with the maps of poverty, malnutrition, ill health, high infant and child mortality rates. Studies indicate that education to some extent compensates the effects of poverty on health irrespective of availability of health facilities (Ratcliffe, 1984). Thus, health is affected by a host of factors – measurable and non - measurable.

This paper attempts to study the pattern of public health expenditure in various states and analyses the extent to which state is fulfilling its responsibility in providing public health facilities. The relation between per capita health expenditure and level of economic development, as measured by per capita net state domestic product (PCNSDP), in various states is studied by using double log regression. The study also analyses the relations between major indicators of health viz. crude birth rate(CBR), crude death rate (CDR), infant mortality rate (IMR), expected life for female (ELF) and expected life for male (ELM) and their major determinants viz. PCNSDP, per capita public health expenditure (PCHE) and Literacy rate (LR). In order to analyze the relationship, simple regression analysis has been applied by taking various health indicators, state wise, as function of PCNSDP and LRs in various states.

II. Inter-State Analysis of Public Health Expenditure

Health care expenditure is a very necessary social expenditure for any country. Whether it is a developing country or a developed one, state's role in developing a good health infrastructure and assuring good health to everybody becomes very critical and important. Public expenditure on health has been grossly inadequate right from 1940's in India, when Bhore Committee Report stated that per capita private expenditure on health was Rs. 2.50 compared to a state per capita health expenditure of just Rs. 0.36. In 1950s and 1960s private health expenditure was 83 per cent and 88 per cent of total expenditure respectively (Bhat and Nishant, 2004). The public health expenditure in the country is very low and as a percentage of GDP has declined from 1.3 per cent in 1990 to 0.9 per cent in 1999 (GOI, 2001).

Inter-State PCHE: The subject matter of health is in the state list of the Indian Constitution. It is important to examine inter state differences in spending patterns, while the central government provides funds to the states under centrally sponsored, schemes based on uniform norms, per capita expenditure in states varies depending upon the prevalence of diseases and utilization of funds allocated. If these are taken into account, the central government expenditure does not show much variation between states.

There are substantial variations in per capita expenditure on health by the states. The states like Bihar, Madhya Pradesh, Uttar Pradesh and Orissa have low per capita expenditure, poor access to health care and poor health indices. However, Rajasthan and Assam continue to have poor health indices in spite of relatively higher expenditure. The inter-state disparities in per capita health expenditure have not changed much over time. During 1991, the states having high per capita health expenditure were Punjab (Rs. 98.47) and Kerala (Rs. 79.97). During 2001, Punjab again had a high per capita expenditure of Rs. 146 and Kerala had per capita expenditure of Rs. 101. Other better performing states are Tamil Nadu, Gujarat and Maharashtra. Low performing states are Bihar, Assam, Rajasthan and Andhra Pradesh (Table 8.1).

There is no major change in the ranking of states during the period 1991 to 2001. Except for Karnataka which slipped down from 4 to 6 and Orissa high slipped down from 9 to 11.5. Gujarat has improved from 6 to 4 and West Bengal from 8 to 7. In all states, patients incur out-of-pocket expenses to meet the health care cost in public and privately – funded hospitals. There are massive differences in private spending on health care services in public and private facilities between states. Patients from Kerala and Punjab spend about four times more on health as compared to patients from Bihar. The high and low spending in private and public sector do not always go hand with each other. In Rajasthan out-of-pocket expenditure in private and government hospitals is almost equal, because the state has been levying user charges and providing drugs at cost price to persons admitted in government hospitals.

Table 8.1: Per Capita Public Health Expenditure

States	1991	Rank	2001	Rank
Andhra Pradesh	53.71	10	082	9
Assam	48.43	12	058	11.5
Bihar	46.80	13	045	13
Gujarat	65.37	6	099	4
Karnataka	68.88	4	096	6
Kerala	79.97	2	101	2
Madhya Pradesh	48.94	11	062	10
Maharashtra	66.06	5	098	5
Orissa	55.31	9	058	11.5
Punjab	98.47	1	146	1.
Rajasthan	62.72	7	088	8
Tamil Nadu	74.78	3	100	3
Uttar Pradesh	39.58	14	043	14
West Bengal	61.56	8	090	7

Source: Calculated by authors on the basis of state level total health expenditure in year 1991 and 2001 as given in CMIE reports.

The public expenditure on health is grossly in adequate in various states. Public have to spent out of pocket to meet there health needs this puts poor people in very vulnerable position and is the main cause of poor health condition specially in poorer states.

III. Health Indicators: Inter-State Disparities

Inter-state analysis shows states like Orissa, M.P., U.P., and Bihar are low performing states whcreas Kcrala, Maharashtra and Tamil Nadu are better performing states (Tables 8.2 and 8.3).

Table 8.2: Health Development Indicators 1991

State	PCHE	PCNSDP	LR	IMR	CBR	CDR	ELF	ELM
Andhra Pradesh	53.71	4722	44.1	73	26.0	9.7	64.48	61.40
Assam	48.43	3427	52.9	81	30.9	11.5	58.48	58.74
Bihar	46.8	2539	38.5	69	30.7	9.8	60.09	60.81
Gujarat	65.37	6060	61.3	69	27.5	8.5	62.74	60.94
Karnataka	68.88	4737	56.0	77	26.9	9.0	65.30	64.15
Kerala	79.97	3843	89.8	16	18.3	6.0	72.37	67.23
Madhya Pradesh	48.94	3814	44.2	117	35.8	13.8	57.96	59.24
Maharashtra	66.06	7409	64.9	60	26.2	8.2	65.06	63.90
Orissa	55.31	3180	49.1	124	28.8	12.8	58.40	60.13
Punjab	98.47	8281	58.5	53	27.7	7.8	66.55	66.61
Rajasthan	62.72	3983	38.6	79	35.0	10.1	61.34	60.50
Tamil Nadu	74.78	4428	54.6	57	20.8	8.8	63.05	62.85
Uttar Pradesh	39.58	3690	41.6	86	36.1	12.7	56.90	58.10
West Bengal	61.56	4673	57.7	56	24.5	8.3	63.60	62.20

Sources: Compiled from GOI (Various Issues); CMIE Reports, various issues.

Table 8.3: Health and Development Indicator 2001

State	PCHE	PCNSDP	LR	IMR	CBR	CDR	ELF	ELM
Andhra Pradesh	82	17932	61.11	65	21.0	8.2	65.00	62.79
Assam	58	11132	64.28	75	27.0	9.6	60.87	58.96
Bihar	45	5445	47.53	62	31.2	8.2	64.79	65.66
Gujarat	99	19607	69.97	62	25.0	7.8	64.10	63.12
Karnataka	96	18196	67.04	57	22.2	7.6	66.44	62.43
Kerala	101	19803	90.92	14	17.3	6.6	75.00	71.67
Madhya Pradesh	62	12125	64.11	87	31.0	10.1	58.01	59.19
Maharashtra	98	24052	77.27	48	20.7	7.5	69.76	66.75
Orissa	58	10021	63.61	96	23.5	10.4	59.71	60.05
Punjab	146	25625	69.95	52	21.2	7.0	72.00	69.78
Rajasthan	88	13621	61.03	79	31.1	8.0	62.80	62.17
Tamil Nadu	100	20315	73.47	51	19.1	7.7	69.75	67.00
Uttar Pradesh	43	9162	57.36	83.89	32.6	10.1	63.54	64.09
West Bengal	90	16146	69.20	51	20.5	6.7	66.08	69.34

Sources: Compiled from GOI (Various Issues); CMIE Reports, various issues.

Basic indicators of health like IMR, CDR, and life expectancy (LE) give broad picture of health status of a country and state. They can be use for assessing specific health care needs and also for evaluating quality of health services and programs. Basic health indicators in various states have improved over time but still far behind developed countries. IMR of 70 per thousand live births and a child mortality rate of 95 per thousand are very high compared with five to six child mortality rate (CMR) in developed country.

IV. Relationship between Health Indicators and PCHE

The results of simple regression between health indicators as dependent variable and PCHE as independent variable for the years 1991 and 2001 are given in the Tables 8.4 and 8.5.

Table 8.4: The Effect of PCHE on Health Simple Regression Result, 1991

No	Independent→ Dependent ↓	Constant	PCHE	R^2	R^{-2}	F
1.	IMR	147.568 (4.902)	-1.164 (-2.543)**	.393	.332	6.465
2.	CBR	39.428 (6.780)	-.18005 (-2.036)**	.293	.222	4.144
3.	CDR	16.270 (7.854)	-.1029 (-3.269)*	.517	.468	10.685
4.	ELF	50.075 (12.966)	.2014 (3.428)*	.540	.494	11.750
5.	ELM	52.065 (27.904)	.158 (5.574)*	.756	.732	31.072

* 99 per cent level of significance. **95 per cent level of significance. *** 90 per cent level of significance.

The result for 1991 show the IMR, CDR, and CBR have significant negative relationship with per capita public health expenditure. Similarly, LE both for male and females has highly significant and positive relationship with per capita state heath expenditure. The regression result for the year 2001 again confirms direct relation between per capita public health expenditure and heath indicators. Values of R^2 and R^{-2} are relatively low because health is multi factorial and is also affected by factors other than per capita health expenditures like gender empowerment, poverty, education, adequate housing, clean drinking water and sanitation etc. Thus public health facilities are crucial for meeting the basic health requirements of masses in India. States which are poorly performing in terms of various health indicators need to make more public investments in health.

Table 8.5: The Effect of PCHE on Health Simple Regression Result, 2001

No.	Independent→ Dependent ↓	Constant	PCHE	R^2	R^{-2}	F
1.	IMR	99.623 (5.431)	-.433 (-2.125)**	.311	.242	4.517
2.	CBR	33.434 (8.309)	-1.07 (-2.401)**	.366	.302	5.767
3.	CDR	11.026 (13.386)	-.0325 (-3.556)*	.558	.514	12.644
4.	ELF	53.922 (14.802)	.1367 (3.376)*	.5633	.486	11.398
5.	ELM	55.710 (17.438)	.0978 (2.756)**	.432	.375	7.594

* 99 per cent level of significance. **95 per cent level of significance. *** 90 per cent level of significance.

V. Relationship between Health Indicators and PCNSDP

The results of simple regression between health indicators as dependent variable and Per Capita Net State Domestic Product (PCNSDP) as independent variable for the years 1991 and 2001 are given in the Tables 8.6 and 8.7. The results for 1991 show that IMR, CBR, and CDR have negative relation with income. LE both for male and female is positively related with PCNSDP. But the relationship has not being found to be significant and value of R^2 and R^{-2} are also very low. Thus per capita income variable is not significantly affecting heath indicators. However the results for 2001 show different picture and income variable is significantly affecting health indicators. All the regression coefficients have desired signs and are statistically significant.

Table 8.6: Effect of PCNSDP on Health Simple Regression Results, 1991

No.	Independent → Dependent ↓	Constant	PCNSDP	R^2	R^{-2}	F
1.	IMR	98.964 (4.079)	-.00554 (-1.138)	.115	.026	1.294
2.	CBR	30.629 (6.772)	-.000584 (-.644)	.039	-.056	.414
3.	CDR	12.576 (7.256)	-.000619 (-1.779)	.240	.164	3.165
4.	ELF	57.998 (16.987)	.00106 (1.548)	.193	.112	2.396
5.	ELM	58.091 (27.487)	.000875 (2.064)	.298	.228	4.261

* 99 per cent level of significance. **95 per cent level of significance.
*** 90 per cent level of significance.

Table 8.7: Effect of Per Capita Net State Domestic Product (PCNSDP) on Health Simple Regression Results, 2001

No.	Independent → Dependent ↓	Constant	PCNSDP	R^2	R^{-2}	F
1.	IMR	97.306 (6.242)	-.00212 (-2.377)**	.361	.297	5.65
2.	CBR	34.026 (11.332)	-.000596 (-3.471)*	.546	.501	12.046
3.	CDR	10.495 (13.360)	-.000138 (-3.063)*	.484	.432	9.381
4.	ELF	55.548 (17.085)	.000615 (3.304)*	.522	.474	10.915
5.	ELM	57.392 (19.256)	.000408 (2.396)**	.364	.301	5.739

*99 per cent level of significance. **95 per cent level of significance.
*** 90 per cent level of significance.

VI. Relation between Health Indicators and LR

The results of simple regression analysis between LR as independent variable and health indicators as dependent variables for the years 1991 and 2001 have been shown in Tables 8.8 and 8.9. The result show that literacy has highly significant relationship with all the health indicators and state having high literacy rates also perform better in terms or health indicators i.e. they have lower child mortality rate lower birth and death rates and higher LE. Regression result for the year 2001 confirms the same pattern. The above analysis shows that economic development, public policy and literacy have direct bearing on health attainment. Development effects health both directly by improving nutrition and access to health facilities, and also indirectly by improving education attainment.

Table 8.8: Effect of Literacy Rate on Health Simple Regression Results 1991

No.	Independent → Dependent ↓	Constant	LR	R^2	R^{-2}	F
1.	IMR	148.549 (5.793)	-1.391 (-3.039)*	.480	.482	9.233
2.	CBR	42.676 (10.258)	-.272 (-3.663)*	.573	.530	13.419
3.	CDR	15.495 (7.829)	-.107 (-3.034)*	.479	.427	9.204
4.	ELF	50.235 (15.699)	.234 (4.105)*	.627	.590	16.848
5.	ELM	54.399 (22.893)	.143 (3.385)*	.534	.487	11.459

* 99 per cent level of significance. **95 per cent level of significance. *** 90 per cent level of significance.

VII. Relation between PCHE and PCNSDP

Public Health is primarily a state responsibility in India and there are wide spread inter-state disparities in PCHE. How growth in state PCNSDP is influencing PCHE can be studied in terms of following function:

Table 8.9: Effect of Literacy Rate on Health Simple Regression Results 2001

No.	Independent → Dependent ↓	Constant	LR	R^2	R^{-2}	F
1.	IMR	159.232 (5.132)	-1.435 (-3.157)*	.499	.449	9.969
2.	CBR	47.846 (7.274)	-.350 (-3.636)*	.569	.526	13.217
3.	CDR	12.083 (5.681)	-.057 (-1.834)***	.251	.176	3.364
4.	ELF	43.419 (5.556)	.329 (2.880)**	.453	.398	8.296
5.	ELM	48.990 (7.128)	.224 (2.227)**	.331	.264	4.960

* 99 per cent level of significance. **95 per cent level of significance. *** 90 per cent level of significance.

$$\ln PCHE = \alpha + \beta \ln PCNSDP + \varepsilon$$

The relationship is specified in log–log form so that the coefficient estimates are elasticities and, therefore, enable us to interpret the relation between PCHE and PCNSDP. Therefore, β will give the elasticity of PCHE with PCNSDP and ε is the residual.

Regression Results for 1991

$$\ln PCHE = 0.13837 + 0.455 \ln PCNSDP + \varepsilon$$

(.253) (3.038)* R^2 =0.479, R^{-2} =0.428, f=9.228

The results show that PCHE has significant relation with per capita income, which means rise in per capita income will lead to rise in per capita health expenditure.

Regression Results for 2001

$$\ln PCHE = 0.997 + 0.696 \ln PCNSDP + \varepsilon$$

(-2.850) (8.330)* R^2=0.874, R^{-2} =0.861, f=69.228

Results for 2001 again show that higher the per capita income of a state, higher will be its PCHE. There is significant relation between the PCHE and per capita income. Values of R^2 and R^{-2} are quite high for the year 2001 indicating that inter-state income disparities are significantly affecting inter-state differences in health expenditure. Elasticity of PCHE with respect to PCNSDP is 0.455 for the year 1991 and 0.696 for the year 2001.This shows that over the years elasticity coefficient for states have increased. Thus, higher incomes potentially permit individuals and society to afford better health care; better health increases productivity and enhances the ability to earn more income. So there is a two way relation between health and income.

VIII. Conclusions

The study shows strong interlink between health and economic development. In order to improve health indicators, the state governments will have to spend more on public health as well as education. In case of poorly performing states in terms of health, country can't wait for the state incomes to rise. States will have to devote more resources to promote basis health facilities especially for poorer section. Health sector can absorbed large quantity of investment, both public and private and yet leave millions of people specially the poor who suffer from high disease burden, uncovered. Public health subsidies are disproportionately distributed in favor of the richer groups and are not well targeted towards poor in India especially those in rural areas and in poorer states (NCAER, 2004).Thus in addition to raising public investment, policy are to be developed to permute equitable access to preventive and curative health services.

References

Bhat, Ramesh and Nishant Jain (2004): Analysis of Public Expenditure on Health Using State Level Data, Working Paper, IIM Ahmedabad, *www.iimahd.ernet.in* accessed on 11th August 2006.

GOI (Various Issues): Health information of India, Central Bureau of Health Intelligence, *www.cbhidgas.nic.in* accessed on 11th August 2006.

Nabuhide, Hatasa (2001): Health and Economic Development: a Cross Country National Empirical Analysis, *Journal of National Institute of Public Health*, Vol. 50, No. 3.

National Council of Applied Economic Research (NCAER) (2004): *Who Benefits from Public Health Spending in India-Results of a Benefit*

Incidence Analysis for India, New Delhi.

Park, K. (1994): *Preventive and Social Medicine*, Banarasi Das Publishers, Jabalpur

Ratcliffe, John (1984): *In Practicing Health for All*, in David Marley et.al. (Eds), Oxford University Press, New York.

9

Health-Development Interface in the Context of Malaria in Orissa

Nirmal Chandra Sahu and Santosh Kumar Bali

I. Introduction

The interface between health and development has been well-documented. Good health is not only an outcome of socioeconomic development, but is also a determinant of the latter. Apart from governing the core of human well-being, health itself promotes development. The improvement in the health status of people is essential to sustained economic and social development. There are thus two-way linkages between the two. Better health status promotes development through many ways. Similarly it is argued that economic development promotes conditions of good health.

From mid-20th century, global public health efforts have vastly improved. Enormous success has been achieved in dealing with several diseases and even eradicating small pox, one of the world's worst health problems. Infant and child mortality have dropped in the face of massive immunization campaigns, food supplements and new treatments for common illnesses. The advent of antibiotics saved million of lives. Life expectancy at birth (LEB) rose dramatically in both developed and developing countries. In India, for example, LEB increased from about 37 years in 1951 to 64 years in 2001.

Further, the health care system has been a major catalyst in the longevity revolution of the human society. There has been a secular decline in mortality and morbidity throughout the world, which has been systematically monitored and explained in the 20th century. Robert W. Fogel, the economics Nobel laureate of 1993, has analyzed and explained these long-period trends through the synergy between biomedical and economic developments. Expansions of health care efforts and economic developments have been reinforcing each other with salutary effects on human welfare.

II. Research Problem

The research problem in this study is formulated from a surmise that the reciprocity between health and development is not always true. While good health has positive effects on development, it's contrary is not true everywhere. Unless well-focused policies are in place, economic development may not imply better health status for the people. This proposition is examined in the context of Malaria in Orissa. In the subsequent three sections, the paper pursues three objectives: (a) It briefly counts the benefits and issues on either side of the health↔ development inter-linkage; (b) the case history of Malaria in Orissa is narrated; and (c) the influence of increase in real income on incidence of Malaria is statistically analyzed using a time-series running for more than four decades since 1961. The study only processes the available secondary materials using standard statistical tools of correlation and regression, with necessary correction for autocorrelation.

III. The Health-Development Interface

It is now strongly claimed that investment in health is justified on purely economic grounds. Improved health contributes to development of an economy in at least ***seven*** ways (World Bank, 1993; and Gupta and Mahajan, 2003):

First, good health reduces production losses caused by worker illness. In other words, there are gains in workers' productivity from better health. For example, as early as in 1936, J. A. Sinton calculated that Malaria caused a loss of Rs. 1,000 crore per annum in India. According to him, "It constitutes one of the most important causes of economic misfortune engendering poverty, diminishing the quantity and quality of food supply, lowering the physical and intellectual standards of the nation, and hampering increased prosperity and economic progress in every way" (Gupta and Mahajan, 2003).

Second, improved health reduces the losses due to morbidity and mortality. These losses are of three types: cost of death (the value of each life saved), cost of morbidity (loss of work days and work efficiency due to sickness) and cost of treatment (money spent on purchase of drugs; medical services, transport to hospital, costs associated with the attendants, etc.).

Third, it permits the use of natural resources that had been totally or nearly inaccessible because of disease. Some health investments raise productivity of land. Areas previously blighted by mosquitoes become attractive for settlement. Migrants move in, which raises output. National productivity also increases when health programs throw open hitherto unavailable avenues of production.

Fourth, better health increases the enrollment of children in school and makes them better able to learn, and thereby contributes to the welfare of the future generation. We all know that like education, health is an investment into the future. There is no dispute that education pays off in higher income. There are many ways to establish that education, particularly of children, is directly influenced by health and nutrition. Thus health care yields significant benefits in the next generation, which promotes an essential condition of sustainable development.

Fifth, it saves resources for alternative uses, which would otherwise have to be spent on treating illness. Health care expenditure that reduces the incidence of disease result in big savings in treatment costs. For some diseases the expenditure pays for itself even if we ignore all the indirect benefits, like increased labour productivity and reduced pain and suffering. In case of health problems like Polio and AIDS, it has been estimated that savings in annual treatment costs far exceed the investment required to eliminate it over a period of time.

Sixth, it makes life more satisfying by contributing to better quality of life. One of the most important social effects of health services is to improve the quality of life. Two of the three determinants of the physical quality of life index, relate to health, viz. infant mortality rate (IMR) and longevity of life, the third being the literacy rate. However, quality of life also depends upon the degree of happiness and security enjoyed by the people. It is undisputed that adequate health services and good health are associated with a state of enthusiasm, vigour and happiness. While IMR is a function of investment in the health sector, longevity is promoted both by health care and happiness of the people. Happiness, being a subjective state, is a function of several factors. But at a more physical and mental level, it is believed that happiness of the people is obtained through a sufficient level of health care in a society.

Seventh, it has been found that the poor die younger and suffer more from disability. They are exposed to greater risks from unhealthy and dangerous conditions, both at home and at work. Malnourishment and the legacy of past illness imply that they are more likely to fall ill and slower to recover, especially as they have little access to health care. Yet another economic dimension in this context relates to the impact on the financial conditions of the family of the poor. When a family's breadwinner becomes ill, other members try at first to cope by working harder themselves and by reducing consumption, even of food. Both the adjustments harm the health of the whole family. If free health care is not available, the costs of treatment may drive a family deeper into debt. Although ill health is only one of the several factors causing financial distress of the poor households, its potential to spell disaster is being increasingly recognized. Thus health development contributes to the goal of reducing poverty. The adverse effects of ill health are the greatest for the poor people. It is not only because they fall ill more often, but also because their income depends exclusively on physical labour and they have no savings cushion. They therefore find it impossible to recover from an illness with their human and financial capital intact. So the social justice dimension of health sector development is prominent, as the different economic gains are relatively greater for the poor people, who are typically most handicapped by ill health.

The above discussion indicates that health and health services do not have adverse effects upon development. However, all types of economic development and the means to attain the same are not necessarily desirable in all circumstances, from the point of view of health promotion. Socioeconomic development may have positive as well as negative consequences upon health.

On the positive side, it has been pointed out that economic development brings about quantitative and qualitative improvement in health services and there by improve the health of people. Being a major objective of development, growth of public investment in human capital promotes the health care delivery system of an economy along with expansion of health education and research, and medical technology. In the private sector, investments in the pharmaceutical industry, hospitals and medical education strengthen the health services. Development of education changes the level of awareness and attitude towards better health. Further, it has been said that development is the best contraceptive and brings about a decrease in fertility. This in turn leads to decrease in infant mortality and bring in associated positive health economic effects. Prosperity also provides the conditions conducive to promotion of longevity.

On the negative side, there is a tendency for excessive economic growth to render development unsustainable. Poverty and inequality linger. It can lead to wasteful consumption and environmental degradation. An example of unsustainable development relate to the intensive use of ground water obtained from tube wells for agricultural and industrial purposes, which adversely affect the availability of drinking water. Environmental degradation ultimately results in ill-health, due to either malnutrition or diseases. There is several adverse health effects associated with air and water pollution.

IV. Malaria in Orissa

Orissa is one of the states with very poor health indicators. So far as mortality rate, a robust indicator of the overall health status of a population, is concerned, the percentage decline in the 1980s as well as in the 1990s has been the least in Orissa as compared to the other states and the level of mortality in Orissa by the end of the 1990s has remained the highest (GOO, 2004). Infant mortality rate (IMR) continues to be the highest in Orissa among all the states. The absolute magnitude of infant and child deaths is very high. The rate of decline in IMR has been rather slow and this is a cause for concern. Between 1981–83 and 1995–97, it declined by 25 per cent, i.e. at the rate of about 1.6 per cent per annum. This is lower than the rate of decline in IMR in other low-income states over the same period (Uttar Pradesh: 44 per cent, Bihar: 35 per cent, Madhya Pradesh: 28 per cent), as well as all-India (33 per cent). Further the morbidity incidence rate is also significantly higher in the case of Orissa. Malaria, tuberculosis, gastroenteritis, and vaccine preventable diseases (VPDs) have significantly contributed to morbidity.

In Orissa, Malaria continues to be the most important public health problem. In 1998, the state, with a share of less than four per cent of all-India population, accounted for 28.6 per cent of the detected cases of malaria in India (two million) and 62.8 per cent of all malarial deaths in the country, as per the National Malaria Eradication Programme Report for 1998 (GOO, 2004). This is mainly due to the predominance of the deadly Plasmodium Falciparum (PF) species responsible for severe (cerebral) malaria. 36.2 per cent of PF cases occur in Orissa. There is a marked endemic nature of malaria in four districts of Orissa, namely Kandhamal, Keonjhar, Sundargarh, and Mayurbhanj. These four districts account for 50 per cent of all PF malarial cases and 40 per cent of the malarial deaths in the state (GOO, 2004).

The available epidemiological data for the period 1961 to 2003 gives us an idea about the level and trend in the incidence of malaria as well as the increase in case-fatality rate (Table 9.1). The percentage of PF cases in the total number of positive cases (PF per cent) is used as a proxy of case-fatality rate. The Slide Positive Rate, being an indicator of incidence shows that the rate has remained at a high level of more than 10 per cent since 1973 and has not declined through the 1980s and 1990s.

Table 9.1: Epidemiological Data on Malaria and Per Capita Income in Orissa, 1961 to 2003

Year	Malaria Slide Positive Rate (Per cent)	Cerebral Malaria – PF Rate (Per cent)	Per Capita State Income at Current price (Rs.)	Per Capita State Income at Constant (1993-94) price (Rs.)
(1)	(2)	(3)	(4)	(5)
1961	1.40	13.30	223.01	2763.71
1966	0.40	71.80	387.37	3127.44
1971	2.60	40.80	478.33	3150.82
1976	15.90	63.80	689.83	2940.85
1981	10.90	78.80	1339.73	3749.22
1986	11.20	80.00	2035.87	3948.61
1991	10.50	84.70	3907.00	4686.84
1992	9.70	84.80	4114.00	4542.39
1993	9.70	84.90	4896.00	4896.00
1994	10.20	85.60	5795.00	5280.08
1995	11.20	85.80	6985.00	5842.51
1996	11.80	86.30	6548.00	5100.12
1997	10.30	86.40	7973.00	5800.14
1998	12.10	85.40	8766.00	5876.07
1999	10.60	84.40	9486.00	6114.14
2000	11.80	84.00	9281.00	5778.41
2001	11.00	83.50	10021.00	6046.40
2002	10.40	83.20	10340.00	5980.81
2003	9.50	83.00	11858.00	6664.85

Note: (1) In case of income, the years are from April 1 to March 31. So 1961 is 1961-62. (2) State income relates to Net State Domestic Product at Factor Cost.
Source: GOO (1991, 2004, 2005) and GOI (2005, 2006)

On the other hand, the PF per cent, has discernibly increased from about 72 per cent in the late 1970s to more than 86 per cent by 1996 (Table 9.1).

The National Anti-Malaria Programme (NAMP), being implemented in the entire state, includes active and passive surveillance of fever cases, presumptive treatment of all fever cases, and presumptive radical treatment of all suspected cases in high endemic areas. Distribution of drugs through Drug Distribution Centers (DDCs) and Fever Treatment Depots (FTDs), management of complicated malaria cases, vector control through insecticides by residual spraying of DDT, distribution of medicated mosquito nets, and anti-larval measures in urban areas are also part of the programme. Since 1997-98, the Enhanced Malaria Control Project (EMCP) has been taken up with the assistance of the World Bank and the Government of India in 158 out of 314 blocks in the state. Recently, two major initiatives - rapid diagnostic kit and simplified treatment regimen - have been launched under the EMCP in Orissa, which, it is hoped, can increase the effectiveness of malaria control by making a dent on both the morbidity and mortality caused by malaria.

V. Why do Income and Malaria Rise in Orissa?

The correlation matrix of measure of income and incidence of malaria in Orissa is shown in Table 9.2, which indicates that the two sets of variables are positively related. In fact, the correlation coefficients of income with cerebral malaria are around 0.6, which is high. Malaria is increasing in Orissa along side economic development, which is frustrating. The generalized Chocrane-Orcutt autoregressive regression models estimated through GRETL software indicates that per capita income of Orissa has an increasing influence on the incidence of Malaria. An increase in current per capita income by Rs. 100 tend to increase the Cerebral Malaria (PF rate) by about a fifth of a percentage point as is evident from the regression equation (R1) given below. The coefficient of real per capita income is even higher (R2).

Table 9.2: Correlation Matrix of Variables Relating to Income and Incidence of Malaria in Orissa, 1961-2003

Variables	Per Capita State Income at Current price (Rs.) (PCYCU)	Per Capita State Income at Constant (1993-94) price (Rs.) (PCYCO)
Malaria Slide Positive Rate (Per cent) (SPR)	0.1610	0.1250
Cerebral Malaria - PF Rate (Per cent) (PF)	0.5593	0.6154

$$PF = \underset{(10.98)}{65.46} + \underset{(1.96)}{0.0022}\,PCYCU \qquad R^2 = 0.687 \quad DW = 1.68 \qquad (R1)$$

$$PF = \underset{(3.42)}{42.41} + \underset{(2.60)}{0.0072}\,PCYCO \qquad R^2 = 0.694 \quad DW = 1.70 \qquad (R2)$$

This is a case which demonstrates that income growth could be insensitive to health issues, if a well-focused health policy is not in place. This has happened in Orissa, because of low public expenditure on education and health. The Human Expenditure Ratio (HER), which is an index of the extent of political commitment of the Government to social sectors, has hovered around 3.5 per cent throughout the 1990s. This is a ratio of social priority expenditure to NSDP, which is recommended to be at least 5 per cent.

VI. Concluding Observation

Health improvement has a number of positive effects on socioeconomic development. However, economic development may not positively promote health. This is evident from the case history of Malaria in Orissa. From a simple time series analysis of incidence of malaria and increase in income of Orissa, it is evident that economic growth could be insensitive to health problems. For development to be helpful to health, well-focused political commitment to social sectors is necessary.

References

Baru, R. V. (1198): *Private Health Care in India: Social Characteristics and Trends*, Sage Publications, New Delhi, p. 184.

Carrin, G. and C. Politi (1997): *Poverty and Health: An Overview of the Basic Linkages and Public Policy Measures*, Health Economics Technical Briefing Note, Task Force on Health Economics, WHO, Geneva, p. 38

Government of India (GOI) (2005): *Economic Survey 2004-05*, Ministry of Finance, New Delhi.

GOI (2006): *Economic Survey 2005-06*, Ministry of Finance, New Delhi.

GOI (1991): *Estimates of State Domestic Product 1950-51 to 1988-89*, Directorate of Economics and Statistics, Planning and Coordination Department, Bhubaneswar.

GOI (2004): *Human Development Report* 2004, Planning and Coordination Department, Bhubaneswar.

GOI (2005): *Economic Survey 2004-05*, Directorate of Economics and Statistics, Planning and Coordination Department, Bhubaneswar.

Gupta, M. C. and B. K. Mahajan (2003): *Textbook of Preventive and Social Medicine* (Third Edition), Jaypee Brothers, New Delhi, p. 609.

World Bank (1993): *The World Development Report, 1993: Investing in Health*, Oxford University Press, New York.

10

Determinants of Nutritional Status of Children in Urban Households

A. Sugirtha Rani

I. Introduction

Human resource is a key factor in development. The formulations of man's physical, mental and social development are laid in early childhood. The quality of future human resource is determined largely by the investment for the development of child population. Children are the budding human resources and future citizens of a nation. Healthy and literate children are not only assets but also the stepping-stones to build a strong and prosperous nation. The morbid or diseased children are not only a burden on their family members, but also on the society.

Of the numerous problems facing the country, growth of children and elimination of malnutrition among the children is the most dominant issues. Nutrition is an integral component of health and well being of all individuals. Good nutrition enables one to lead a socially and economically active life. On the other hand, malnutrition adversely affects health, which is reflected in the incidence of sickness among children and life expectancy. An individual's nutritional level is determined by a number of factors acting directly or indirectly such as, levels of employment, food availability, food consumption pattern, purchasing power of the people, distribution of income, intra-household food distribution, levels of nutritional knowledge, literacy, availability of government schemes and awareness.

Childcare is a good investment in the future productivity or human capital of the labour force. Investment on childcare today will enhance the economic well being in the future. The "Human Capital" metaphor emphasizes the cumulative and structural nature of human development.

II. Need for Special Nutrition Programmes

A question has been raised whether a government should take care of the problems of children, along with the general developmental effort, the government should go in for direct intervention strategies for child health. Experience in many developing countries indicates that, economic development does not necessarily improve lot of the well being of children through well designed income distribution policies and it takes a long time for the benefit from the fruits of economic development.

Several nutritional programmes were implemented at state, national and international level. Nutrition programmes are implemented by the state government viz., MGR Nutritious Noon Meal Programme (NMP) and Tamil Nadu Integrated Nutrition Programme (TINP) which provides supplementary nutrition to antenatal and postnatal women. At national level, *Balwadi* Nutrition Programme (BNP), Crèche/Day Care Centre, Mid-day Meal Scheme and Integrated Child Development Services Scheme (ICDS) are functioning. Apart from state and national level, some programmes are sponsored through international organizations like Co-operatives for American Relief Everywhere (CARE) and Danish International Development Agency (DANIDA). Out of which the national level nutrition scheme ICDS aims at providing a package for early childhood services to children below 6 years, expectant and nursing mothers. The package of services consists of supplementary nutrition, immunization, health checkup, referral services for children and mothers, non-formal pre-school education for children in the age group of 3-5 years, nutrition and health education to mothers. The services are delivered through an *anganwadi* is a grass root level institution among as a focal point for childcare services.

III. Measurement of Nutritional Status

The nutritional status can be assessed by using clinical signs of malnutrition, biomedical indicators and anthropometry measures. The anthropometry measure has an important advantage over other nutritional indicators, whereas biomedical and clinical indicators are useful only at the extremes of malnutrition, body measurements are sensitive over the full spectrum.

Malnutrition refers to a number of diseases each with a specific cause related to one or more nutrients, protein, iodine, Vitamin-A or iron. In the present context malnutrition is synonymous with protein-energy malnutrition, which signifies an imbalance between the supply of protein and the body's demand for them to ensure optimal growth and functions. This imbalance includes both inadequate and excessive energy intake. The former leading to malnutrition in the form of wasting, stunting and underweight, and the latter resulting in overweight and obesity.

Human nutrition is not simply intake of food. Good nutrition and malnutrition are the end results of many interacting factors operating simultaneously and concurrently on the individual in the physical, ecological and cultural environment of the community. The amount of various foods and nutrients reaching different segments of the population depends on food production and its availability logistics of distribution, cultural and economic systems, educational levels and food habits of the people. All these factors contribute towards the total health status. Nutrition is closely to several aspects of human life. Integration of educational, medical, nutritional and public health, including family planning services is therefore imperative for better health and ultimately human development.

Child Growth Indicators and Standard Deviation Classification System

In children there are three commonly used anthropometric indices, such as: weight-for-height, height-for-age and weight-for-age to assess their growth status.

There are three different systems by which a child or a group of children can be compared to the reference population; Z-scores (standard deviation scores), percentiles and per cent of median.

For population based assessment including surveys and nutritional surveillance the `Z' score is widely recognized as the best system for analysis and presentation of anthropometric data because of its advantages compared to the other methods (WHO Global Database on Child Growth and Malnutrition, Geneva).

In database, weight-for-height, height-for-age and weight-for-age are interpreted by using `Z' score classification system. The `Z' score system expresses the anthropometric value as a number of standard deviations or `Z' scores below or above the reference mean or median value. A fixed `Z' score interval implies a fixed height or weight difference for children for a given age. For population-based uses, a major advantage is that a group of `Z' scores can be subjected to summary statistics such as the mean and standard deviation. Formula for calculating the `Z' score is:

Z-score (or SD score) =	Observed Value – Median Value of the reference population
	Standard deviation value of reference population

The three nutritional status indices are expressed in standard deviation units (Z scores) from the median for the international reference population. Children who fall more than two deviations below the reference median are considered to be undernourished, while those who fall more than three standard deviations below the reference median are considered to be severely undernourished.

Each of the indices provided somewhat different information about the nutritional status of children. Children who are more than two standard deviations below the median of the reference populations in terms of height-for–age are considered short for their age or stunted. The per cent in this category indicates the prevalence of chronic under nutrition which often leads to chronic diarrhoea. Stunting is typically associated with inadequate food intake resulting from poor feeding practices or from the lack of sufficient food as well as existence of adverse environmental conditions for an extended period of time. Height-for-age is a measure of the long-term effects of under nutrition.

The weight-for-height index measures body mass in relation to body height children who are more than two standard deviations below the median of the reference population in terms of their weight-for-height are considered to be wasting. The per cent in this category indicates the prevalence of acute under nutrition.

Weight-for-age is a composite measure which takes into account both chronic and acute under nutrition. Children who are more than two standard deviations below the reference median on this index are considered underweight.

IV. Empirical Evidence

Before analyzing the nutritional status of children, it is worth to look at some of the important empirical studies, which are closely related to this study.

It is found that, the works of the following researchers Mathews and Benjamin (1980), Knudson (1981), and Bhargava (1983) studied how far the intervention of government or supplemental programmes improve the nutrition and health status of children. They found that there is positive correlation between programme intervention with nutrition and health status of children. Further, some of them have suggested that nutrition education and regularity of continuous medical care would be complementary to any intervention programme.

Studies other than the above reviewed had explained the determinants of nutrition and health status of children. Some explored that the effect of nutrition (Jesudason and Ambujadevi, 1980), effects of socio-economic status and mothers education (Khanna et al., 1984), effect of birth weight, birth spacing and breast feeding and the impact of mother's work pattern (Khan, 1980) on nutrition and health status of children. Child's age, gender, and birth order were the determinants of nutrition and health status of children.

From the empirical evidences it is found that many studies

have dealt with either intervention programmes or the factors, which are influencing the nutritional and health status of children. But this study has been linked with the impact of government-sponsored scheme on mother's participation in economic activity specifically. And how far this female participation has its influence on two aspects such as nutritional and health status of children those who are in the age group between 2 to 5 years. Further in this study, it is hypothesized that mother's earning positively influences the nutrition and health status of children. Main objective of the study is that how far mother's labour force participation enhances the nutritional and health status of children.

V. Methodology

To carry out this study primary data was collected in Coimbatore City Corporation limit. The scheme offered by government and provides a package of services for the targeted group who are economically deprived. ICDS is one such programme which takes care of the nutritional requirement as well as health education to children and mothers. According to 1991 Census, five wards were selected, which had higher percentage rate of female labour force participation. The sample size had been restricted to 483 households (242 were working mothers and 241 were non-working mothers), having children in the preschool age. In each ward, the ICDS centers as well as households were randomly selected and primary data was collected by using interview schedule technique.

The schedule contained information on demographic socio-economic profile of the households as well as data on family size, income and expenditure of households. In addition to this, data were also collected from mothers about the children's age, feeding practices, immunization of the children, birth order, birth interval, mother's age at the time of child birth, consumption expenditure on food items and mother's time allocation on different activities. As the children are too young the mothers were asked to recall the food provided to the children for the previous day and data were recorded accordingly. The quantum of food intake of the children was calculated by collecting the intake of food and this has been converted into raw ingredients of the food item.

In order to get information on incidence of illness and access to health care, mothers were interviewed on the incidence of sickness for the past 90 days and the choice of health care system; they have taken to cure the disease. To study the nutritional and health status of children three months weights were recorded for each and every child. Among the three months, the first two months data related to weights of children were recorded at the Integrated Child Development Scheme (ICDS) center and the third month data was collected at the time of interview and the height of the children were also measured. Simple statistical and econometric tools such as Ordinary Least Square (OLS) were used to study the determinants of nutrition and health status of children.

Factors Determining Nutritional and Health Status of Children

The World Health Organization (WHO) has recommended weight-for-age, height-for-age and weight-for-height as measures to assess the nutritional status. Using these measures the nutritional status of children are assessed all over the world. This is supported by the fact that World Family Health Surveys and National Family Health Surveys (NFHS) in India also followed the same measures. Further, a scientific report from the Nutrition Foundation of India has concluded that the WHO standard is applicable to Indian children as well.

In this analysis, the variables selected in the equations are parental age, education, earnings, mother's age at the time of giving birth of the child, birth order of the child, birth interval maintained from one child to another, child age, sex of the child, number of days the child has suffered from any illness and quantum of per day food intake of children at home and household expenditures on food items. These variables have been identified as exogenous variables based on past empirical evidences.

Following function has been drawn with the assumption that these variables are determinants of nutritional status (NS) of children.

NS = f(AGE_F, EDU_F, EARN_F, AGE_M, EDU_M, EARN_M, MAGE,
BO, BI, CHI_AGE, MORBI, F_HH, SEX, EXP_FOOD)

Based on the functional relationship between nutritional status of children and explanatory variables in the equation, following models were derived for the three indices of nutritional status of children.

$$NS = b_0 + \sum_{i=1}^{N} b_i X_{ij} + u_1 \quad \text{.....(1)}$$

$$NS_{n-1} = b_o + \sum_{i=1}^{N} b_i X_{ij} + u_2 \quad \text{.....(2)}$$

$$NS_{n-2} = b_o + \sum_{i=1}^{N} b_i X_{ij} + u_3 \quad \text{.....(3)}$$

$$NS_4 = b_o + \sum_{i=1}^{N} b_i X_{ij} + u_4 \quad \text{.....(4)}$$

$$NS_5 = b_o + \sum_{i=1}^{N} b_i X_{ij} + u_5 \quad \text{.....(5)}$$

In these five models, NS, NS_{n-1}, NS_{n-2}, NS_4, NS_5, are dependent variables. Where;

NS - Weight-for-age at the time of interview.

NS_{n-1} - Weight-for-age index one month prior to the time of interview.

NS_{n-2} - Weight-for-age index two months prior to the time of interview.

NS_4 - Height-for-age index at the time of interview.

NS_5 - Weight-for-height index at the time of interview.

'i' stands for a variable and 'j' stands for a child.

X_{ij} stands (i = 1...n) n – independent variables, either continuous or dummy.

b_o and b_i – parameters to be estimated.

$u_1 \ldots u_5$ - random unobserved variables.

Following listed variables were introduced as categorical or dummy from the above said regression models to estimate the nutritional status of children.

EDU_M_1 = 1; Education of mother – illiterate = 1; otherwise = 0.

EDU_M_2 = 1; Education of mother – primary level = 1; otherwise = 0.

EDU_M_3 = 1; Education of mother – higher secondary level = 1; otherwise = 0.

EDU_M_4 = 1; Education of mother – higher level = 1; otherwise = 0.

Similarly in case of father's educational level also,

EDU_M_1 = 1; Education of father – illiterate = 1; otherwise = 0.

EDU_M_2 = 1; Education of father – primary level = 1; otherwise = 0.

EDU_M_3 = 1; Education of father – higher secondary level = 1; otherwise = 0.

EDU_M_4 = 1; Education of father – higher level = 1; otherwise = 0.

SEX_CHI = 1; Male = 1; otherwise = 0.

Besides these variables all other variables in these models were introduced as continuous explanatory variables.

VI. Result Analysis

Descriptive Statistics of Explanatory Variables: With a view to analyze the factors, which determine the health status, selected variables were presented in Table 10.1. For this study, the standardized 'Z' scores of weight-for-age for three months, height-for-age and weight-for-height were used as dependent variables. The variables in Table 10.1 were selected as exogenous factors, which influence the nutritional status of children.

Table 10.1: Descriptive Statistics of Explanatory Variables

Variables	Mean	SD
Age of father (in years)	31.75	4.80
Education of father – illiterate	.12	.32
Education of father – primary	.24	.43
Education of father – higher secondary level	.51	.50
Education of father – higher level	.04	.21
Earning of members in the households (in Rs.)	1685.91	760.27
Age of mother (in years)	27.17	3.97
Education of mothers – illiterate	.39	.48
Education of mother – primary level	.31	.46
Education of mother – higher secondary level	.07	.26
Education of mother – higher level	.20	.40
Monthly earnings of mother (in Rs.)	427.44	475.21
Mothers age at the time of giving birth (years)	24.23	4.12
Birth order	1.76	.78
Birth interval (in months)	21.37	22.72
Child age (in months)	40.49	9.19
Length of morbidity (in days)	4.29	3.06
Hospital expenses per child (in Rs.)	46.70	89.56
Average income loss for each day of sickness (Rs.)	41.66	76.42
'Z' score of weight-for-age prior to two months at the time of interview	.0056	1.0002
'Z' score of weight-for-age prior to one month at the time of interview	.0078	1.0037
'Z' score of weight-for-age at the time of interview	.004	1.0016
'Z' score of height-for-age at the time of interview	.000038	.9981
'Z' score of weight-for-height at the time of interview	.0001	1.000
Per day quantum of food intake in household (gms)	.227	0.786
Amount spent on food items (Rs. Per month)	757.10	329.82

Note: SD stands for Standard Deviation

Factors Determining Nutritional and Health Status of Children: Table 10.2 reveals how far the explanatory variables are influencing significantly either positively or negatively on nutritional status of children. In this analysis, same sets of explanatory variables were used by using three indices of anthropometry measures of nutritional status of children as a dependent variable. So this will be useful to compare the factors determining nutritional status of children. It is to be noted that the caregiver's (mother's) information namely, Body Mass Index (BMI) other than age and education has not been used. Due to time and resource constraints it was not possible to collect the BMI of mothers. Further, it is a tough job for an individual researcher and hence the study includes only mother's age at the time of interview as well as mother's age at the time of birth giving, and birth order of the child and interval time.

Using the above listed variables different specifications were made and regression analyses were made. The results of the regressions are presented in the following Table 10.2. The model covered the parental basic human capital characteristics such as age, education and economic variables were introduced. Besides these parental human capital variables as well as variables like, quantum of food intake, birth order, birth interval and mother's age at the time of birth, length of the morbidity, age and sex of the child were also introduced. It was hypothesized that these variables have a direct bearing on the nutritional status of children. The outcome regression co-efficient were provided in the Table 10.2. In each equation same sets of variables were used but the dependent variable say, nutritional status of measurement is different. Results indicate that only age of the child has emerged significantly in all the equations. To study the nutritional status, age of a child is an important requirement. Further an attempt has been made to study the impact of the age of child on nutritional status. Because when the number of year increases, the children may understand the health and nutrition education, which is provided in the ICDS center and adopts her/him for betterment. So there is a positive relationship between children's age and their

Table 10.2: Factors Influencing Nutrition and Health Status of Children

Independent variables	Weight-for-age at the time of interview	Weight-for-age prior to one month at the time of interview	Weight-for-age prior to two months at the time of interview	Height-for-age at the time of interview	Weight-for-height at the time of interview
	Co-efficient (t values)	Co-efficient (t values)	Co-efficient (t values)	Co-efficient (t values)	Co-efficient (t values)
Constant	-1.196 (3.457)	-1.367 (3.842)	-1.065 (2.919)	-.636 (1.679)	-3.607 (13.888)
Age-f	.0053 (.368)	.013 (.896)	.0063 (.412)	.024 (1.560)	.027** (2.524)
Edu_f_2	.055 (.511)	.047 (.427)	.116 (.720)	-.152 (1.288)	-.051 (.635)
Edu_f_3	.046 (.303)	.019 (.127)	-.023 (.134)	.080 (.483)	.063 (.554)
Edu_f_4	.032 (.196)	.018 (.109)	.025 (.222)	.106 (.091)	.077 (.622)

Contd...

Earn-oth	.0002* (3.600)	.0002* (4.006)	.00021* (3.035)	-.00006 (.938)	-.0001 (.349)
Age_m	-.045 (1.593)	-.041 (1.431)	-.050*** (1.689)	-.080** (2.590)	-.061* (2.859)
Edu_m_2	.146 (1.418)	.132 (1.251)	.075 (.697)	-.073 (.661)	-.011 (.148)
Edu_m_3	.015 (.086)	.010 (.056)	-.034 (.187)	.009 (.048)	-.034 (.261)
Edu_m_4	-.114 (.824)	-.117 (.824)	-.136 (.933)	.055 (.367)	.072 (.694)
Earn_m	.075*** (1.931)	.074*** (1.840)	.067 (1.620)	.061 (1.426)	.054*** (1.835)
Mage	.044** (1.975)	.033 1.443)	.038 (1.625)	.053** (2.173)	.036* (2.184)
BO	-.187* (2.686)	-.187* (2.608)	-.166** (2.253)	.0267 (.351)	.020 (.383)
BI	.0034 (1.547)	.0039*** (1.713)	.0031 (1.348)	.0002 (.083)	-.001 (.645)

Contd...

Chiage	.0149* (3.090)	.0156* (3.130)	.017* (3.361)	.0162* (3.057)	.084* (22.470)
Morbi	-.082* (5.276)	-.0466* (2.884)	.0011 (.067)	-.0008 (.050)	.003 (.260)
F_hh	1.539* (2.735)	- -	- -	.705 (1.145)	.703*** (1.663)
Sex_chi	.159** (1.991)	.146*** (1.779)	.161*** (1.912)	-.027 (.319)	-.026 (.442)
Food_exp	.0005 (3.137)*	.0004 (2.213)**	.00041 (2.24)**	.000014 (.072)	-.000012 (.088)
R^2 F Ratio	.208 7.961	.165 6.022	.117 4.045	.431 1.369	.555 37.902
Degrees of freedom	18	16	16	18	18
Total	543	543	543	543	543

Note: Figures in parentheses indicate absolute't' values. * Significant at 1 per cent level, ** Significant at 5 per cent level, *** Significant at 10 per cent level.

nutritional status. In support of this view, the result shows that child age positively emerged at 1 per cent of significant on all the indices of anthropometry measures.

The results reveal that while father's age has positively influenced at 5 per cent level of significance on weight-for-height. But the mother's age influenced negatively on height-for-age, weight-for-age prior to two months and weight-for-height has emerged significantly at 1 per cent level. This may be inferred that if mother's age increases, the nutrition growth of children fallen may be due to the fact that mother may be unable to provide better care to the child who is first in the birth order when compared to the last child. Moreover when the interval is narrowed down from one child to next childbirth the problem further gets aggregated and the attention of the mother gets divided.

While talking about the impact of variables related to parents on nutritional status of children, earnings of parents plays a predominant role. Because earnings directly influence the resource availability and thereby consumption pattern of households, and which in turn affects the nutritional status of family members including children. In the case of earnings of father which influences positively and significantly at 1 per cent level on index of weight-for-age 'Z' score of three months alone, not on other indices of anthropometry measures of child. Because as is known more income ensures obviously nutritious food. Similarly, the mother's earning, positively influences the weight-for-age at the time of interview and prior to one month as well as weight-for-height at 10 per cent level of significance. This shows that the nutritional status of children and parental earnings have positive association, albeit the earnings of father may not be sufficient one. The addition of mother's earning might enhance the probability of purchase of nutritious food for the children. As far as Indian social system is concerned, the mother's care is essential for child growth and whenever they get earnings, proportionately spends the amount on childcare.

Another variable related to age of mother at the time of birth of a child has positively emerged significant at the anthropometry measure at 5 per cent level of significance and for weight-for-height at 1 per cent level of significance. If the mother bears a child at the average age of 24 or so the child is in better health status. Additionally Indian women around 25 years are very active in taking up domestic chores along with childcare.

With regard to birth order of the children, it is found that it negatively influenced the weight-for-age at the time of interview and weight-for-age one month prior to the interview at 1 per cent level and weight-for-age two months prior to the interview at 5 per cent level of significance. From this it is inferred that, there is a negative relationship between birth order of the child and nutritional status of children. The same factor did not influence other indices of anthropometry measures of children. This indicates that, if mother goes for higher birth order, the weight-for-age of the children may be affected. Also this leads to another due that while the mother bears children with short gestation, she will not have energy to take care of the children more intensively.

The variable birth interval of one child to other was identified as one of the determinant factors of nutritional status of children. This factor positively influenced at 10 per cent level of significant on weight-for-age of child prior to one month only. As a matter of fact for all other measures of health status this variable has not played a significant role.

Similarly, it is assumed that the length of morbidity also influenced negatively the nutritional status of children. In order to test this assumption, the number of days of illness as one of the factors which may determine the nutritional status of children. The regression results supported the hypothesis and the length of morbidity negatively emerged at 1 per cent significance on the weight-for-age. When the number of days of illness is higher, then it is reflected negatively on weight of the children. One has to note here, that the length of morbidity influences weight-for-age at the time of interview and weight-for-age 'Z' scores prior to one month alone not all other indices of anthropometry measures. This is one of the reasons cited already about the need for taking three months weight to measure the nutritional status. The results justified the need for taking at least three months weight to measure the nutritional status. So in weight-for-age 'Z' scores of prior to two months, it has no effect for the introduction of length of morbidity.

Food is one of the important inputs for better nutritional and health status for human being. Keeping this idea in mind, the quantum of food intake of sample children on the previous day to the time of interview from their mothers was collected. The information was converted into grams of that raw ingredient. The quantum of food intake in household showed a positive impact on weight-for-age and weight-for-height significantly emerged at 10 per cent level on nutritional status of children. Further it shows that, follow-up of nutrition and health education indirectly helps to better nutritional status of children. Better nutrition intake reduces the occurrence of illness for the child which in turn has no effect on weight of the children also. Expectedly the quantum of food intake from the household shows a positive and significant influence on nutritional status of children.

Another dimension is to study, whether the gender of the child has anything to do with the nutritional status of children. So the sex of the child introduced as one of the exogenous dummy variable in the equations. From the result it is inferred that gender of the child positively influenced at 5 and 10 per cent levels on weight-for-age at the time of interview and weight-for-age prior to one and two months to the interview respectively. This can be interpreted that male children have better nutritional status than the female children and it may be due to sex discrimination in the household level in providing nutritious food and health facilities etc. In India often felt that males do have preference than their counterparts and this has resulted in widening gender gap in terms of spending on health care similar to education.

Apart from these variables household expenditure on food items introduced as one of the explanatory variables. Because better consumption of food products helps to promote better nutritional status of the children. In this study, it has been introduced household expenditure on food as an explanatory variable. It emerged positively at 1 per cent and 5 per cent level of significant on weight-for-age at the time of interview as well as weight-for-age prior to one month and weight-for-age prior to two months respectively.

It can be summarized that explanatory variables positively influenced nutritional status of children were; father's age, father's earning, mother's earning, mother's age at the time of birth giving, birth intervals between one child to other, age of the children, sex of the children, quantum of food intake in household and household expenditure on food items. Similarly variables, which influences negatively are; mother's age, birth order of the child and length of morbidity on different indices of anthropometry measures of nutritional status.

It is necessary to point out the fact that the education level of both mother and father has not emerged significant in this analysis. On the contrary in many other studies related to human investment education has emerged significant. In the present study it has not supported the same characteristics, which is difficult to understand.

VII. Conclusion

Based on the analysis, it may be concluded that, children in the sample area were not affected seriously by any illness during the reference period, may be due to periodical immunization provided at the centers, follow-up of nutrition and health education taught to children and mothers. Such programme, reduced the occurrence and prevalence of illness for more number of days. In case of factors influencing nutrition and health status of children, the result revealed that father's age, earning, mother's earning, mother's age at the time of birth giving, birth interval, child age, sex were positively emerged while, others like mother's age, education, birth orders and length of morbidity were emerged negatively on the nutrition and health status of children. In this study it was hypothesized that the mother's earning positively influences the nutritional and health status of children in the household. This hypothesis is supported by the regression analysis and the hypothesis is accepted.

References

Akin, S. John, Griffin C Charles, K. David Guilkey and M Barry Popkin (1985): Determinants of Infant Feeding: A Household Production Approach, *Economic Development and Cultural Change,* 34(1), pp.57-81.

Alderman, Harold, Pierre-Andre Chiappori, Lawerence Haddad, John Hoddinott and Ravi Kanbur (1995): Unitary Vs Collective Models of the Household: Is it Time to Shift the Burden of Proof? *The World Bank Research Observer,* 10(1), pp. 1-19.

Behrman Jere R. and Anil B. Deolalikar (1987): Will Developing Country Nutrition Improve with Income? A Case Study for Rural South India, *Journal of Political Economy,* 95, pp. 1108-138.

Bhargava, A. and Sualabh Sharma (1983): Importance of Regularity in Nutritional Intervention of Severly Malnourished Rural Pre-School Children, *Archives of Child Health,* 25(6), pp. 143-47.

Chakravarthy, Archana and Shukla Annapurna (1989): An Evaluation of Weight Standards and Recommended Nutrient Intake in the First Year of Life, *Journal of Family Welfare,* XXXV (5), pp. 26-33.

Chandra P and Venkatasamy (1986): Health and Nutritional Status of Pre-school Children in Rural Tamil Nadu, *Indian Pediatrics,* Vol. XV, No. 6, pp. 499-504.

Claeson, Mariam and J. Ronald Waldman (2000): The Evolution of Child Health Programmes in Developing Countries from Targeting diseases to Targeting People, *Bulletin of World Health Organization,* 78(10), pp. 1234-1245.

Franke, W. Richard (1993): Feeding Programs and Food Intake in a Kerala Village, *Economic and Political Weekly.* Vol. XXVIII, No. 8 and9, pp. 355-360.

Friedman, Debra, Michael Hechter and Kanazawa Satoshi (1994): A Theory of the value of Children, *Demography,* 31(3), pp.375-401.

Haddad, Lawrence, Kennedy Eileen and Sullivan Joan (1994): Choice of Indicators for Food Security and Nutrition Monitoring, *Food Policy,* 19(3), pp. 329-343.

Haddad, Lawrence, Ravi Kanbur, Bouis Howarth (1995): Intra-household Inequality at Different Welfare Levels: Energy Intake and Energy Expenditure Data from the Philippines, *Oxford Bulletin of Economics and Statistics,* 57(3).

Jesudason, Voctor and K. R. Ambujadevi (1980): Effect of Intervention on the Nutritional Status of Young Children: A Longitudinal Study", *Social Action*, 30(1), pp. 50-61.

Kennedy, Eileen, Bouis Howarth and Braun Von Joachim (1992): Health and Nutrition Effects of Cash Crop Production in Developing Countries: A Comparative Analysis, *Social Science Medicine* 35 (5), pp. 689-697.

Khan, M. E., Dastidar Ghosh and Singh Ratanjeet (1986): Nutrition and Health Practices Among Rural Women – A Case Study of Uttar Pradesh, India, *Journal of Family Welfare*, Vol. XXXIII, No. 1.

Khanna, Sushma; B. Renu Patel and Udani H Rekha (1984): A Comparative Study of Effects of Socio-Economic Status and Mother's Education on Child Care and Feeding Practices in Normal and Malnourished Children in Urban Slums of Bombay", *Souvenir Nepas Journal*, 3(1),pp. 53-60.

Knudsen, K. Odin (1981): Economics of Supplemental Feeding of Malnourished Children: Leakages, Costs and Benefits, World Bank Staff Working Paper No.451, World Bank, Washington, D.C.

Mathews, C. M. E. and V. Benjamin (1980): Health Education Evaluation and Belief and Practices in Rural Tamil Nadu-3: Diet and Weaning, *Social Action*, 30, pp. 171-180.

Maxwell, G. Daniel (1995): Alternative Food Society Strategy: A Household Analysis of Urban Agriculture in Kampala, *World Development*, 22,(10), pp. 1669-1681.

Mehta, Jaya (1982): Nutritional Status and Measurement of Malnourishment and Poverty, *Economic and Political Weekly*, Vol. XVII, No. 33, pp. 1332-1340.

Millman, R. Sara, and Cooksey C Elizabeth (1987): Birth Weight and the Effects of Birth Spacing and Breast Feeding on Infant Mortality, *Studies in Family Planning*, 18(4), pp. 202-121.

Mishra, C. P., D. C. S. Reddy and I. C. Tiwari (1987): Nutritional Status of Pre-school Children in Backward Community, *Indian Journal of Pediatrics*, 54, pp. 29-35.

Okyere, Asenso W. K., F. A. Asante and M. Nube (1997): Understanding the Health and Nutritional Status of Children in Ghana, *Agricultural Economics*, 17, pp. 59-74.

Onis, de Mercedes (2000): Measuring Nutritional Status in Relation to Mortality, *Bulletin of World Health Organisation*, 78(10), pp.1271-280.

Onis, de Mercedes, A. E. Frongillo and Monika Blossner (2000): Is

Malnutrition Declining? An Analysis of Changes in Levels of Child Malnutrition Since 1980, *Bulletin of World Health Organization,* 78(10), pp. 1222-1223.

Osmani, S. R. and A. Bhargava (1986): Health and Nutrition in Emerging Asia, *Asian Development Review,* 16(1), pp. 31-71.

Rajasekar, D. (2002): Economic Programmes and Poverty Reduction: NGO Experiences from Tamil Nadu, *Economic and Political Weekly,* Vol. XXXVII, No. 29, pp. 3063-3068.

World Bank (2000): India: Reducing Poverty, Accelerating Development, Oxford University Press, New York.

11

Status of Health and its Determinants in North East India

Keya Sengupta

I. Introduction

Health is recently being recognized as a crucial determinant of economic development. Role of health sector is an important component of new development economics, because this new branch of economies is guided by new sets of priorities. This is mainly because the most important objective of development economics is to raise per capita income and distribute it more equitably by an overall transformation of the structure of demand, trade production and employment (Chenery, 1981). New development economics also emphasizes socio-economic change, by transforming not only the economic variables but also social variable such as improving the health and education status of the less privileged sector of the society. Pareto optimality of the neo-classical school had so far totally excluded such vital factors from the preview of economic growth and development.

Consideration of efficiency excluded the role of the market in such matters and the provision of these necessities was the sole responsibility of the individual, whatever may be his level of income. The result was the emergence of acute form of social inequality, in terms of wide divergence in achievement with regards to health and educational status leading to social inequality in those societies, which adopted neo- classical models of growth for economic development. Such strategies of growth, which ignores the vital issues of social infrastructure would be more disastrous for backward regions, for long-term sustainable development.

It is, therefore, left to the state to assume these responsibilities for the deprived and poverty-stricken people of the society. "It is a patently unsatisfactory social philosophy which in the process of securing individual freedom for the few deprives of our compassion towards the withered lives of the underclass and which in the blind pursuit of economic efficiency is incapable of providing answers to the obvious questions that the voiceless millions ask. A clearly social philosophy would accord centrality to such life and death issues and emphasize entitlements as much as achievements" (Naqvi, 2002).

It has now being accepted by economists of all nations that health is a basic pre-condition for raising the productivity of a nation. It is only labourers who are healthy physically as well as mentally who are capable of working hard for raising productivity. Consequently, health is definitely a crucial input to aggregate production function.

It is therefore extremely important that diseases and various types of illness which affect normally the poor and impoverished due to lack of clean and unhygienic living condition, unsafe drinking water and problems of sanitation be eradicated and reduced. This will bring down the mortality rate so that every person in the economy is able to lead a life free from the fear of illness and death. The poor left on their own to fend for these health problems are often unable to do so. This may raise the level of maternal, child and general mortality rates. Market economy of Pareto optimality, which believes in optimal utilization of resources; do not prescribe resource allocation on health sector for the poor.

The present study is thus an attempt to examine the health status of the people of the north eastern region. The study seeks to make a detailed analysis of the various indicators affecting health condition of the people of the region across different social, religious, and linguistic groups, in view of the significant inter-state, rural, urban and group differential in standard and quality of life characterizing the region. It will perhaps be for the first time that such a microscopic study on health condition of the people of the region will be made in the present study.

The study is based on primary data collected from the sixteen districts of the various states of the region (Six districts from Assam, two each from the smaller states except Manipur), through multistage stratified sampling method. The Sample Size is 350. It needs to be mentioned here that data could not be collected from Manipur due to the socio economic turmoil prevailing in the state at the time of data collection.

II. Status of Health Across Different Religious, Social and Income Groups

The main aim of examining the health status across various socio economic groups is that it will provide a detailed analysis of health status at the micro level. Added to this is a fact that belonging to a certain advantageous social group, May also opens greater accessibility to social opportunities. Religious norms and bindings may also influence attitudes and beliefs, due to which certain religious groups may take greater advantage of the health care facilities, and thereby witness better health record. For exactly the opposite reasons certain social, religious and economic groups may be deprived of the accessibility and a good number facilities. It is due to this reason that macro-level data for the above region or even for the whole state may not convey the true micro-level picture on various indicators of health status.

In an attempt to outline the true picture at a disaggregate level, this section makes a tabular analysis of the data on health condition for different groups. Rest of the sections make an attempt to identify the pivotal factors that determine the health status of the various individual groups through the use of the regression models.

Examination of the above table reveals that health status across various religious, social and economic groups of the population of the region. Among the religious groups, the Buddhists have the highest infant mortality rate, which is as high as 11 per thousand. This may be due to the fact that major sections of the population, belonging to the Buddhist religion, are inhabitants of the remote places of Arunachal Pradesh. The state already has a very poor record of health status, which is true for most religious and social groups. Over and above this, a large section of the population belonging to this religious group resides in very remote and far flung areas, where accessibility to health facilities in an already backward state, is far more inferior.

Table 11.1: Infant Mortality (in Thousand): Different Groups

Religious Groups	Hindus	Christians	Muslims	Buddhists	
	4.29	5.00	5.28	10.50	
Social Group	GC	SC	ST	OBC	
	4.18	5.71	5.00	3.62	
Economic Group (Annual income in Rs.)	Below 20,000	20,000 - 40,000	40,000 - 62,000	62,000 - 86,000	86,000 above
	8.18	6.50	4.87	2.50	1.00

Note: GC – General Category, SC – Scheduled Caste, ST – Scheduled Tribe, OBC – Other Backward Classes.
Source: Compiled from Primary Data.

Table 11.2: Life Expectancy (in Years)

Religious Group	Hindus	Christians	Muslims	Buddhists
	57.02	59.25	59.63	54.00
Social Group	GC	SC	ST	OBC
	58.67	57.00	58.28	57.8

Source: Compiled from Primary Data.

Among the other religious groups, Muslims have a relatively higher infant mortality rate which is not surprising in view of the fact that female literacy which is an important determinant of infant mortality is the lowest among this group. Medical expenditure per head is also the lowest among this group. This may also be a possible explanatory factor for high infant mortality. Whether this is due to the inability to spend or due to the lack of the desire to spend is of course a different issue, which falls outside the purview of our discussion. A disturbing factor; relating to this observation is also the fact that percentage of children immunized is the lowest among this religious group. Lower literacy rate in general and female literacy in particular, among this group is integrally related to this phenomenon.

The Christian community according to our study has a marginally higher infant mortality than the Hindu community. This is a little surprising, because on the whole per capita medical expenditure among the Christians is higher than the Hindus. The literacy rate as well as the female literacy rate among the Christians is slightly higher than their Hindu counterpart, and thus higher infant mortality among them is slightly surprising.

Examining infant mortality across social groups, it is revealed that the population belonging to the SC group has the highest rate of infant mortality followed by ST group. Analyzing the figure for medical expenses per head, it is observed that the SC group records the lowest per capita medical expenditure, which could be a possible explanatory factor for their high infant mortality rate (IMR). However, the same may not be true, for the ST group of the population, whose per capita spending is higher than most other social groups. The fact that medical expenditure per head may not be the possible explanatory factor explaining infant mortality is further revealed by the fact that the general category group witnesses the highest per capita medical expenditure, but do not record a similar satisfactory figure with respect to infant mortality rate. In contrast, the OBC group of the population has the best figure with respect to medical expenses.

Another feature that emerges from the study is that, infant mortality is governed in a very important manner by the income level of the group concerned, irrespective of the social or the religious group, they may belong to. Among the five income groups into which population have been divided, it can discern a clear pattern of declining rate of infant mortality along with rising income level. An inverse relationship between income level and infant mortality can clearly be identified. The reasons may not be too far to seek. Poverty leads to lower literacy rate and lower literacy rate increases ignorance, which decreases the level of awareness relating to child care, benefits of immunization et cetera. All these factors combine to increase the infant mortality rate, among the lower income groups. It needs to be noted that though income group determines infant mortality, yet it is not lower medical expenditure of lower income groups, which govern infant mortality but through unhygienic living condition, less attention in terms of time, nutrition and care for the infants of the family that emerges to be the crucial determinants of infant mortality.

Medical expenditures, therefore, do not emerge as a determinant factor of infant mortality, though level of income emerges as an important one. Higher literacy rate, among the general category population may explain lower infant mortality though the same do not seem to be true for the other social groups. However, the level of child immunization across different socials groups may be an important factor. In an attempt to know the exact quantitative impact of these various determinant factors, the study tried the regression models outlined above.

In a further attempt at evaluating the health status of the region, the study has tried to examine the life expectancy of the various religious and social groups of the region. It is revealed very interestingly that the section of the population belonging to the Muslim community have the highest life expectancy of 60 years. This is surprising because the group of population belonging to this religion, not only experiences the lowest medical expenses per capita, but the lowest literacy rate as well, factors which were considered crucial as determinants of health status. Infant mortality, as well as poverty is high among this group. Perhaps inherent physical traits, may explain the reason for their better life expectancy. Life expectancy is about 59 years among the Christian community, which may perhaps be explained by better performances in terms of literacy rate, medical expenses and lower level of mortality among them. All these factors taken together may explain a satisfactory level of human development among this group. Life expectancy among the group of population belonging to the Hindu community is only 57 years, in spite of better performance with respect to the other determinants. The Buddhist community has the lowest life expectancy of only 54 years, which is not only the lowest in the region, but much below the national average as well. The reason for this poor record may be similar poor record of other determinants of health as well as remoteness of the place of residence of the Buddhist Community.

Among the social groups; population belonging to the general category has the highest life expectancy followed by the ST group. The lowest life expectancy among the social groups is recorded by the SC group preceded by the OBC category. Taking an overall view, life expectancy for most of these social groups is shaped by the determinants which are identified, though the exact quantitative relationship can be discussed only through the use of regression models.

III. Empirical Estimation of the Determinants of Health Status

In the above analysis, inferences have been drawn about the health status of different social, religious and economic groups. Attempts also had made to identify the broad reasons for the same. However, to know the exact quantitative relationship among the various indicators of health status and their determinants, various models have been fitted below. The results of these models are expected to have very important implications for policy considerations in the health sector for this region. The reason for this is that the results of these functions are expected to focus attention to the various ways in which different factors affect the health condition of different groups.

Firstly, literacy rate is regressed on IMR for various social and religious groups, the results of which are presented in Table 11.3.

The results revealed that R^2 is not satisfactory for any of the social or religious groups, though the figure and sign of the regression coefficient is satisfactory in most cases, with the only exception of the Muslim, Christian and the general category group. However, none of the coefficients are statistically significant, except for the ST groups and the general category. In view of the lower explanatory power of the equation, we do not accept this model even for this group. Consequently, the model is not acceptable for any of the groups of the region.

Table 11.3: Literacy Rate Regressed on IMR (IMR = a – b Lit)

Parameters		A	B Lit	R^2	F
Religious groups	Hindus	10.56 (3.640)	- .457 (-1.921)	.209	3.689
	Muslims	1.531 (.294)	.308 (.729)	.095	.524
	Christians	4.055 (.842)	.064 (.129)	.004	.017
Social groups	General Category	8.410 (4.922)	-.558 (-2.515)	.311	6.232
	ST	10.189 (4.615)	-.573 (-2.425)	.329	5.880
	SC	.886 (3.959)	-.075 (-.150)	.006	.022
	OBC	8.507 (2.865)	-.560 (1.655)	.313	2.739

In the next model, female literacy is adopted as an important explanatory variable, since numerous studies have highlighted the role and significance of female literacy rate in determining health condition (Table 11.4).

The function seems to be accepted only for the Christian community and the ST group. The explanatory power of the variable is as high as 626 and the variable explains 80 per cent of the variation in infant mortality.

This indicates that literacy rate occupy a very important place among the Christian Community and its favourable impact is felt directly on infant mortality. Similar is the case with the ST group for whom the explanatory power of the variable though not too high, yet the regression coefficient of the independent variable, is significant both on statistical as well as on theoretical grounds. One reason for the significance of this model for both the groups could be that most of the Christian community belongs to the ST category in this region. Almost 60 per cent of the variation in IMR is explained by female literacy. However, this is not to suggest that female literacy do not have any impact on IMR but the fact is that the impact of female literacy may be felt over a period of time, as female literacy affects other socio-economic variables in a favourable manner, and the overall impact of this may be felt only after a time gap. Studies of similar nature all over the world have revealed that female literacy is the single most important factor for reducing infant mortality.

Table 11.4: Female Literacy Rate Regressed on IMR ($IMR = a - b\ Lit_F$)

Parameters		A	b Lit_F	R^2	F
Religious groups	Hindus	7.833 (3.355)	-.370 (-1.434)	.137	2.057
	Muslims	1.531 (.294)	.308 (.724)	.095	.524
	Christians	13.733 (4.49)	.791 (-2.890)	.626	8.354
Social groups	General Category	7.720 (1.717)	-.489 (-.484)	.239	4.396
	ST	10.569 (4.371)	-596 (-2.567)	.355	6.590
	SC	5.791 (4.159)	-.045 (-.091)	.002	.09
	OBC	6.463 (2.657)	-.434 (-1.180)	.188	1.393

In fact female literacy has always been considered as a better "predictor" of child mortality than per capita expenditure on health. The correlation between infant mortality and female literacy is 0.8 in comparison to 0.4 correlation coefficient between infant mortality and per capita expenditure. Studies have revealed with respect to other states (Murty et el, 1995), that after controlling for female literacy, per capita expenditure has no significant association with child mortality. Therefore, diversity in the magnitude of influence of female literacy across different groups on infant mortality, do not reduce the role of female literacy in the region. Social development among the Christian Community, majority of whom in this region belong to the ST social group, has been much better than the other groups in the region for a considerable longer period. Greater social opportunities, among them has been due to greater spread of literacy among them, better status of women, lower gender gap, which has a reflection on widespread and equitable health care including child care and infant mortality.

In this context, Kerala experience deserves reference. The early promotion of basic education, particularly female education, in the state has lead to important social achievements, including that of the various aspects of health status. In contrast, in Uttar Pradesh where half of the female population never goes to school, female literacy is extremely high, which is turn has its reflections on lower levels of social achievement including high infant mortality rates.

In the next model per capita medical expenses is taken as an explanatory variable.

$$\mathbf{IMR = a - b\ Md_{exp}}$$

Religious Group

Hindus:

$IMR = 9.866 - 0.622\ Md_{exp}$

$R^2 = 0.387$, $F = 8.825$

t – Value (5.699) (-2.971)

Muslims:

$IMR = 2.919 - 0.484\ Md_{exp}$

$R^2 = 0.235$, $F = 1.535$

t – Value (3.034) (-1.238)
Christians: $IMR = 2.020 - 0.672\ Md_{exp}$
$R^2 = 0.451, F = 4.112$
t – Value (4.423) (-2.028)
Social group
GC:
$IMR = 7.594 - 0.667\ Md_{exp}$
$R^2 = 0.445, F = 11.223$
t – Value (7.194) (-3.350)
ST:
$IMR = 9.544 - 0.629\ Md_{exp}$
$R^2 = 0.396, F = 7.867$
t – Value (5.613) (-2.805)
SC:
$IMR = 6.70 - 0.375\ Md_{exp}$
$R^2 = .141, F = .656$
t – Value (5.176) (-.810)
OBC:
$IMR = 8.293 - 0.506\ Md_{exp}$
$R^2 = .256, F = 2.067$
t – Value (8.540) (-1.438)

The model is satisfactory on theoretical account for all social and religious groups. However, the function is acceptable only for the Hindu and Christian community among the religious groups and ST and general category, among the social groups. For these groups, the explanatory power of the function is also high. About 62 to 67 per cent of the variation in infant mortality is explained by medical expenses. Insignificance of this variable among the other categories may be explained by the fact that a major segment of these population may belong to lower income group, who may not have the ability to spent and thus depend more on government health services.

To capture the essence of all these factors in a composite manner, I have included all the above mentioned variables in a single function. Though the explanatory power of the function is as high as 0.765 to 0.711, in certain cases as revealed by the value of R^2, yet multi-collinearity is very high in all cases, which is observed through the change in the sign of the regression coefficients of almost all the independent variables in all cases. However, this is not surprising, since these are all socio-economic variables whose degree of interrelationship is bound to be very high. As a result of all these reasons, none of these models can be accepted from our point of view. It may thus be inferred from this analysis of regression model, that though the operation of all the factors affecting infant mortality identified are important, yet none of these factors affect the various socio-economic and religious group in an identical manner. For some female literacy has a direct impact, whereas for the others it has an indirect impact. Medical expenses assume importance for some groups, whereas general education is important for the rest. Consequently, the composite function is not effective and acceptable.

The above findings have important policy implications, in so far as it reveals that attempt to raise the health status of the population of this region, may necessitate tackling these problems differently at different socio-economic levels. As far as provision of government health services at the supply side is concerned, some kind of uniformity may not be undesirable for all socio-economic and economic groups. On the demand side however, tackling the problem at a heterogeneous level is called for. Provision of health services by the state uniformly irrespective of any groups or community is extremely essential particularly in some districts of the region. Some of these districts are the Tirap and Itanagar districts of Arunachal Pradesh, Cachar, Karimganj and Barpeta districts of Assam, and East Garo Hills of Meghalaya, where the state of health of all the groups is a matter of serious concern. This is important, not only from the point of view of improving the quality of life, but also for long term economic development, since high infant mortality rates, low life expectancy, high mortality and under nourishment, can act as serious barriers to labour productivity and thereby economic development (Dreze and Sen, 2002).

An important indicator of good quality of life is long and

healthy life. Longevity is the combined effect of a good number of factors working together. Inherent physical characteristics, literacy rates, economic status which has its impact on medical expenditure per capita and the ability to satisfy the required nourishment are some such factors. It is already highlighted that in North East India, like the rest of the country, medical expenditure per head, increases along with income level, in all the states. This implies that level of income, determines medical expenditure per capita. Therefore, it is considered as pertinent to regress per capita medical expenditure on life expectancy for all the groups in the region. This can also relate life expectancy to economic well-being, since it is a common experience that longevity is lower among low-income groups and higher among the high-income groups. Higher medical expenditure implies greater ability to fight illness and diseases as well as the capacity to prevent them, resulting in longer life span.

The results of the estimation of the values of model, in which I have taken medical expenses per capita as independent variable and life expectancy as a dependent variable reveal that the explanatory power of the function is satisfactory in almost all cases, and the regression coefficients are theoretically as well as statistically significant. In case of the SC group almost 82 per cent of life expectancy is explained by medical expenses. For the population group belonging to the Muslims and Hindu religious community almost 67 per cent of longevity is explained by medical expenses. Only in the case of the Christian community and ST social group, who in most cases are the same group in this region, the function is not satisfactory on any account and therefore unacceptable for this group. It may thus accept per capita medical expenses (or economic well-being) as an important determinant of life expectancy in this region. Similar are the findings of studies conducted by Anand and Ravillion, (1993) who maintain that nearly half the variations in life expectancy can be attributed to difference in GNP per head. These findings therefore establish beyond doubt that the value of higher real income, enhances the possibilities of improving the quality of life, which are not possible at lower level of income. Anand and Ravillion in their work further point out that the relationship between per capita income and life expectancy is established via public action. Higher GNP enables reduction of poverty and increasing public expenditure on health, via appropriate public policies, which in turn increases life span of the common man.

It has also been noted earlier that economic well-being is a direct determinant of infant mortality as well, as in the case of life expectancy. Therefore improvement of quality of life is crucially dependent on per capita income.

Table 11.5: $Lif_{exp} = a + b\ Md_{exp}$

Religious and Social Groups	A	b (Md_{exp})	R^2	F
Hindus	50.844 (26.402)	.662 (3.307)	.439	10.938
Muslims	49.975 (10.853)	.678 (2.063)	.460	4.254
Christians	59.260 (14.390)	-.0012 (-.001)	.002	.004
General Category	53.528 (19.569)	.463 (1.953)	.214	3.815
ST	55.665 (19.317)	.259 (.929)	.067	.862
SC	44.74 (11.654)	.823 (3.234)	.677	10.458
OBC	45.372 (6.706)	.602 (1.847)	.363	3.413

It is here that the role of economic development assumes importance in enhancing health status of the people, so that the two cannot be viewed in isolation. In fact only a satisfactory level of economic development can ensure a better quality of life, which has already been highlighted as the real criteria of success of economic development. Therefore, the traditionally accepted criteria of development through GNP cannot be discarded in an outright manner. One has to bear in mind that GNP per head by itself is not important. What is necessary to remember here is how higher GNP achieved through economic development can raise the quality of life. HDR of 2003 also focuses attention to the fact that failed economic growth lies believed the failure of Human Development Index and the inability of many countries and regions to reduce income and human poverty. Income poverty cannot be reduced in stagnant economy, and the development experience of recent years reveal that poverty can be reduced only in a fast growing economy. Therefore, the report maintains that growth is essential for reducing income poverty.

In view of the important role of education and its relationship with health, the function is estimated, in which literacy rate is accepted as an independent variable. Though theoretically the regression coefficients are satisfactory in almost all cases, yet statistical insignificance of the coefficients and lower explanatory power of the function judged by the value of R^2 compels us to reject the model for all religious and social groups. Attempt also made to test the multiple regression models, in which per capita medical expenditure, literacy rate and female literacy as independent variables. This model too is not acceptable on either theoretical or statistical grounds. Medical expenditure which emerges as a crucial determinant of life expectancy becomes insignificant, since its coefficient changes its sign indicating the presence of multi-collinearity. As indicated earlier, multi collinearity is not surprising in case of socio-economic variables, where there is an interrelationship among the independent variables identified.

This is not to suggest the insignificance of these variables operating to influence life expectancy at the individual level. It also needs to be noted that the composite operation of these variables become more effective via public action on health care. For instance, it is only the educated people, who are aware of the government health facilities and are more conscious of the ways in which the facilities can be availed of. Medical expenses can become meaningful, only with the existence of medical infrastructure. These infrastructures may be private or state for ownership and operates in the form of dispensaries, hospitals, doctors, medicines et cetera all of which provides the avenues medical expenses. All these features associated with state of health condition, are the result of public action, all of which can have an important influence on health status of the common man. Variables like education, medical expenses and others seem to have a direct impact on the various components of health status of the region taken individually. It is due to this that the composite influences of these factors taken together do not seem to be too effective.

IV. Conclusions

It is, therefore, evident that intra-regional variation, in North Eastern Region and variation among various social, religious and economic groups relating to the various indicators of health is determined not by one single factor. Different factors lie behind behaviourial pattern of health status across various socio economic and religious groups. Consequently viewing the problems of this region from a macro point may not provide the true microscopic scenario of the exact dimension of the problem. Decades of literacy among some groups against new generation learners for others might have resulted in various behaviourial traits in health awareness, or knowledge of public health services. Differences in economic well-being irrespective of all other factors also result in different levels of health status. Minor health problems which when neglected leads to serious complications and resultant high mortality rates. Such problems however, occupies a lower position in the list of priorities for the poverty stricken section of the population. In contrast, among the higher income groups, health along with food occupies, equal position in the list of priorities on which expenditure has to be incurred. All these variations in the behavioural traits in health condition of the population in the north eastern region, only goes to indicatc that the region cannot be treated as a homogeneous unit as far as policy action is concerned.

In view of the remoteness of some of the districts of the region, and the extremely sensitive nature of the tribal population who occupy a dominant place in the region, policy action cannot be like the rest of the country. Minute and careful variation is called for, even within the region itself. Detailed statistical enquiry and scrutiny of our study at the micro-level is therefore expected to be extremely helpful to raise the quality of life via sensitive public action. The findings will go a long way in explaining the casual factors leading to differences in health status of different groups in the region at a disaggregate level. At the same time, some integrated understanding of the whole region is also expected to be extremely helpful and useful. On the whole the study reveals that some districts of the region, some income groups and certain special groups, perform much better than the all India performance level, whereas the record of the others is much below the national average, and may take several years, before they can reach the national average. The historical factors responsible for the socio-economic growth of the community and their consequent behavioural traits also assumes crucial importance in this region.

References

Anand, S. and Martin Ravallion (1993): Human Development in Poor Countries: On the Role of Private Incomes and Public Services, *Journal of Economic Perspectives*, 7

Chenery (1983): Interaction between Theory and Observation in Development, World Development, 10:11, 856-861

Drenze, J. and A. Sen (2002): *India Development and Participation*, Oxford University Press, New Delhi

Murty, M., A. C. Juio and J. P. Drez (1995): Mortality, Fertility and Gender Bias in India, *Population and Development Review*, Vol. 35, No. 1.

Naqvi, S. Q. H. (2002): *Development Economics: Nature and Significance*, Sage Publications, New Delhi.

12

Health Care Delivery System in Orissa

Rabi N. Patra

I. Introduction

Health is a state of complete physical, mental and social well-being and not merely the absence of disease and infirmity (WHO, 1992). It is a socio-physical good and a major determinant of human resources so vital for enhancing productivity, accelerating economic development and improving the quality of life and the level of social welfare. It is believed that children who enjoyed better health and nutrition in the pre-school years and are healthy and well-fed in their years of education, usually achieve higher success rates at both education and work. Hence the adage goes 'Health is wealth'. However, health not only aids economic development but is facilitated by it as well. Economic development brings persistent increases in income and improvements in health status and helps movement of individuals and social groups towards a situation of materially and spiritually better conditions of life.

Concern for health is relatively recent. It was accorded priority only in the 1970s as part of the equity-oriented development strategies particularly in the developing countries. It attracted special attention of the policy makers and planners with United Nations Development Programme (UNDP)'s annual series of Human Development Reports (HDRs) initiated since 1990 which emphasizes Human Development Index (HDI) as a holistic measure of economic development. Health also finds a place of prominence in the UN's Millennium Development Goals (MDGs) which, among other things, includes reducing child mortality, improving maternal health and combating HIV/AIDS, malaria and other diseases. In the contemporary society health is an end in itself.

Health is a public good in the sense that in many cases one person's use of health information and health services does not leave less for others. For example, it is not possible to limit the benefit of malaria control programmes to only one individual. It also has strong positive externalities. For instance, immunizing one against measles may benefit others by way of slow/non-transmission of the disease to them. Penetration of health centres into the rural areas and free delivery of health care facilities to the poor can be instruments for reducing regional disparities and poverty while free/below-cost provision of warranted health services can overcome the problem of moral hazards in the health sector. These characteristics of health point to market failure in the provision of health care to the people and make a strong case for active state intervention in the health sector as also for regarding government spending on health as a form of social investment.

Right from the First Five Year Plan, the government endeavoured to improve the quality of life of the people through, among other measures, a well defined health care system. The massive increase in public financed extensive health care facilities and programmes during the Plan period has, no doubt, brought good dividends in terms of near total eradication of mass killing diseases (cholera, plague, smallpox etc.), substantial control over other fatal diseases (tetanus, tuberculosis, rabies, malaria etc.) and reduction in deaths and disabilities caused by injuries and vaccine preventable diseases (accidents, polio etc.), yet India lags far behind many other developing countries in terms of health status. The UNDP HDR-2006 contains a Health Index for 177 countries of the world in which India has a poor 126th rank, much worse than Srilanka's position at 93. India's public health spending as percentage of GDP is one of the lowest in the world (0.9) which is lower than China's 1.9 and even lower than Malayasia's 1.5. The health status of Orissa is gloomier. She compares very poorly with the performance at the national level in terms of basic health indicators such as death rate, infant mortality rate, life expectancy at birth and per capita per annum public expenditure on health except birth rate where Orissa's position is little better compared to the all India figure (Table 12.1).

The mushrooming of private sector super speciality health centres, polyclinics and nursing homes in the urban areas and a large number of small clinics in the rural hinterlands of the state along with the aforestated health status is a matter of serious concern. It is indicative of the inadequacies of the public health care system in fulfilling the expectations of the people in general and of the poor in particular.

In this back drop the present paper is a humble attempt at analyzing the health care delivery system, examining the issues of accessibility and financing health services and spelling out their implications for policy making and programme implementation in the context of Orissa. The study is based on both primary and secondary data. Simple statistical tools are used to interpret data and draw conclusions there from. The paper is designed in four sections. Section I is introductory. Section II discusses the health care delivery system and infrastructure, accessibility to health facilities and financing of health expenditure in Orissa. Results of an empirical health survey are analyzed in section III and section IV presents a summary of observations and some workable suggestions for improving the system.

II. Delivery, Accessibility and Financing

Delivery: Health care delivery system includes all the actors and activities designed to promote, restore or maintain health. The structure of health care delivery system in the state of Orissa is largely complex and multidimensional characterized by pluralism. Broadly speaking it consists of two main components: (i) a formal segment comprising the public health department, hospitals, clinics and residences of doctors and paramedics and (ii) an informal network of traditional healers. The formal component encompasses a near universal highly expensive western allopathic mechanism and the conventional modes of health services such as ayurveda, homoeopathy, unani and physiotherapy. The informal

Table 12.1: State of Health Care: Orissa versus India

Nation/ State	Public Expenditure on Health 2002-03			Birth rate per 1000 in 2001	Death rate per 1000 in 2001	Infant mortality rate per 1000 in 2001	Life Expectancy at Birth in 2001
	Per capita expenditure on Medical PH and FW	As per cent of Domestic Product	As Per cent of Overall Public Expenditure				
India	179.23	0.9	4.55	25.4	8.4	66	63
Orissa	160.65	1.0	4.25	23.4	10.2	91	61

PH = Public Health; FW = Family Welfare.

Sources: GOI (2004): Economic Survey, 2003-04; Census of India (2001) and **GOO** (2005): Economic Survey, 2004-05.

segment has health providers like siddha, yoga, herbal and quack healers, black magic and spirit worship faith-healers.

The conventional and informal components of the health care system have always been dominated by private practitioners. Of late the government has shown interest in establishing ayurvedic and homoeopathic health centres in different areas of the state. The state has 527 ayurvedic health centres including 5 hospitals, 484 homoeopathic centres inclusive of 4 hospitals, one unani hospital and three physiotherapy centres attached to the three allopathic medical colleges as on 2005. The allopathic segment of the health care delivery system in the state mostly remains in the public sector. In the year 2005, this segment has 179 hospitals including the three medical colleges, 202 community health centres (CHCs), 141 public health centres (PHCs), 1166 new PHCs, 13 mobile health units and 13,886 beds. However, the majority of qualified allopathic doctors and surgeons, more than 80 per cent, are serving in the private sector. This includes many government doctors and surgeons who practice privately after/during government duty hours either in their own clinics/nursing homes or as consultants in privately runs health centres. The health care delivery system in the state is, thus meaningfully based in the private sector.

From the analytical point of view, the health care system in Orissa is quite segmented. The public sector is prominent in highly expensive secondary and tertiary health care than in primary health care. The specialist/super specialist orientation of patients coupled with lack of dedication at the primary public health care delivery level with the staff at this level referring the patients to hospitals and specialists at the earliest opportunity has resulted in, what is known as the tragedy of primary public health centres. The public sector reins supreme in the field of preventive care. But in the case of curative and ambulatory care the private sector has gone retail in the state.

In Orissa, public Sector health infrastructure in the allopathic segment is overburdened (Table 12.2) with a very large population served per health centre (21,580), per doctor (7,423) and per hospital bed (2,643). The average coverage of square kilometer area per health centre (91.5), per doctor (31.5) and per bed (11.21) also remains high in the state. With inadequate health infrastructure it is naïve to expect proper health care delivery.

Table 12.2: State of Allopathic Health Infrastructure in Orissa, 2001

Particulars	Average Coverage Per Health Centre	Average Coverage per Doctor	Average Coverage per Hospital Bed
Population	21580	7423	2643
Square KM Area	91.5	31.5	11.21

Source: GOO (2005): Economic Survey, 2004-05.

The quality of public sector health care in Orissa is rated low. Operation theatres with leaking roofs, poor equipment and unwilling personnel are common in the government hospitals. Long queues for surgery are another disheartening matter. In 2005 the government established eight regional diagnostic centers (RDCs) in the state amidst high expectations for providing round the clock state-of-the-art diagnostic services at cheaper rates. But many of the equipments supplied to the eight RDCs have either not been installed or diverted to hospital departments or even lying defunct. Most of the RDCs lack qualified personnel to handle the sophisticated equipments or do not have the required floor space for installing the machines for which they are rusting in the store without use. Even after more than a year and half of establishment the RDCs fail to deliver.

Accessibility: Potential and Effective Accessibility

In the context of health services, accessibility has two dimensions – potential and effective. Potential accessibility involves access to physically existent health care facilities and is a necessary condition of meaningful health care. Effective accessibility denotes the level of actual access of the patients to the health provider. It requires that the health service centre is (i) located at a reasonable distance, (ii) functioning with appropriate working hours, (iii) operating with desired inputs, and (iv) using all the personnel and materials optimally to the full benefit of the patient(s). Needless to say effective accessibility is one of the sufficient conditions of meaningful health care. The public health services sector in Orissa most often remains in the news for the wrong reasons – lack of effective accessibility.

Three more aspects of accessibility are worth noting. They are: geographical accessibility, socio-economic group-wise accessibility and gender accessibility.

Accessibility: Geographical Accessibility

It is no gainsaying that while 85 per cent of the state's population lives in the villages, 55 of its 179 allopathic, 5 ayurvedic, 4 homeopathic and the lone unani hospitals are located in the urban centres. The public health infrastructure and the quantity and quality of health services in the state run rural health centres is one of the worst in the country. In the remote areas and backward tribal pockets the public sector allopathic health care units run with skeleton and unwilling staff and irregular timings offering slip shop and half hearted treatment. In some cases the nurse, the pharmacist and the doctor are seen attending the health centre alternately for a short time twice/thrice a week. Long periods of unauthorized absence are not uncommon too. In many villages consulting a doctor in emergencies is a luxury. Provision of public health service in the state thus has an urban bias.

The situation is no better at the district level. For purposes of comparison, a constructed composite health development index (CHDI) of health infrastructure is constructed for each of the 30 districts of the state on the basis of five indicators viz., number of persons served per health facility, number per doctor and number per bed, and area served per health centre and per doctor. Each of these five indicators is assigned equal weight for the sake of simplicity. The coefficient of variation is calculated in respect of these indicators and composite index values as a measure of inequality to show the disparity in health services across districts in the state.

The coefficient of variation is found to be very high for the number of population covered per health centre (17.16 per cent), per doctor (36.18 per cent) and per bed (59.38 per cent) and for average area covered per health centre (56.13 per cent) and per doctor (63.92 per cent). It is also very high (37.56 per cent) in the case of the composite index. Looking at the composite index values for different districts, it is found that out of the 30 districts in the state only 13 have index values of more than 100 and hence may be termed as developed districts so far as the public health care facilities are concerned. They are Cuttack, Sambalpur, Khurda, Ganjam, Kandhamal, Jagatsinghpur, Puri, Balasore, Malkangiri, Nayagarh, Bhadrak, Jajpur and Kendrapara in the descending order. It is disheartening to note that barring only three i.e. Sambalpur, Kandhamal and Malkangiri, the rest ten are parts of the four erstwhile coastal districts and are also easily accessible to the two medical college hospitals located at Cuttack and Berhampur. Of the three other districts in the medically developed category, Sambalpur has a medical college hospital and Kandhamal and Malkangiri are very thinly populated. The remaining 17 districts are less developed with very low composite index values. Boudh, Angul, Nuapada, Deogarh and Nabarangpur are found to be the least medically developed districts in that order.

Western and central districts have less than average access to health infrastructure. The health infrastructure coverage is also non-uniform across the coastal and hilly districts of the state. The coastal districts are in a relatively favourable position in respect of area coverage while coverage of population is comparatively better in the case of hilly districts.

Thus the health service system in the state exhibits large disparities across districts. Like most low income countries of the world, the capital city, the millennium city, and other major and minor urban areas and towns in the state usually have several times as many doctors and public health facilities relative to the rural areas, highland villages and tribal pockets in Orissa.

Accessibility: Accessibility and Socio-Economic Classes

Disease knows no law it affects all sections of the population indiscriminately irrespective of wealth, social status and political power. But with globalizations and WTO-led rise in pharmaceutical prices, economic reforms directed users' fees in the public health services sector and privatization induced unregulated growth of the private health care centres, health has become commoditized and is exposed to the vagaries of market forces in Orissa as elsewhere. While the overall willingness to pay for health services remains low in the state it is not uniform across high and low income groups as also across different social classes. The operations in the health sector thus restrict the already limited access to health services for the vulnerable sections and hence accentuate the inequalities in access to health facilities.

Public health care facilities are, no doubt, cheaper than private provisioning yet, the 'private ness' in public services are no less stringent. Those who are better off socially, politically and economically use their clout to ensure the public health services for them, while others who are in the lower echelons are denied effective access. Besides, the patients have to 'please' and 'grease' the public health personnel from top (the surgeon) to bottom (the peon and sweeper), and may be in advance, for treatment. This obviously limits poor people's access to public health care facilities.

Gaps in patients' expectations and perceptions also affect effective accessibility. Over the years, the public health service system in Orissa has earned a bad name for it on account of poor quality care. The causes are many. Centralized decision-making, badly deployed and wrongly supervised personal and their commercial mindset, inadequate contact and history taking, a total lack of personal touch and missionary zeal and dysfunctional infrastructure are some of the reasons for poor health services and lower patient satisfaction. In the context of the socio-economically disadvantaged population the expectation-perception divide is wider and quality of care worse for which access to public health care facilities remains low; they not only get less but also receive low quality care. It thus follows that health subsidies are not well targeted and that the public health care system remains in the outreach of the very people it is expected to serve.

Accessibility: Gender Discrimination

Gender relations are basically linked to inequality and subordination and have, of late, been incorporated in development analysis. In matters of concern for health the fair sex is discriminated against in a variety of ways. As fetus they are killed in the womb itself; as girls they are given less vaccination and less nutrition and bear the brunt of child marriage which deprive them of the gains from health; as women they carry the entire burden of contraception, conception, child bearing and rearing, shoulder all household responsibilities, eat last and low quality diet, and neglect their sickness until they fall too ill to do household chores; and in old age they are prone to a number of ailments and ill treatment , more so if they are widows. Women are a repository of many diseases mainly because they are exposed to heavy smoke in the kitchen and are susceptible to gynaec and maternal disorders. But they are also the last to get the benefits of health care as in most cases their ill health and disease(s) are not considered as a problem by themselves.

Women's access to health care is not a question of mere availability of such facilities. Much depends on social, cultural, psychological and attitudinal conditions. Reproductive health problems and gynaecological diseases are a matter of private affair and they remain as unspoken diseases. Factors like geographical distance, lack of freedom to go out and seek medical help, hesitation to consult a male doctor etc. explain poor accessibility of women to health care facilities.

Low female-male ratio and life expectancy at birth for females as well as high female infant mortality rate compared to males in Orissa and relative to the national average are (Table 12.3) the crucial manifestations of the prevailing gender disparities in access to health care services in the state. The problem is more serious when looked at the innate biological advantages which females are endowed with relative to their male counterparts. With health care services becoming more expensive under the impact of the new economic policy and globalization, women are going to be further marginalized in the health care sector in a very poor state like Orissa.

The Private Health Care System

In Orissa health care is also provided by the private sector the operations of which are highly diverse in methods and quality. The traditional system of health care consisting of ayurveda, homoeopathy, siddha, faith-healing, naturopathy and yoga have largely been dominated by private practitioners and private financing. In addition most of the doctors and many of the nurses and sub-staff working in and retired from the public health service system and all those qualified allopath who are in and out of employment in other sectors are based in the private health sector in the state. Only a handful of health personnel employed in the public sector who are principled and / or are not well marketable do not engage themselves in 'private practice'. But health statistics in the state are limited mostly to the public sector because most of the private sector health centres are not registered nor do they document their activities well. Hence the size of the private health sector, though enormous, is not amenable to exact measurement.

Now-a-days the patients in the state are showing a strong preference for the private health care system particularly for ambulatory and curative care. The evils of the public health care facilities, viz. unenthusiastic and heartless health personnel, long waiting period, marginal consultancy time with history skipping and emphasis on tests, nonfunctional diagnostic centres, ill-equipped operation theatres etc. along with the 'user fees' and the need of 'pleasing' the health personnel involve a kind of double taxation of the patients for which they are averse to this system. The private system, on the other hand, is relatively caring and better mannered, involves negligible waiting time and appropriate appointment scheduling and is rated high in terms of client perceptions of providers' skills and efficiencies. It, therefore, enjoys the confidence of the people and has become popular.

But all is not well with the private sector health care in the state. Although this sector enjoys a virtual monopoly in a commoditized health system, the main source of its strength i.e. supplier induced demand for health care and doctor shopping is sinisterly defective. It has the dubious distinction of (i) working hand in glove with brokers, diagnostic laboratories and pharmacos and (ii) administering over-treatment with a strong tendency to over-refer, over-test, over-operate, over-inject and over-medicate. Besides, it also promotes inappropriate factor substitution. When charges of physicians, surgeons and other technical staff rise, it responds by substituting away from them and towards less qualified and lower skilled staff, e.g. from professional nurses to nurse aides, resulting in poor quality care and adverse outcomes including increased risk of mortality. Thus in the guise of timely and quality care, the private system has become a vicious exploitation trap and a necessary evil.

III. Empirical Findings

Profile of Area and Households: Comprehensive studies on the working of the health care system in Orissa are conspicuous by their very absence. No wonder then that very little is known about the health providers, delivery of health care, accessibility to alternative health care facilities and financing of health expenditure in the state. On the basis of a census survey of 90 households in three adjacent villages in Oupada Block of Balasore district in Orissa are studied. The villages were selected just for convenience and the household survey was conducted in January, 2007. Only those households were surveyed which visited a health provider at least once during December, 2006. Of the 90 households covered in the survey 36 (40.0 per cent) are agricultural labour and casual labour households including 21 (23.33 per cent) Scheduled Caste households. They come under the below-the-poverty-line (BPL) category. Among the rest 54 (60 per cent) households placed in the above-the-poverty-line (APL) group, 39 (43.3 per cent) are not really rich. The findings of the survey are presented in Table 12.3.

Table 12.3: Health Status of Women 2001

Nation/ State	Female-Male Ratio	Life-Expectancy at Birth		Infant Mortality Rate (2003)	
		Male	Female	Male	Female
India	933	62.8	64.2	64	68
Orissa	972	62.13	61.15	90	93

Sources: GOI, Census 2001; SRS Statistical Report No 3, 2004.

Health Care System: The villages are served by a public health sub-centre with one Auxiliary Nurse Midwife (ANM) and one anganwadi worker operating in one of the villages, a CHC at a distance of one Kilometer and a public hospital which functions in a town nine kilometers away from them. These villages are well connected by all weather roads and with the CHC and the hospital through convenient private transport service. The ANM who is supposed to stay in the ANM centre actually operates from near the CHC and the two doctors posted in the CHC attend their duties alternately 3 days a week with most of the health service provided by the pharmacist, the lady health visitor and two nurses. In times or need the people consult the doctor in the CHC, if available, of for minor ailments they take the help of the pharmacist and/or chemist shops near the CHC. For serious and little bigger ailments they go to the public hospital or the private practitioners operating around the public hospital. In life threatening cases the villager(s) take treatment with the health personnel in the district head quarters hospital/private health providers in the district town.

Accessibility: On an average a person belonging to the BPL category visited a health facility 1.11 times during the month of which 0.87 visits or 78.4 per cent were to a public provider and 0.24 or 21.6 per cent were to a private facility. In the case of the APL group these figures are 0.38 (28.1 per cent) and 0.97(71.9 per cent) respectively. Looking at major ailments requiring surgery, more or less same pattern is observed. It follows that poor people access the public health facilities more than the rich.

The survey does not reveal serious gender gaps in access to health care in the case of major ailments. Adult women (18-32 years age group) are not discriminated against. Rather they get preferable treatment. The modal age of a woman at marriage and that of having the last child are found to be 19.8 and 26.3 years respectively. Corresponding to the women in the age group 18-32 years, men are at the prime age of 26-40 years with high market value. It is rational for the family to keep woman healthy for a presentable physique to facilitate marriage and for bearing and rearing a healthy child such that the number of man's trips to the health centres can be reduced and the loss of current income can be minimized. Women also co-operate as they are more mindful in avoiding loss of working time on seeing a doctor. However, in the case of minor ailments women's access to formal health facilities are found to be low because they manage with naturopathy. But girls are discriminated against. Their curative health expenditures are responsive to parents' education, family income and wealth holdings. For the boys such responses are weak. Besides it is known for certain that girls will contribute less to the family after getting married. Hence girls have little chance of getting treated than boys except in highly critical and life threatening situations.

The survey reflects limited effective accessibility for the poor and females in terms of quality care in public health facilities and affordability in private health centres relative to non poor and males.

Health Financing: For the individuals health financing is a private issue. Evidently the BPL category spends less on health

(Rs.85.73) than the APL category (Rs. 241.90) even though the share of health expenditure in total expenditure is approximately the same for both the groups. In the case of major ailments similar results have been observed. Expenditure in getting treated in a public health care centre is substantially lower compared to a private provider. In 3 of the 5 cases (60 per cent) of major ailments noticed for the BPL group, households reported to have borrowed from money lenders at 48 per cent interest to meet the cost of hospitalization while in the balance 2 (40 per cent) cases they said to have sold their assets, gold and landed property for the purpose. For the APL group the financing sources have been own savings, borrowings and sale of wealth for 2 (25 per cent), 5(62.5 per cent) and 1 (12.5 per cent) cases respectively.

Patients and their attendants revealed that the hospital supplies of drugs and consumables are very marginal and they had to buy almost everything from bandage cloth and saline to injection and to pay all the health personnel. 'Pleasing' sub-staff has also spread to the private sector health providers. It is thus clear that hospitalization can cause indebtedness, loss of wealth and impoverishment.

Choice of Health Provider: The results of the survey are puzzling and beg the question as to why even poor people are moving away from the public care centres. The revelations are startling. Two main issues have surfaced. Firstly, the quality of care is worse in the public health care centres. It is reported that during delivery the nurses hit the mother and the sweepers and hospital staff ridiculed their attendants for not having brought clean clothes. Most of the time the health personnel including the doctor behave in a rude manner and even do not care to reply to the patient's / attendant's queries. Secondly, the public care system is not cheap as is understood in common parlance. Public health care involves waiting and associated wage costs , user fees and the costs of 'pleasing' and 'greasing' in addition to treatment costs. Respondents were of the view that if allowance were made for everything the private health care facilities would not be too costlier than the public ones. In course of discussion it came out that a bleeding delivery patient died while waiting for treatment, sometimes the illness heals on its own in the waiting process and after a period of waiting the patient prefers to accept the illness. He also exits the public system and enters the domain of private health care because he cannot afford to trade between his health and ability to pay. But everything is not rosy with the private system either. It was reported that in the private nursing home(s), the surgeon insisted on expensive tests with a particular laboratory most of which may be unnecessary, over operated and vanished after surgery and offered only tele-advice. The patient finds him crushed between extreme commercialization and deteriorating standards as the iron between the hammer and the anvil.

However, people who availed of health service facilities from both public and private sectors are divided with regard to their choice between these two systems. Some say that the quality of care offered by the private providers is better while some others held the opposite view.

V. Conclusions and Implications for Policy Observations

The paper reveals the poor state of health care system in Orissa. Firstly, the Public sector health care facilities are inadequate, inappropriate, and not less expensive in comparison to the private providers and by the criterion of quality they are worse. Treatment of serious patients on the floor is a naked scene in the public hospitals. The quality of care in the private sector is not very encouraging either. Secondly, the private alternative has undermined the public system and in view of preferential treatment to the relatively well to do in the latter, inequality in access to health care facilities is increasing. Thirdly, concern for health has increased and hospitalization has become quite costly pushing many to debt trap and poverty. Fourthly, people are willingness to pay even for public health services on quality considerations. However, the economically weaker sections exhibit a low willing to pay compared to the better off. Fifthly, cost recovery through user fees hardly amounts to one per cent of public expenditure on health and there is no mechanism to review user charges and to ensure its utilization.

The note is clear: the health care system is not working the way as it desired to. It is a good thing that, of late, the health system in the state is showing the signs of slow improvement. The Government of Orissa (GOI) is implementing some innovative people friendly health programmes in recent years. Two such programmes deserve special commendation. The first is the system of health auxiliaries under which the village health workers, the anganwadi workers and the ANMs are operating as '*barefoot doctors*' for providing preventive care, treatment for minor ailments and disseminating health information. The second is the five disease treatment programme, known as '*Panchavyadhi Chikitsa Vyabastha*'. Under this programme the government is distributing free drugs/ reimbursing medicine costs for five common diseases, such as acute respiratory infection, diarrhoea, leprosy, malaria and scabies. The two programmes are doing well in the rural areas.

Policy Implications

In the contemporary society the health sector is faced with the following five major challenges: (i) what can be done to ensure quality care? (ii) How can public and private health facilities be made more responsive to the needs of the people? (iii) Can patients'/attendants' perceptions be incorporated into teaching, training and supervision programmes to reverse poor treatment? (iv) what steps can the government take to improve performance of the private health care sector? (v) how can pro-poor health policy measures be implemented?

India was a signatory to the Alma Ata declaration: 'Health for all' by 2000 AD and is committed to achieving the MDGs by 2015. It has certainly not achieved 'Health for all' but is trying hard to reach the target given in the MDGs. The case of Orissa is bleaker.

There is an urgent need to improve the quality of public health care services as well as putting the private providers under regulatory cover. The following measures may be tried for ensuring a better performing health system.

The fact remains that the public health care facilities cannot do away with. In addition to its monopoly in the field of preventive care, the experience with this sector in the aftermath of the 1999 Orissa super cyclone, things are highly encouraging. Once epidemics commenced the private practitioners fled while the public sector medical staff did miracles with lack of funds, dearth of staff and inadequacy of medicines notwithstanding.

The need is to reorient this sector. But this involves financial costs and motivation of personnel. The government should earmark at least six per cent of NSDP for the health sector and think of alternative sources of financing public health. It may be noted that the GOO has tried the users' fees strategy as a supplementary source of public health financing. But given the low ability and willingness to pay on the part of the vulnerable group, a uniform policy seems unjustified. It is, therefore, necessary to adopt a price discriminatory user charges policy with exemptions for the poor because this would help cross subsidization and work toward better targeting of health subsidies. Regarding quality of health care, strict discipline needs to be administered in the hospitals and in no case private practice during duty hours is permitted.

The government may permit private practice in hospital premises under which subsidized health care will be provided to the people on payment basis during off hours and the receipts be shared between the government and the health personnel on a 70:30 basis. Client perceptions of providers' skills may be incorporated into the medical education and training system in line with '*Munna Bhai MBBS*' type of ideology. This way the system can be made more responsive to patients' needs and people's expectations.

Unregulated and uncontrolled growth of private sector health centres has to be brought under regulation. Rules have be provided and implemented for clinical establishments and a system of accreditation in line with National Assessment and Accreditation Council scheme for colleges and universities be evolved for the private health sector to ensure quality health care at reasonably affordable prices.

A bottom up approach to health planning and policy with emphasis on PHCs as provider of preventive and curative care and first referral services would be the right strategy. It is, therefore, imperative to provide adequate funds for this component of public health services in the state.

In this juncture, the onus of improving the health care system lies with the government, the civil society and the people themselves. But given the type of political economy and the nature of governance which we have, reforms in the health sector are really a Herculean task and our aim of providing 'Health for all from womb to tomb' is difficult but not impossible.

References

Gillis Malcolm, et. al. (1996): *Economics of Development*, W.W Norton and Company, London and New York.

Government of India (GOI) (2005): *Mid-Term Appraisal of Tenth Five Year Plan*, Planning commission, New Delhi.

GOI (2003): *Economic Survey 2003-2004*, Economic Division, Ministry of Finance and Company Affairs, New Delhi.

GOI (2004): *Economic Survey 2004-2005*, Economic Division, Ministry of Finance and Company Affairs, New Delhi.

GOI (2005): *Economic Survey 2005-2006*, Economic Division, Ministry of Finance and Company Affairs, New Delhi.

GOI (2002): *Orissa Development Report 2004*, Planning Commission, New Delhi.

GOI (2002): Statistical Abstract of Orissa 2003, Directorate of Economic and Statistics, Bhubanewar.

GOI (2003): *Economic Survey 2003-04*, Directorate of Economic and Statistics, Bhubanewar.

GOI (2004): *Economic Survey 2004-05*, Directorate of Economic and Statistics, Bhubanewar.

GOI (2005): *Economic Survey 2005-06*, Directorate of Economic and Statistics, Bhubanewar.

Mahal, A. et.al. (2001): Who Benefits from Public Health spending in India, *World Bank Working Paper on Health, Nutrition and Population*, World Bank, New Delhi.

Park, J.E (1986): *Text Book of Preventive and Social Medicine*,

Banarsidas Bhariot Publishers, Jabalpur, India.

Peters, David H. et. al. (2002): *Better Health systems for India's Poor, Findings, Analysis and Options*, World Bank, Washington.

World Health Organization (1992): *Basic Document*, 39th Edition, Geneva.

13

Use of Primary Health Care Services among Rural Population

R. Annapoorani

I. Introduction

Health is important in every individual's life and so we call it as 'Health is Wealth'. Health is defined by World Health Organization (1948) as 'a state of complete physical, mental and social well being and not merely the absence of disease or infirmity'. In the process of economic development, health is identified as one of the paramount indicators. According to Reddy (1995), improved health contributes to economic growth in four ways: it reduces production loss caused by worker's illness; it permits the use of natural resources that had been totally or nearly inaccessible because of disease; it increases the enrolment of children in school and it frees for alternative use of resources that would otherwise have to be spent on treating illness.

Since the prevention of diseases promotes health, emphasis was laid on provision of health care facilities. The term 'health care' has been used to denote wide variety of types of health care, ranging from public health services (such as environmental sanitation) through personal preventive services (such as immunization) to personal curative services.

There are different levels of health care. World Health Organization (1973) defined three levels of health care and they are primary care comprises general health practice services which are offered to the population at the point of entry into health care system; secondary care comprises the care provided through specialized services on referral from primary care services; and tertiary care includes highly specialized services and eventually the super specialties such as plastic surgery, neurosurgery and heart surgery.

Of the different levels of health care, primary health care was concerned as a development movement which embraced the social and economic aspects. Primary health care approach advocates provision of health care services to the people nearest to their home and at a cost within their reach. The first International Conference on Primary Health Care defined it as 'essential health care based on scientifically sound and socially acceptable methods and technology made universally acceptable to individuals and families in the community through their full participation and at a cost that the community and country can afford to maintain at every stage of their development in a spirit of self reliance and self determination'. Alma Ata Declaration (1978) stressed that the primary health care approach is based on five basic principles: equitable distribution of health services; community involvement in health decision; focus on preventive and promotive services rather than curative services; appropriate technology to make the health system acceptable and relevant and a multi sectoral approach making health as part of total care including nutrition, education, water supply, shelter, etc.

Though primary health centers provide free treatment for rural population, sometimes people visit private hospitals for treatment. The inpatients and outpatients of primary health centers also face problems in using health care facilities. As such, a research study on 'Extent of use of primary health care services among rural population' was under taken with the following objectives:

- to study the organization and management of selected primary health centre.
- to study the beneficiary assessment of people utilizing primary health care services.
- to study the efficiency of health care services provided by primary health centre.

II. Methodology and Database

The research study was confined to a primary health centre in Perumanallur village, Tirupur block, Coimbatore district in

Tamilnadu. For the study purpose, 50 beneficiaries were selected by random sampling method. The study had used both secondary and primary source of data. For studying the organization of primary health centre, the information about the patients treated, number of doctors and nurses, facilities and equipments available were compiled from the records maintained by the medical officer for the period 2000-2005. The data were collected during December 2005. For analyzing the data collected, the study used the quantitative tools – coefficient of variation, growth rate, Chi – square analysis, simple regression and multiple regression analysis.

III. Findings of the Study

The major findings of the study are as follows:

A. Analysis about the Organization and Administration of the Selected Primary Health Centre: Firstly, in the selected primary health centre, the number of inpatients treated increased from 15,000 to 31,776 representing 111.84 per cent increase during 2000-2005. Among the inpatients, females were availing the treatment to a greater extent. On an average, in a year, the selected primary health centre provides inpatients treatment for 8,456 males, 10,343 females and 3,362 children. The number of outpatients increased from 30 to 122 representing 306.6 per cent increase. On an average, in a year, the selected primary health centre provides outpatients treatment for 19 males, 32 females and 11 children.

Secondly, in the reference period, the number of doctors, nurses, laboratory technicians and the pharmacists remained constant. There existed demand supply gap in the provision of health care facilities, since the doctor pupil ratio increased from 1,875 to 2,130 during 2000-2005.

Thirdly, the selected primary health centre is equipped with essential infrastructure - laboratory room, casualty room, office room; review meeting hall, furniture, ambulance and equipments like generator, electric autoclave, oxygen cylinder, D and C set.

B. Beneficiary Assessment of People Utilizing Primary Health Care Service: Firstly, the study found that 48 per cent of the selected respondents were using the service of primary health centre alone and 52 per cent were using both primary health centre and private hospitals for treatment. Further, 64 per cent were getting the treatment regularly and 36 per cent were getting the treatment occasionally.

As compared to joint families, more of nuclear families were using the services of primary health care services. The analysis of chi-square indicated that there was association between the type of family and the use of primary health care services since the calculated $\chi^2 = 1.03 < \chi^2_{.05} = 3.84$. However, there was no association between the size of the family and the use of primary health care services since the calculated $\chi^2 = 6.98 > \chi^2_{.05} = 3.84$. The study also noted that low income people made use of primary health care as compared to high-income group, since with improvement in income, people shift their health care to other private hospitals.

Secondly, the reasons stated by the respondents for the use of primary health centre were free treatment, free accessibility of doctors and nearness to the place of residence.

Thirdly, in order to find out the differences in the use of health services by different income groups, the study fitted the following multiple regression equation.

$Y = a + b_1X_1 + b_2X_2 + b_3X_3 + e$

Where Y = Total expenditure of the household;

X_1 = Expenditure on food;

X_2 = Expenditure on health;

X_3 = Expenditure on housing, clothing and education and

e = Error term

The estimated equation for the high income group was

$$Y = 0.141 + .900X_1 + .0670X_2 + .148X_3 \quad .....(1)$$

$$(.231)\ (8.511)^{**}\ (1.081)\ (2.071)^{*}$$

$R^2 = .89$, $F = 51.03$, $N = 23$

The estimated equation for the low income group was

$$Y = 1.055 + .610X_1 + .116X_2 - .278X_3 \quad .....(2)$$

$$(3.064)(10.754)^{**}\ (3.561)^{**}\ (5.053)^{**}$$

$R^2 = .93,\ F = 105.68,\ N = 27$

To find out the beneficiary assessment by education, the multiple regression equation was fitted. For the literary sample, the estimated equation was

$$Y = .428 \quad + .740X_1 + .103X_2 \ + .257X_3 \qquad .....(3)$$
$$(1.139)\ \ (9.348)^{**}\ \ (3.323)^{**}\ (5.674)^{**}$$

$R^2 = .99,\ F = 191.89,\ N = 12$

For the illiterate group, the estimated equation was

$$Y = .674 \quad + .794X_1 + .107X_2 \ + .137X_3 \qquad .....(4)$$
$$(1.573)\ (11.478)^{**}\ (2.466)^{**}\ (1.840)^{*}$$

$R^2 = .88,\ F = 82.96,\ N = 38$

Equation (1) implies that for high income group people an increase in health expenditure by one per cent brings out an increase in total expenditure by 6 per cent. But from equation (2) it is evident that for low income group, the impact of health expenditure on total expenditure was to the extent of 11 per cent. However, equation (3) and (4) makes it obvious that the impact of health expenditure on total expenditure was equal (10 per cent) for the literate and illiterate sample.

Fourthly, the major problems stated by the respondents in using the service of primary health centre were waiting in long queue. There was non-availability of cesarean facilities. For patients taken to primary health centre in case of emergency, only the first aid was given. For getting injections, the doctors use only ordinary syringe and not disposable syringe.

Fifthly, to improve the operational efficiency of primary health centre, the respondents recommended that there is a need for arranging for the visit of a specialist once in a week, construction of operation theatre, providing better medicines and provision of super specialty beds.

IV. Conclusion

From the research study, it is emanating that the health care sector should be accorded the status of a core sector. To reduce the demand and supply gap with regard to primary health care, it is necessary to increase the number of doctors, nurses and health assistants in the primary health care unit.

References

Emmel, N.D. (1998): Health For-All for 21st Century: Demise of Primary Health Care, *Economic and Political Weekly*, Vol. XXXIII, No.11, pp.577-580.

Hadded (1998): Community Perceptions of Primary Health Care Service in Guinea, *Social Science and Medicine*, Vol. 47, No.3, pp.381-394.

Johnfry and John Hasler (1986): *Primary Health Care 2000*, Churchill Livingstone, Edinburgh, pp.17-27.

Mukhopadhyay, Alok (1998): Revamping Primary Health Care, *Yojana*, Vol. 42, No. 8, pp.69-75.

Reddy, Ranga (1993): *Health Care Services Management for under Privileged*, Delta Publishing House, New Delhi, pp.135-141.

Sharma, B.B., and P. P. Talwar (1990): Health for All and Population Stabilization in India, *Journal of Rural Development*, Vol.10, No. 6, pp.779-793.

The Business Line (1999): Accord Health Care Core Sector Status, March 17th.

Verma, K.K. (1990): *Health and Family Welfare*, Mittal Publication, New Delhi, pp.94-105.

14

Health Care and Awareness among Urban Educated Females

Shweta Upadhyay and A.K. Jain

I. Introduction

Health is multi-dimensional and holistic, embracing all aspects of individual and collective existence. A healthy person is one who enjoys a harmonious existence within themselves and within their societal context (Hunter, 2003). Health care awareness is necessary but not sufficient for good health. For practicing health care awareness everybody should join in mediation, yoga, physical activity, diet control and go for normal health check-up. Good health of the girls would contribute towards improvement in educational achievements; higher income generation and overall improvement in the status of the girls in particular and their families in general. But this is possible only if and when the girls are made aware about health care and its importance.

The health of a community is intimately related to its economic status and its social and political organization. To improve health, health care is the most essential and basic requirement for all (Park, 2000). The present study considers the health awareness among female students in the University of Allahabad, India.

An increase in the health care and awareness of the girls shall go a long way for improvement in health status, reduction in infant mortality rate (IMR) and the maternal mortality rate (MMR) because these very girls shall marry and have their own family. No doubt the IMR in India shows a consistently decline from 146 in 1951 to 72 in 1998 and 66 in 2002 with the projection for 2010 being 30, as per the national population policy 2000. In the same way, improved health status of the girls would also lead to decreasing trend in the MMR which is 540 in 2003 against the target of 100 by 2010 as per the national population policy 2000 and the MMR at U.P. is 707 in 1997. At the same time, once these girls accept the importance and relevance of health awareness, this can percolate to the various strata of society, both in rural as well as urban area. It may be argued that reduction in IMR and MMR would lead to an increase in the population and which is contrary to the policy of controlling population growth. However, the paper has not taken up this matter. The National Rural Health Programme is welcome steps towards health but it is beyond the scope of this paper.

II. Objectives of the Study

The main objective of the study is to assess the health care and awareness among urban educated females. The specific objectives are:

- to assess the perception of health level among the respondents.
- to assess health promotional activities.
- to find out periodicity of health check-up.
- to find out health care awareness by consultation with doctor, when ill.
- to assess the awareness towards need for group health insurance.

III. Methodology

The study is based on primary data collected from the girl students of Arts Stream of University of Allahabad, India for convenience and purposive sampling method is adopted. The survey is done in the month of February 20-28, 2006. Total 100 girl students are selected on the basis of random sampling method, in which 50 girl students are from undergraduate classes, 30 post graduate and 20 D.Phil. scholars based on proportional representation, covering five departments selected at random: Economics, Urdu, Ancient History, Geography and Psychology from Arts block of University of Allahabad.

A structured, closed-ended schedule containing 10 questions on personal information (Schedule 1), 13 questions on health information (Schedule 2) and 22 questions on Institutional health services (Schedule 3) is used and information is asked from the respondents on interview basis. In the presence study, however, questions from schedule-1, 2 and 3 have been considered.

The sample is further divided class wise: out of 50 Undergraduate girls, there were 10 girls from B.A. I, 13 from B.A. II and 27 from B.A. III. Similarly, out of 30 postgraduate students, 17 girls were studying in M.A.I while 13 were in M.A. II. The remaining 20 girls were D.Phil. scholars. The study examines the health perception, health promotional activity, time-period of health check-up, consultation with doctor, and awareness for group health insurance. χ^2 – Test has been used to analyze the data.

IV. Results and Findings

Table 14.1 shows class-wise perception of girls for health rating on ten points scaling ascending order. Out of 50 Undergraduate girls, 2(4 per cent) girls gave the response between 1-3, which indicate the unhealthy position, 33 (66 per cent) gave between 4-7, which represents normal health and rest 15(30 per cent) girls gave the response between 8-10, which indicates the healthy position in girls. Out of 30 P.G. girls, 1(3.33) is in the category of 1-3, that reflects the perception of the girl as unhealthy, 13(43.33 per cent) girls were in normal health position, which is between 4-7, and 16(53.33 per cent) girls showed healthy with the range between 8-10.

Regarding 20 D.Phil. scholars, 10(50per cent) were in the normal health position (4-7) and 10(50per cent) girls were healthy (8-10). At the U.G. level almost three-fourth of the girls were conscious about the health, while at the P.G. level the same is 60 per cent, at the D.Phil. stage 80 per cent of the girls were found to include in same health promotional activity. The lower percentage at the P.G level may be attribute to the fact that more than 50 per cent of the respondents were residing in university hostel and as reported by them, they had little time and money for these activities, specially time. Since there were seriously involved in building their carrier prospects.

Table 14.1: Perception of Girls for Health Rating on Class-Basis

Class	Health perception			
	1-3	4-7	8-10	Total
B.A.I	-	7(70)	3(30)	10(100)
B.A.II	-	11(84.62)	2(15.38)	13(100)
B.A.III	2(7.41)	15(55.56)	10(37.04)	27(100)
U.G.	2(4)	33(66)	15(30)	50(100)
M.A.I	1(5.88)	7(41.18)	9(52.94)	17(100)
M.A.II	-	6(46.15)	7(53.85)	13(100)
P.G.	1(3.33)	13(43.33)	16(53.33)	30(100)
D.Phil	-	10(50)	10(50)	20(100)
Total	3	56	41	100

Notes: 1. Unhealthy (1-3), Normal healthy (4-7) and healthy (8-10).
2. Figures shows in parenthesis are in percentage of horizontal totals.

According to the overall responses of girls three per cent and 56 per cent showed that they are unhealthy and normal healthy respectively based on their own perception of health and 41per cent girls in the category of healthy. Thus, only 3 per cent of the girls perceive themselves to be unhealthy while the remaining 97 per cent feel or believe that their health is good or normal. However, comparing the results obtained from Table 14.2, it is found that 30 per cent of the girls did not think for their health. This shows that the perception of the girls towards their health may be biased. The χ^2 – test also shows the independence between health perception and class. Other indicators have to be considered to assess the correct situation. To test the independence between health perception and class, the χ^2 – test has been applied to the above data. The null hypothesis has been framed that the health perception and class are independent of each other. The alternative hypothesis is that health perception and class are dependent.

At 5 per cent level of significance and 2 degrees of freedom: χ^2 cal = 4.79, χ^2 tab = 5.991 since χ^2 cal < χ^2 tab, the null hypothesis is accepted, which shows the health rating and class are independent of each other.

Table 14.2 shows the distribution of health promotional activity on class basis. Out of 50 undergraduates, 5(10 per cent) girls do meditation for their health care, 5(10 per cent) are yoga, 4(22 per cent) girls do physical activity, 10(20 per cent) girls take nutritious food, 4(8 per cent) believe in diet control, 1(2 per cent) girl has health check-up, and 14(28 per cent) girls do not do anything for their health. Out of 30 postgraduate girls, 1(3.33 per cent) girl do meditation, 1(3.33 per cent) yoga, 6(20 per cent) girls physical activity, 7(23.33 per cent) girls were taking nutritious food, 1(3.33 per cent) believe in diet control, 2(6.67 per cent) normally go for health check-up and rest 12(40 per cent) girls do not do anything. If the analysis of 20 D.Phil. scholars states that 1(5 per cent) girl does meditation, 3(15 per cent) did yoga, 7(3 5per cent) girls were physical active, 5(25 per cent) girls were taking nutritious food and rest 4(20 per cent) girls were not doing anything for their health.

Overall, 70 per cent girls were aware about their health by taking some care. This may be due to at U.G, P.G. and D.Phil. level girls were contact with different people with different perception, and they gave some new direction to their thinking for health awareness. Amongst the 70 girls who were aware and care for the health, 24 undertook some from of physical activity like walking, jogging etc. 22 of the respondents were particular about eating nutritious food to look after their health, 7 and 9 girls undertook meditation and yoga respectively. As regard diet control there were 5 girls who exercised this as the means of maintaining/reducing weight, which is an important aspect of health. The remaining 3 girls were reported that they went for medical check-up as a precaution against ill health. Overall, out of

Table 14.2: Promotional Health Activities on Class Basis

Class	Promotional Activities								
	a	b	c	d	e	f	g	h	Total
BA I	1(10)	1(10)	3(30)	3(30)	-	-	-	2(20)	10
BA.II	1(7.69)	1(7.69)	4(30.77)	3(23.08)	2(15.38)	-	-	2(15.38)	13
BA III	3(11.11)	3(11.11)	4(14.81)	4(14.81)	2(7.41)	1(3.70)	-	10(37.04)	27
U.G.	5(10)	5(10)	11(22)	10(20)	4(8)	1(2)	-	14(28)	50
M.A.I	1(5.88)	-	4(23.53)	3(17.65)	1(5.88)	1(5.88)	-	7(41.18)	17
M.A.II	-	1(7.69)	2(15.38)	4(30.77)	-	1(7.69)	-	5(38.69)	13
P.G.	1(3.33)	1(3.33)	6(20)	7(23.33)	1(3.33)	2(6.67)	-	12(40)	30
D.Phil	1(5)	3(15)	7(35)	5(25)	-	-	-	4(20)	20
Total	7	9	24	22	5	3	-	30	100

Notes: 1. Figures shows in parenthesis are percentage horizontal totals. 2. (a) Meditation, (b) Yoga, (c) Physical activity, (d), Nutritious food, (c) Diet Control, (f) Health check up, (g) Any other, (h) Nothing.

70 girls 46 i.e. about two-thirds in favour of physical activity/nutritious food as a promotional health care measure.30 per cent girls were not aware for their health. Class wise analysis indicates that, in U.G. 14(28 per cent), P.G. 12(40 per cent) and D.Phil. 4(20 per cent) girls were not aware. There is a decrease in the number of girls who do nothing for health as educational level increases; this may be due to that they are getting familiar with the University atmosphere and the area of their knowledge become board with the time. So the number of girls is decline that shows they were not aware. To test the independence between health awareness and class, the χ^2- test has been applied to the above data. The null hypothesis has been framed that the health awareness and class are independent of each other. The alternative hypothesis is that health awareness and class are dependent.

At 5 per cent level of significance and 2 degrees of freedom: χ^2 cal = 2.11, χ^2 tab = 5.991. Since χ^2 cal < χ^2 tab, the null hypothesis is accepted at 5 per cent lever of significance & 2 degrees of freedom, which shows that health awareness and class are independent of each other.

Table 14.3 shows the health care awareness by time period of health check-up on class-basis. Regarding 50 undergraduate girls, 3(6 per cent) girls normally go for monthly health check-up, 1(2 per cent) six monthly, 1(2 per cent) yearly and 45(90 per cent) girls go for a health check up when they needed. Out of 30 postgraduates, 1(3.33 per cent) girl goes for monthly health check-up and rest 29(96.6 per cent) girls were go when they feel need. In the case of 20 D.Phil. scholars, 1(5 per cent) girl goes for monthly health check-up and rest 19(95 per cent) girls go for health check-up when they need it. If class-wise analysis states that, in B.A. I, out of 10 girls, 90 per cent girls were not aware, for their health, they prefer health check-up when they feel need. Health check-up without need shows a sign of awareness about health. In B.A. II, 76.92 per cent girls and in B.A.III, 96.30 per cent girls preferred check-up when they feel sick. At the postgraduate level, in M.A.I 100 per cent girls go for health check-up when they feel need and 92.31 per cent in M.A. II. 95

per cent D.Phil. scholars favour health check-up when they feel need.

Table 14.3: Time Period of Health Check-Up on Class- Basis

Class	Time Period					
	Monthly	Quarterly	Half Yearly	Yearly	When Needed	Total
B.AI	-	-	1(10)	-	9(90)	10(100)
B.AII	2(15.38)	-	-	1(7.69)	10(76.92)	13(100)
B.AIII	1(3.70)	-	-	-	26(96.30)	27(100)
U.G.	3(6)	-	1(2)	1(2)	45(90)	50(100)
M.A I	-	-	-	-	17(100)	17(100)
M.A II	1(7.69)	-	-	-	12(92.31)	13(100)
P.G.	1(3.33)	-	-	-	29(96.67)	30(100)
D.Phil.	1(5)	-	-	-	19(95)	20(100)
Total	5	-	1	1	93	100

Note: Figures shows in parenthesis are percentage of horizontal totals.
Source: Compiled from primary data

Overall 93 per cent girls showed acute indifference in the context of health awareness for time period of health check-up. These 93 per cent girls were not taking check-up as a preventive aspect, they only believe in curative aspects, which show when they become ill than they will go for check-up. This may be due to financial problems as some girls cannot afford health check-up and some parents do not prefer health check-up of their daughters due to gender bias. A measure response included as a reason for health check-up failure is the fear of some illness/diseases being diagnosed during check-up and hence the respondents avoided regular medical check-up. This clearly reflects the ignorance on the part of the respondents that the earlier an illness/diseases is diagnosed, the better are the chances of it being cure or control through proper treatment. Thus the girls do not conceive the preventive aspect in the health check-up. Some respondents reported that going for medical check-up is completely wastage of time this could utilize in a better way. The above appears to be consistence with the approach of a common person in our society that a health check-up becomes important only when needed or prescribed by a doctor.

Table 14.4 shows consultation with doctor (always) on class-basis when illness occurs, which is also a part of health care awareness. Out of 50 Undergraduate girls, 17(34 per cent) always consult with doctor for all illness and 33(66 per cent) girls said that they do not always consult with doctor for all illness, but only sometimes consult with doctor for their illness.

Table 14.4: Consultation with Doctor (Always) on Class Basis

Class	Consultation with doctor			
	Yes	No	Sometimes	Total
B.A.I	2(20)	-	8(80)	10(100)
B.A.II	5(38.46)	-	8(61.54)	13(100)
B.A.III	10(37.04)	-	17(62.96)	27(100)
U.G.	17(34)	-	33(66)	50(100)
M.A I	3(17.65)	-	14(82.35)	17(100)
M.A.II	6(46.15)	-	7(53.85)	13(100)
P.G.	9(30)	-	21(70)	30(100)
D.Phil.	2(10)	-	18(90)	20(100)
Total	28	-	72	100

Note: Figures shows in parenthesis are in percentage of horizontal totals.
Source: Compiled from primary data

Regarding 30 P.G. girls, 9(30 per cent) girls always consult with doctor for all type of illness and 21(70 per cent) girls sometimes consult with doctor for their all illness. Out of 20 D.Phil. scholars, 2(10 per cent) girls always and 18(90 per cent) sometimes consult with doctor for their illness.

Overall, 28 per cent girls are aware of health importance because they are always consulting with doctor for all types of illness. This may be due to high consultation charges of doctors, lack of trust on diagnostic reports which are also expensive and probability of serious problem diagnosis which may create terror in girls. Some girls believe in self-treatment for illness, so they do not consult with doctor. However, almost three-fourth (72 per cent) of the respondents reported that they consult a doctor only sometimes when they are ill, which reflects a high degree of indifferences regarding health care. Because an illness which appear to be minor may turn out to be or get converted into a serious illness. This means that the girls do not believe in the saying that "prevention is better than cure".

Table 14.5 shows the responses for provision of group health insurance on class-basis. Out of 50 undergraduate girls, 23(46 per cent) girls said yes, that there should be a provision of group health insurance for girls in the institution, 22(44 per cent) said no and rest 5(10 per cent) girls said cannot say, that mean they are not aware of group health insurance.

Out of 30 P.G. girls, 14(46.67 per cent) girls agreed with the group health insurance, 12(40 per cent) were not agreeable and 4(13.33 per cent) girls cannot say anything.

Regarding 20 D.Phil. students, 15(75 per cent) girls show favorable awareness for group health insurance and rest 5(25 per cent) were not in the favour of it.

Table 14.5: Provision for Group Health Insurance on Class-Basis

Class	Provision for group health insurance			
	Yes	No	Cannot say	Total
B.A.I	4(40)	3(30)	3(30)	10(100)
B.A.II	5(38.46)	6(46.15)	2(15.38)	13(100)
B.A.III	14(51.85)	13(48.15)	-	27(100)
U.G.	23(46)	22(44)	5(10)	50(100)
M.A.I	8(47.06)	7(41.18)	2(11.76)	17(100)
M.A.II	6(46.15)	5(38.46)	2(15.38)	13(100)
P.G.	14(46.67)	12(40)	4(13.33)	30(100)
D.Phil.	15(75)	5(25)	-	20(100)
Total	52	39	9	100

Note: figures in parenthesis are in percentage of horizontal totals.
Source: compiled from primary data

Overall 52 per cent girls were in favour of group health insurance, 39 per cent girls did not want group health insurance, and nine per cent girls have no idea about group health insurance. Class-wise 27 girls at U.G., 16 at P.G., and 5 at D.Phil. level were not in favor. This may be because the girls do not know, what group health insurance is and family atmosphere of the girls create lack of awareness for group health insurance. Sometimes family members of the girls do not want health insurance for their daughters due either to gender bias or ignorance about the benefits of group health insurance. It would be relevant that out of the 52 girls who were in favour of health insurance, 48 were willing to contribute 10 per cent of the applicable premium, while the remaining 4 girls could contribute 25 per cent, the rational being that the reminder would be borne by the institution.

With regard to awareness about health care, 36 per cent girls of Undergraduate classes, 18 per cent at postgraduate level, 16 per cent at D.Phil. level girls were aware of the need for health care and they do meditation, yoga, physical activity, diet control and health checkup for their health. 30 per cent girls were not aware and so they were not doing anything for their health care. The class-wise distributions of these students are 14 per cent, 12 per cent, and 4 per cent girls at U.G., P.G. and D.Phil. level respectively. The study finds overall positive response by the female students for awareness about health care which is a good sign. The χ^2- test shows the health awareness and class are independent of each other.

In the context of awareness of girls for health rating, it found that three per cent girls perceived being unhealthy, 56 per cent were normal and 41 per cent were healthy on the basis of health perception given by girls. The χ^2- test shows the health rating and class are independent of each other. With regard to health awareness by time period of health check-up, it is found that only seven per cent girls were aware of the need for health check-up and rest 93 per cent girls showed indifference. Only 28 per cent girls regularly consult doctors for their health problems where as 72 per cent girls casual. This shows lack of health care awareness.

For group health insurance scheme only 48 per cent girls agreed where as 52 per cent girls are not in favour of it.

Thus, on the basis of findings of the study, it has to be said that health care awareness in the female students in the University is not adequate. Since the sample shows lack of awareness among the university female students it can be concluded that the overall level of awareness among the educated females in the urban area is very low and this also leads us to believe that the level of health care undertaken by the females leaves much to be desired. It can also be inferred that the level of awareness and health care among the uneducated or less educated urban females would not be more than that of the educated females. Thus the implication is that health appears to be in the hands of god, which is highly fatalistic attitude among the females.

V. Suggestions

On the basis of this study it appears that necessary direction should be provided to increase awareness regarding health and maintain good health through proper health care. The educational institutions should generate health awareness amongst the students through appropriate campaigns which can include the benefits of good health and as well as the drawbacks of ill health.

Health camps should be organized where free or subsidized health check-ups can be made to identify any ailments especially regarding hemoglobin, iron content, glucose along with routine pathological tests. This is necessary because timely treatment is an important aspect of health care.

There should be provision for health consultation where the girls can discuss their medical problems with qualified professionals so that they may obtain proper and correct advice. Lastly, there should be a provision for individual or group health insurance on subsidized basis which would helps the girls and the families in meeting medical expenses if any. Especially because medical treatment has become very expensive over the year and may be beyond the reach of the average family.

VI. Limitations of the Study

There are some limitations in our study. The sample size for the study should have been larger for a better analysis. It considered only the Arts students having excluded the other stream students. The health perception in the study may not reflect the true health status of the students. The major reason for the above limitations is paucity of funds and the timing of the survey in the February when most of the female students were concerned about their examinations.

References

Bennett, S., and V.R. Muraleedharan (2000): New Public Management and Health Care in third world, *Economic and Political Weekly*, Vol. 35, No. 1-2, pp. 59-68.

Bhatt, Ramesh, K. S. Basu (2004): Health Insurance and Third Party Administration, Issues and Challenges, *Economic and Political Weekly*, Vol. XXXIX, No. 28, pp. 3149.

Crew, F.A. (1986): *Health Awareness, Its nature and conservation*, 'Pergamon Press, London.

Culyer, J.A. (1990): *Competition in Health Care Reforming the NHS*, Macmillan Press, p. 252.

Hunter, David J. (2003): *Public Health Policy*, Blackwell Publication Ltd.

Narayan, V.K. (2003): Changing Health Care System, *Economic and Political Weekly*, Vol. XXXVIII No. 12 -13, p. 1230.

Park, K. (2000): *Preventive and Social Medicine*, Simplex Printing Press, Jabalpur, pp. 12, 631.

Sharm B. B. L., J. P. Gupta and R. Kumar (1994): Health Economics in University, Medical College and Management Institution, National Institute of Health and Family welfare, New Delhi.

15

Determinants of Health and Medical Care in India

Dastageer R. Myageri

I. Introduction

The basic objective of the healthcare system is to cater to the health needs of the people in the country in a cost effective manner. Generally, as countries move on the path of progress Gross Domestic Product (GDP) increases and the public expenditure on health also concurrently increases. Many times even when public expenditure on health is higher the performance of the health status seems to be low. This paper aims to examine the performance of healthcare system as a whole by measuring the trends of health indicators, determinants and the effect of the determinants of health status on each of the health indicators.

The engine of development in the broad sense is the quality of life; the people enjoying better quality of life generally fall in higher income groups. Such a group benefits from better education, high quality of health facility, nutrition and lives in a clean environment etc. Health is an important constituent of well being and acts as a foundation for prosperity and development of a country (Rao, 2004). WHO defines "Health is a state of complete physical, mental and social well being of the individuals in a society"? In the present days health has been considered as a right of every citizen in the countries (Rao, 2004).

The historical evidence of several nations revealed that better diets, housing, and control of communicable diseases have raised the quality of life everywhere (World Bank, 1991). The age standardized death rates (ASDR) in developing countries declined from 40 per cent per thousand to 5 per cent in the last two centuries. Life expectancy has also increased from 50 years to 68 years (Rao, 2004). This is mainly due to the important role played by the disease control measures and improvement in the medicine supply, nutrition level, educational level, and public expenditure on health and family welfare, health education and per capita income as a result of which there is increase in the living standard of the population and they are enjoying their long life.

II. Statement of the Problem

In 1957 the World Health Organization (WHO) study group on "Measurement of Levels of Health" pointed out that, the comprehensive health indicators are (1) crude birth rate (2) death rate and (3) infant mortality rate. It is recognized that health status is related to and determined by numerous factors such as, per capita income, way of life, marital status, housing, water supply and sanitation, infrastructure, social organization, structure of the economy, nutrition, education, health services provided by government, political and administrative setup, geography, climate, religious beliefs, et cetera (Rao, 20004).

On the basis of the existing literature, the proposed paper has however, considered the indicators such as; (1) public expenditure on health and family welfare (2) number of hospitals and (3) bed strength per million population in the hospitals are selected to analyze the health status of the people in India. In this background, the main objectives of the study are to examine the trends in the indicators and determinants of health status in India; and to estimate the effects of determinants of health on the indicators of health status namely (a) Birth rate (b) death rate and (c) infant mortality rate.

The paper is divided into five sections the 1st section deals with introduction. A brief review of literature is presented in 2nd section The 3rd section deals with model specification and database. Section 4 deals with results and analysis of health status in India and summary and conclusion is presented in 5th section.

III. Literature Review

Studies on Relationship between Health Expenditure and Income: The relationship between health expenditure and income has played a significant attention. Important finding in earlier studies has been documented that the ratio of healthcare expenditure to GDP increases as the countries developed economically and industrially. Abel-smith (1963, 1967) found that after adjusting for inflation, exchange rates and population, GDP is a major determinant of health expenditure. In a seminal paper, Newhouse (1977) raised the question about what determines the quantity of resources a country devotes to medical care and suggest that per capita GDP of the country is the single most important factor. This study found a positive linear relationship between the percentage of health care expenditure to GDP and GDP. Gardham et al (1992) used a single cross-section of 19 OECD countries. They found per capita income (PCI), urbanization and the share of public financing in to health expenditure as positive and significant variables. Hitris and Posnett (1992) used 560 pooled time series and cross section observations from 20 OECD countries over the period 1960-87 and found a high positive correlation between per capita health expenditure and GDP. The other similar studies, such as of Hansen and King (1996), McKoskey and Selden (1998), Gerdtham and Lothgren (2000), Karatzas (2000) agree that healthcare expenditure is dependent on the GDP of the country.

Studies Relating to Elasticity of Health Expenditure and Income: Whether health care is a luxury or necessity is important from the viewpoint of predicting the future expenditure on health and medical care. If the health care is luxury product it will consume an every increasing share of national income. Newhouse (1977) argues that since income elasticity of health care expenditure is more than one, it could be treated as a "Luxury" good. A number of studies analyzing international cross-section or pooled cross-section data on health care expenditures pointed out that health care are luxury. i.e., the demand for health care seems to have income elasticity in excess of unity (Blomqvist and Carter, 1997). Some studies like (Newhouse, 1997: Gerdtham et al, 1992) found the elasticities greater than one while many studies (Manning et al, 1987, Mc Laughlin, 1987; Dimattero and

Dimatteo, 1988) found that it is much less than one. Getzen (2000) in his paper analyses the literature and concludes that, healthcare is neither "a necessity" nor "a Luxury" it is "both" since the income elasticities varies with the level of analysis. With insurance, individual income elasticities are typically near zero. While national health expenditure elasticities are commonly greater than one. The debate over whether health care is or is not a luxury good arises primarily from the failure to specify levels of analysis clearly so as to distinguish variation within groups from variation between groups.

Studies Relating to Determinants of Health: On what factors does health depends? Since the health depends upon both subjective perception and also on objective assessment, it might be difficult to identify all the determinants of health, for some of them might simply be part of the subjective domain, not easily discernible and quantifiable (Panchamukhi, Year is not mentioned). The defined and quantifiable factors are nutrition, economic condition of the family, size of the family, life style, family environment, sanitation, education and availability of good medical and public health services determine the health status of individual and the community as a whole. Birth-weight of babies, childhood nutritional status, sex of the child and mother's parity and age are said to be the major determinants of health of children in developing countries (Winikiff and Brown, 1980).

The macro indicator of health status is measured in terms of specified health indicators. As health is defined also in negative terms as the absence of the ability to resist disease or death, some of the generally used indicators of health are expressed in terms of the absence of the extent of ill health. Negative health indices have been thus used to through light on the health status. Overall mortality rate, age specific mortality rate, infant mortality rate and prevalence and incidence of morbidity are some of such negative indicators (Panchamukhi, Year is not mentioned). In 1967, WHO itself came out with a Report on National Planning in Developing Countries, wherein it suggests two types of health indicators such as indices of resources as health manpower and indices of ill health and disease such as mortality rates.

WHO in its 1981 document entitled Development of Indicators in Monitoring Programmes towards Health for all by the year 2000, considers health for all in terms of a level of health that enables all people to live socially and economically productive life. From this point of view a global indicators may have to refer to the nutrition status, psychological development, mortality related indicators, morbidity related indicators, facilities and resources for health such as hospitals, doctors, auxiliary health and medical care personnel, material supply and also availability of finances.

High fertility among the poor households particularly in the low-income developing countries is the main cause of crowded housing, which in turn gives rise to increased problems of insanitation and high incidence of disease (Carrin, 1984).

Gulati (1998) used simultaneous equations to highlight the interaction between the fertility and mortality and his empirical findings demonstrate significant interaction between fertility and infant mortality. Also he finds that the cost effectiveness of health and family welfare programs improves substantially. Alternatively, the cost per unit of effect of health and family welfare programs in terms of prevention of additional death or additional birth respectively, reduces significantly.

Rao (2004) studied the trends of health indicators (CBR, CDR and IMR) and determinants (PCI, PHEXP, HOSPITALS, and BEDS) by using linear trend method. And in order to estimate the effect of determinants of health status on each of the indicators of health status a multiple regression was used. Empirically he found that there is a decline in the birth rate and death rate, however the stagnant or marginally negative infant mortality during 1990-2000, particularly in rural areas. Per capita income increased over a period leading to an increase in the expenditure on public health; however the growth rates of the number of hospitals and beds are not proportionate to the rate of the growth of population in Andhra Pradesh. The growth rate of expenditure on public health and the number of hospitals did not succeed in reducing the birth rate particularly in rural areas of Andhra Pradesh, as there budget allocations are found proportionally inadequate. The influence of per capita income and number of hospitals in Andhra Pradesh on infant mortality rate (IMR) though not significant is debatable the IMR is high in rural areas, which implies that the availability of medical services are inadequate and unsatisfactory.

IV. Model Specifications and Data

The determinants of health and family welfare can be broadly classified as economic and demographic variables. The existing literature highlights the significant role played by income in determining health expenditure. The economic variable, per capita income and health expenditure are the measures, which influence performance of the health indicators. As there is a high positive correlation between per capita income and public expenditure on health and family welfare leading to the problem of multicollinarity, we drop the variable per capita income in the mode. Only public expenditure on health and family welfare is considered as the major determinant of health status. Number of hospitals and bed strength per million populations is also considered as the determinants of the health indicators. The demographic variables CBR, CDR and IMR are considered to measure the performance of the health status in India.

To understand the health performs and the movements of the health indicators are examined by fitting a semi log model $LnY_t = \alpha + \beta t + u_t$ for each of these indicators and determinants of health. Assuming that, the three indicators of health are influenced by the three determinants selected in the study.

Dependent variable (Indicators of health status)	Independent Variables (Determinants of health status)
Birth rate (Y_1)	Expenditure on public health (x_1)
Death rate (Y_2)	Number of hospitals (x_2)
Infant mortality rate (Y_3)	Beds per lakh population (x_3)

In order to estimate the effect of determinants of health status on each of the health indicators, a linear multiple regression is used.

$$Y = \alpha + \beta_1 x_1 + \beta_2 x_2 + \beta_3 x_3 + u_t$$

Where α is the intercept and β_1, β_2 and β_3 are the regression coefficients, u_t is error term assumed to be normal with mean zero and variance one.

Data Base: The data on the health indicators for the year 1985 to 2002 is collected from the various issues of Health Monitor, number of hospitals, hospital bed strength per one lakh population, are collected from the Health Information of India 2003. The expenditure on public health and family welfare is collected from various issues of RBI Bulletins and CMIE. The GDP is collected from the Hand Book of Statistics on the Indian Economy 2004-05.

V. Results and Analysis of Health Status in India

Demographic Features of India: According to the 2001 census, total population of India is 1028.61 million. And world population is 6130 million. India accounts for 16.77 per cent of total population of the world, with a density of 324 persons per sq. km. India accounts for 2.4 per cent of the world surface area of 135.79 million square kilometers. The decennial growth is 21.34 per cent. About 742 million (72.2 per cent) live in rural and 285 million (27.8 per cent) live in the urban areas. The percentage decadal growth rate composition in rural and urban areas in the decade ending 2001 was 17.9 per cent and 31.2 per cent respectively. There was a net increase of 2.1 per cent in the urban population of the country during the preceding decade. The sex ratio for the country as a whole was at 933 as against 927 in the previous decade. The literacy rate among the population is 65.38 per cent, female literacy rate is 54.16 per cent and male is 75.84 per cent. Male life expectancy at birth (2000-06) is projected at 63.87 while life expectancy of female is 66.91 years. The crude birth rate and crude death rate during 2002 is 25.0 and 8.1 respectively. The infant mortality rate is 63 and couple protection rate is 48.2 per cent. Health services are covered through a wide network of 16319 sub centers/public health centers/community health centers, 38031dispencires and hospitals, 914543 beds, 836000 nursing personals and 625131 doctors in the country.

Trends in Public Expenditure on Health and Family Welfare: The allocation for health care expenditure shows that, there is rise in health expenditure from 0.8 per cent of GDP in 1980-81 to 0.9 per cent in 1989-90. During the reform period the expenditure on health sector increased from 0.83 per cent of GDP in 1991-92 to 0.89 per cent in 1992-93 and settled down at 0.76 per cent of GDP in 1997-98. The government is contributing just 0.9 per cent of GDP to health sector at present. In the new health policy 2001 there is a proposal to raise it to 2 per cent of GDP by 2010 (Table 15.1).

Table 15.1: Percentage of Health Expenditure To GDP

Year	Per cent to GDP
1980-81	0.80
1989-90	0.92
1990-91	0.88
1991-92	0.83
1992-93	0.89
1993-94	0.79
1994-95	0.73
1995-96	0.73
1996-97	0.72
1997-98	0.76
2001	0.90

Source: Joshi, 2006.

The pattern of public expenditure on Health and Family Welfare has increased during the year 1980-81 to 2004-05. The exponential growth for the state government is 3.46, central government 6.95 per cent and total expenditure of state and central government combined is 3.85 per cent per annum. This increase in expenditure on public health by the state and central government indicates the efforts made to control the disease, eradication of cholera, malaria etc., and to reduce the death rates and control the birth rate and hence to make India a disease free.

Before reforms the annual exponential growth rate was 2.43 per cent by state government, central government and combined state and central expenditure was 3.65 and 2.49 per cent, per annum respectively (Table 15.2).

During the reform period i.e. 1991-92 to 2004-05 the states government growth rate is 4.54 per cent the central government growth rate is much higher as it is 10.47 and combined growth rate is 5.28 per cent per annum. This indicates during reform period the central and state government spending is more on health. This is a healthy indication of welfare state.

Table 15.2: Exponential Growth Rates of Public Expenditure on Health and Family Welfare (1980-81 to 2004-05)

Year	State Expenditure	Central Expenditure	Total Expenditure
Over all Period 1980-81 to 2004-05	3.464 (3.525)	6.95 (7.20)	3.85 (3.928)
Before Reform 1980-81 to 1990-91	2.43 (2.46)	3.65 (3.719)	2.49 (2.523)
During reform 1991-92 to 2004-05	4.54 (4.65)	10.4 (10.96)	5.28 (5.42)

Note: The values in the parenthesis indicates the Compound Growth Rate CGR= [Antilog (β)-1] x 100.

A number of studies analyzing international cross section or pooled cross section data on health care expenditures point out that health care is a luxury i.e. the demand for health care seems to have income elasticity in excess of unity (Blomqvist and Carter, 1997). The empirical investigation in Indian context indicates that elasticity (η) = 0.7. For the year 1980-81 to 2004-05 also we computed the elasticities i.e. log health care expenditure is a function of log GDP. Before reform it is found that $\eta = 0.483$ and after reform it turns out 0.91. It indicates that with increase in income of the country the health expenditure also increases.

Trends in the Indicators and Determinants of Health Status in India: The semi log model is fitted to the data on the indicators of health status and determinants of health status in India during 1985-2002. Birth rate declined at a rate of 1.63 per cent per annum on an average while the infant mortality rate declined on an average of 2.47 per cent per annum. This can be attributed to the effective implementation of family planning programmes and women and child care programmes in India. A decline in the average annual death rate of 1.96 per cent indicates the improvement in the medical and health facilities provided in the country.

The trend relating to the per capita income is positive and significant at an annual average of Rs 347.45 crore (3.722 per cent per annum). The raise in the per capita income indicates that, with an improvement in the economic status there is increase standard of living of the people in the country.

In the similar path, expenditure on public health moved an upward trend at an annual average of Rs. 365.38 crore (4.53 per cent per annum). This increased expenditure on medical and public health indicates the government efforts to improve the medical facilities to control the birth rate, reduce the death rate and IMR and to increase life expectancy and thus to make a healthy society.

A. Birth Rate: Birth rate = f (Health expenditure, Number of hospitals, Beds per lakh population)

It is found that an increasing expenditure on public health has reduced the birth rate in India during 1985-2002 (Table 15.3). In other words, there is a inverse relationship between public health expenditure and birth rate. This expected trend in the birth rate may be due to effective implementation of birth control programmes, better infrastructure and health services provided by increased expenditure on hospitals, increasing per capita income and literacy rate. In the pre reform and during reform period expenditure on health continued to reduce the birth rate. Access to hospital facility plays an important role in lowering the birth rate.

Table 15.3: Multiple Regression Results: CBR is the Dependent Variable

Independent Variables	Over all period	Pre reform period	Reform period
(Constant)	44.9923 (11.37)*	44.3510 (21.077)*	27.2869 (3.1534)*
Health expenditure	-0.0007 (-5.64)*	-0.0005 (-1.346)	-0.0006 (-4.596)*
Hospitals	-0.0004 (-4.20)*	-0.0003 (-2.536)	-0.0001 (-1.281)
Beds per lakh Population	-0.0645 (-1.47)	-0.0769 (-2.986)	0.0774 (0.935)
R square	0.97	0.99	0.96

Note: The figures in the parentheses indicate t values and
*indicates the values are significant at 5% level or more

Expenditure on medical and public health, number of hospitals and hospital beds per lakh population, have influenced the death rate negatively leading to decrease in the death rate. This expected result is due to the effective control of communicable diseases and preventive measures on public health. Also the decrease in death rate probably due to improved standard of living condition. The increased per capita income enabled the people to take the preventive measures. Further, the increasing expenditure on public health ensured better medical and health services and supply of medicine and mobile medical facilities, which reduced the death rate. The number of hospitals and beds per lakh population contributed significantly to reduce the death rates during year 1985-2002 as well as pre-reform and during reform period.

B. Death Rate: Death Rate = f (Health expenditure, Number of hospitals, Beds per lakh population) (Table 15.4).

Table 15.4: Multiple Regression Results: CDR is the Dependent Variable

Independent Variables	Over all period	Pre reform period	Reform period
(Constant)	18.8603 (8.419)*	27.2394 (6.811)*	7.8178 (1.572)
Health Expenditure	-0.0002 (-3.07)*	-0.0005 (-0.728)	-0.0001 (-1.071)
Hospitals	-0.0002 (-3.878)*	0.0002 (0.844)	-0.0002 (-3.372)*
Beds per lakh Population	-0.0550 (-2.216)*	-0.1679 (-3.433)	0.0501 (1.053)
R square	0.95	0.96	0.91

Note: The figures in the parentheses indicate t values and * indicates the values are significant at 5% level or more.

C. Infant Mortality Rate: IMR = f (Health expenditure, Number of hospitals, Beds per lakh population)

It is observed that health expenditure and IMR are inversely related but not significant. IMR decreases as the hospitals and beds per lakh population increase significantly. More interestingly during reform period number of hospitals increases and IMR decreases significantly (Table 15.5).

VI. Summary and Conclusion

The public expenditure on health and family welfare has increased during the year 1980-81 to 2004-05. The trends of pre-reform and reforms period revealed that, the central and state government spending on public health much higher during reform period, than pre-reform period. The allocation for health rises as GDP increases. There is a rise in percentage of health care expenditure to GDP over the year1980-81 to 2000-01.

Table 15.5: Multiple Regression Results: IMR is Dependent Variable

Independent Variables	Over all Period	Pre reform period	Reform period
(Constant)	152.895 (5.204)*	230.816 (3.271)	27.4938 (0.655)
Health Expenditure	-0.002 (-1.627)	-0.017 (-1.461)	-0.0005 (-0.819)
Hospitals	-0.003 (-3.838)*	0.004 (0.959)	-0.0013 (-2.621)*
Beds per Lakh Population	-0.328 (0.33)	-0.773 (-0.895)	0.7210 (1.795)
R^2	0.92	0.85	0.90

Note: The figures in the parentheses indicate t values and * indicates the values are significant at 5 per cent level or more

During the period 1985-2002 the birth rate and death rate decreased 1.63 per cent and 1.96 per cent per annum respectively, however the infant mortality rate has declined 2.47 per cent per annum.

There is an inverse relationship between public health expenditure and birth rate. It implies that, public health expenditure on health plays an important role in bringing down the birth rate. This is true in both the pre-reform and reform period. Access to hospital facility also plays a significant role in reducing the birth rate.

Expenditure on medical and public health, number of hospitals and hospital beds per lakh population has influenced the death rate negatively, leading to decrease in the death rate. The increased per capita income and expenditure on public health, ensured better medical and health services and supply of medicine reduce the death rate. The number of hospitals and beds per lakh population contributed significantly to reduce the death rates during pre-reform and reform period. Health expenditure and IMR are inversely related but not significant. However, IMR decreases significantly as hospitals and beds per lakh population increase.

References

Abel-Smith, B. (1963): Paying for Health Services, *Public Health Papers No. 17*, World Health Organization, Geneva,

Abel-Smith, B. (1967): An International Study of Health Expenditure, *Public Health Papers No. 32*, World Health Organization, Geneva.

Bhatt, R and N. Jain (2006): Analysis of Public and Private Health care Expenditures, *Economic Political Weekly*, Vol. XLI, No. 1.

Blomgrist, A. G. and R.A.L Carter (1977): Is health care really a luxury?, *Journal of Health Economics*, Vol. 16, No. 2, pp. 207-229.

Carrin, Guy (1984): *Economic Evaluation of Health Care in Developing Countries Theory and Applications*, Croom Helm, London.

Chakrabarti, A. and R. Joglekar (2006): Determinants of Expenditure on Education: An Empirical Analysis using state level data, *Economic Political Weekly*, Vol. XLI, No. 15.

Dimatteo, L, and R. Dimatteo (1998): Evidence on the Determinants of Canadian Provincial Government Health Expenditures: 1965-1991, *Journal of Health Economics*, Vol. 17, pp. 211-228.

Gerdtham, U. G. and M. Lothgreen (2000): On Sstationality and Cointegration of International Health Expenditure and GNP, *Journal of Health Economics*, Vol. 19, pp. 461-475.

Gulati, S.C. (1998): Cost effectiveness of Health and Family Welfare Programs in India', Demography India Vol. 27, No. 1, pp 167.

Hansen, Paul and Alan King (1996): The Determinants of Health Care Expenditure; A co-integration approach, *Journal of Health Economics*, Vol. 15, pp. 127-137.

Hitris, T and J. Posnett (1992): The Determinants and Effects of Health Expenditure in Developed Countries, *Journal of Health Economics*, Vol.11, pp. 173-181.

Joshi, Seema (2006): Impact of Economic Reforms on Social Sector Expenditure in India, *Economic and Political Weekly*, Vol. XLI, No.4.

Karatzas, G. (2000): On the Determination of thc USA Aggregate Health Expenditure, Applied Economics, Vol.32, pp. 1085-1099.

Manning, W. et. el. (1987): Health Insurance and the Demand for Medical Care Evidence from a Randomized Experiment, *American Economic Review*, Vol. 77, No. 3, pp. 251-277.

Manonmoney, N. (1994): An Economic Analysis of Health Status in Tamil Nadu, IEA Conference Volume, Bombay.

McCoskey, S. K. and T. M. Selden (1998): Health Care Expenditure and GDP: Panel Data Unit Root Test Results, *Journal of Health Economics*, Vol. 17, pp. 369-376.

Newhouse, J. P. (1977): Medical Expenditure: A Cross National Survey', *Journal of Human Resources*, Vol. 12, pp. 115-25.

Panchamukhi, P R. (Year is not mentioned): *Economics of Health an Introductory Review*, CMDR, Dharwad.

Rao, K. Nageswara (2004): Trends in the Health Status in Andhra Pradesh: An Empirical Analysis, *Indian Economic Journal*, Vol. 51, No.1.

Reddy, K. N. and Selvaraju (1994): Determinants of Health Status in India: An Empirical Verification, IEA Conference Volume, Bombay, p-31.

Sing W. K. (2006): Over estimation of Fertility Rates in Manipur, *Economic and Political Weekly*, Vol. XLL, No.15.

Winikoff, B. and G. Brown (1980): Nutrition, population and health: Theoretical and practical Issues, *Social Science and Medicine*, Vol. 14, pp. 171-176.

World Bank (1991): World Development Report, Oxford University Press, New York, p.4.

16

Rural Primary Health Centres in Andhra Pradesh

S. Radha Krishna

I. Introduction

The rights to basic education and primary health care have been recognized as human rights in the UN charter of Human Rights prepared in 1948. India being signatory to the UN convention on Human Rights, it is the duty of the Government to Provide Primary health care to every citizen of the country. The rural areas are lagging much behind the urban areas, so it becomes imperative on the part of the policy makers to focus much attention on the rural health. In this paper an attempt is made to examine some of the issues related to health care of the rural people in Khammam District of Andhra Pradesh (A.P.). The paper is divided into four sections. Section I introduces the paper along with database. Section II presents the status of health infrastructure and public health expenditures pattern in A.P. It also focuses much light on the health condition prevalent in Khammam District. Section III examines the utilization and functioning of the Primary Health Center (PHC) in Khammam district in particular. Suggestions to improve the health care in rural areas are presented in Section IV.

Database: The data pertaining to the status of health infrastructure and the availability of health facilities in Andhra Pradesh in general and Khammam district in particular has been collected from the PHC of Gandhampally; the District Medical and Health Officer (DM and HO), Khammam; A.P. Statistical abstracts; Health Information India and other related Journals. Apart from this, the primary data has also been collected by interviewing the DM and HO of Khammam, Medical Officers, inpatients and out-patients of the PHC Gandhampally, Bayyaram (M), Khammam district.

II. Health Infrastructure and Expenditure Pattern in A.P.

Bed strength, doctor population ratio, PHC Hospital Population ratios, is some of the physical indicators to assess the progress of health care in rural areas. The data pertaining to these indicators of A.P is presented in Table 16.1 and analyzed below.

Hospital Population Ratio

- The State average of General Hospital population ratio in the state of A.P is 1:2, 13,300.
- In region wise analysis, it is paradoxical that Telangana (excluding Hyderabad) is in relatively better position with 1:1,99,610, followed by Rayalaseema (1:2,01,373) and Andhra (1:2,32,691).
- In Andhra, the districts which are less than the state average of hospital population ratio are Srikakulam (1:1, 58,250), East Godavari (1:2, 12, 956), Nellore (1:2, 05,000). However, it can be noted that with regard to East Godavari and Nellore there is marginal variation when compared to state average of hospital - population ratio. The reason for having relatively less hospital population ratio may be perhaps due to the government initiatives taken in recent times to establish more number of hospitals to provide health facilities in tribal district.
- In Rayalaseema region, Kurnool (1:1, 76,200) Ananthapoor (1:1, 81,950) and Chittoor (1:2, 07,611) are have relatively less than state hospital population ratio. Hence, Kadapa district (1:2, 88,000) needs Government support as the ratio is marginally low.
- In Telangana region, Khammam (1:1,42,722), Adilabad (1:1,77,786), Nigamabad (1:1,80,000), Mahaboob Nagar (1:1,94,944), Medak (1:2,04,923) and Ranga Reddy (1:2,11,508) districts have less than the state average in so for as the of hospital population ratio is concerned. Thus, in this region about 66 per cent of the districts have relatively better

Table 16.1: Health Infrastructure in Andhra Pradesh

Sl. No	Districts	No. General Hospitals	General Hospital Popu. Ratio	No. of PHCS	PHC Population Ratio	Beds	Beds Population Ratio	No of Doctors	Doctor Population Ratio
1.	Srikakulam	16	1:1,58,250	61	1:41,508	934	1:2,711	214	1:11,832
2.	Vijayanagaram	10	1:2,24,300	53	1:42,320	620	1:3,618	225	1:9,969
3.	Vishakapatnam	16	1:2,38,562	64	1:59,640	2637	1:1,447	632	1:6,040
4.	Est. Godavari	23	1:2,12,956	72	1:68,028	2153	1:2,275	594	1:8,246
5.	West Godavari	12	1:3,16,583	63	1:60,302	918	1:4,138	219	1:17,347
6.	Krishna	18	1:2,32,278	64	1:65,328	1528	1:2,736	493	1:8,480
7.	Guntur	17	1:2,62,176	66	1:67,515	2263	1:1,969	566	1:7,873
8.	Prakasham	11	1:2,77,727	72	1:42,430	824	1:3,707	231	1:13,225
9.	Nellur	13	1:2,05,000	62	1:42,984	1297	1:2,055	234	1:11388
	Sub Total	136	1:2,32691	577	1:54,846	13,174	1.709722	3408	1:9,286
10.	Chithuru	18	1:207611	71	1:52,634	1844	1;2,026	593	1:6,302

Contd...

11.	Kadapa	9	1:2,88,000	85	1:30,494	828	1;3,130	**244**	1:10,623
12.	Ananthapuram	20	1:1,81,950	62	1:58,694	1120	1;3,250	**410**	1:8,875
13.	Karnul	20	1:1,76,200	72	1:48,944	2083	1:1,692	**560**	1:6,293
	SubTotal	67	1:2.01.373	290	1:58,660	5875	1:2,296	**1807**	1:7,466
14.	Mahabub Nagar	18	1:1,94,944	75	1:46,786	1,067	1:3,288	**260**	1:13,496
15.	Rangareddy	17	1:2,110058	35	1:1,0251	1275	1:2,775	**202**	1:17,762
16.	Medak	13	1:2,04,923	61	1:43,672	978	1:2,902	**221**	1:12,054
17.	Nizam	13	1:1,80,000	40	1:58,900	974	1:2,402	**169**	1:13,846
18.	Adilabad	14	1:1,777862	64	1:38,890	962	1:2,587	**221**	1:11,262
19.	Kareem Nagar	15	1:2,33,4008	65	1:53,861	1044	1:3,353	**222**	1:15,770
20.	Warangal	13	1:2493859	60	1:54,033	1531	1:2,120	**458**	1:7,078
21.	Khammam	18	1:1,4,722	53	1:48,472	765	1:3,358	**185**	1:13,886
22.	Nalgonda	15	1:2,16,333	66	1:49,166	892	1:3,638	**235**	1:13,808
	Sub Total	136	1:1,99,610	489	1:56,205	9428	2880	**2173**	1:12,493
	Grand Total	339	1:2,13,300	1386	1:54,914	28477	1.804167	**7388**	1:9,784

Source: Statistical Abstract of A.P. various issues

position with regard to number of hospitals. Hence, Warangal, Karimnagar and Nalgonda districts need attention of the government.

PHC Population Ratio

- The State average of PHC population ratio in A.P. is calculated at 1:54,914.
- In region – wise analysis, Andhra (1:54,846) is in better position with regard to PHC population ratio as it is almost equal to state average. In this indicator also Srikakulam (1:41,308) is in better position, followed by Vijayanagaram (1:42,320), Prakasham (1:42,430), Nellor (1:42,984). Hence, the tribal populated district of East Godavari (1:68,028) needs attention. With regard to rich district like Guntur even though it had fewer ratios (1:67,515) it has teaching hospitals of its own reputation. The same situation can be seen with regard to Krishna and Visakhapatnam districts where Health University and teaching hospitals are available. Hence, it can be said that the relatively developed districts with good social infrastructure have a less PHC population ratio.
- In Rayalaseema region, Kadapa (1:30,494) Kurnool (1:48,944) aid Chittoor (1:52,634) have less than the state average. By and large the PHC population ratio in this region excluding Ananthapoor (1:58,694) is less than average of Andhra region (1:54,846), as well as the state.
- In Telangana region Adilabad (1:38,890), Medak (1:43,672), Mahabood Nagar (1:46,786) Khammam (1:48,472), Nalgonda (1:49,166) and Karimnagar (1:53,861) have less than the state PHC population ratio. Warangal district stands at equal ratio to state average. Hence, Nizamabad (1:58,900) needs more PHCs and with regard to Rangareddy (1:1,02,514) district, even though the ratio is high, the availability of health facilities are more as this district is adjacent to Hyderabad.

Bed Population Ratio

- The state average of bed population ratio is (1:2,538). The region – wise analysis shows that Rayalaseema (1:2,296) has less than the state average followed by Andhra (1:2,402),

Telangana (1:2,800) excluding Hyderabad has more than the state average.

- Though Rayalaseema region had in better position in this aspect, Ananthapoor (1:32,250) and Kadapa (1:3,130) district have relatively less bed-population ratio to the state average.
- In Andhra region, Visakhapatnam (1:1,447), Guntur (1:1,969), Nelloor (1:2,055), East Godavari (1:2,275) are in relatively better position with high ratios compared to state average. On the other hand, Srikakulam (1:2,711), Krishna (1:2,726), Vijayanagaram (1:3,618), Prakasham (1:3,707) and West Godavari (1:4,138) districts have fewer ratios. Thus, the Government should take steps in providing more beds in Srikakulam and Vijayanagaram districts in view of low socio – economic conditions of the people.
- In Telangana region, Warangal (1:2,120), Nizamabad (1:2,402), are in a better position though less than the state average, Adilabad (1:2,587) is almost equal to state average. All other districts have low bed population ratio. In this aspect, the district of Nalgonda which had low bed – population ratio needs support.

Doctor Population Ratio

The doctor-population ratio being considered as an important indicator to ascertain the service available to the people. The state average of doctor population ratio is (1:9,784). The region wise data shows that Rayalaseema had highest doctor-population ratio with (1:7,466) stands relatively in better position followed by Andhra with (1:9,286). Telangana is in bad position with less doctor population ratio (1:12,493).

Though the Rayalaseema region has a whole has high doctor - population ratio, Kadapa has less ratio (1:10,623) to state average. In Andhra region, out of 9 districts, 4 districts (West Godavari, Prakasham, Srikakulam, Nelloor), have low doctor – population to state average. Hence, there is a need to create improved facilities in backward districts of Srikakulam, where the people recently affected Malaria at a large scale. In Telangana region, except Warangal district, all other Districts have low doctor population ratio, particularly, the district of Karimnagar, where nearly 80 per cent of people living in rural areas need to seek special attention by providing more doctors.

Expenditure on Health Sector in A.P

The per capita public expenditure on health at constant (1993-94) prices was about Rs. 58 during fifth five year plan. During the Seventh Five year plan it has increased to Rs. 85 per capita and during 1990's it declined to Rs. 73 (in the 8th five year plan period). It can be seen from Table 16.2 that the public expenditure on social services were less when compared to economic services, further it is also observed that there has been a declining trend in health care in social services since fifth plan period to 2004-05. The share of health sector in SDP increased from 1.09 per cent in the fifth plan to 1.29 per cent in the seventh plan. But during 1990's a declining trend can be seen. During 2001 to 2004-05 the share has further declined from 1.03 to 0.82.

The share of social services in SDP increased 5.7 to 8.5 per cent during seventh plan period. From then onwards the share is continuously declined from 6.9 (1990-91) to 5.80 per cent (2004-05). Though the share of economic services is relatively more from fifth plan period to 2000-01, later during 2001-02 to 2004-05 the economic services have been marginally declined when compare to social services. Thus, it can be concluded that due to the impact of structural adjustment programme there was a fall in allocations to healthcare services in A.P. However, a positive sign can be observed with regard to social services allocations from 2001-02 onwards.

III. Health Infrastructure in Rural Areas of Khammam District

At *mandal* level, availability of medical facilities in public sector is mostly PHCs. Latest data of 2004-05 shows that nearly 75 per cent of (50 in number) PHCs are located at agency area, where, the villages are scattered widely. The PHC population ratio in these areas is less than the district average. However, nearly 75 per cent of PHC's in agency areas are being run without doctors. In plain areas, nearly 25 per cent (15 mandals) of PHCs have low PHC population ratio and it is in the range of 32,543 – 62,220 population per PHC.

Table 16.2: Share of Public Expenditure in SDP (Per Cent)

Year	Health Services	Social Services	Economic Services	Total Expenditure
5th five year Plan (1974-79)	1.09	5.7	7.2	16.8
1979 - 80	1.20	7.3	8.7	20.5
6th five year Plan (1980-85)	1.25	8.1	7.6	20.2
7th five year Plan (1985 -90)	1.29	8.5	8.5	22.3
1990 - 91	1.06	6.9	7.2	19.1
1991 -92	1.00	6.5	6.9	18.4
8th five year Plan (1992 - 97)	0.94	6.3	6.9	18.4
1997 -98	0.99	6.5	6.1	18.2
1998 - 99	1.00	6.9	5.2	17.6
1999 - 00	1.04	6.7	5.0	17.9
2000 - 01	1.03	6.7	7.0	20.7
2001 - 02	0.91	5.9	4.7	16.61
2002 - 03	0.83	5.3	3.9	17.35
2003 - 04	0.91	5.8	4.2	16.77
2004 - 05	0.82	5.8	4.4	17.15

Sources: 1. Government of A.P, Budget Estimates, Detailed Demands of Grants, Bureau of Economics and Statistics, A.P, Estimates of SDP Quoted in K.V. Narayana (2003). 2. Statistical Abstracts of A.P, various issues

It can be noted that though the PHC population ratio of Khammam District is higher than the state average, mandal – wise PHC population ratios shows that about 25 per cent of them are with low PHC population ratio.

Hence, it could be concluded that there are variations in respect of PHCs in terms of doctor population and bed ratios at regional level and also in different districts of the regions and also at the district level among some of the areas.

The presence of the Medical Officer at the PHC Utilization and functioning of PHCS in Khammam District is indispensable in so far as providing proper medical aid to the villagers. If the medical officer is not available at any of the PHCs, it would be of no use to have the required equipment, staff and other things. They remain un- utilized because there is no scope to take care of the patients in the absence of a doctor at a PHC. As per DM and HO, Khammam, at present there is a shortage of 30 per cent of the doctors in different PHCs.

There is a general misconception that treatment will be given to people for all diseases at the PHCs. The aim of a PHC is to provide primary health service to the people. As a doctor working in a PHC is not confined to a particular PHC only, providing medical aid to one and all has become a difficult task. As a doctor s/he has to impart medical education and explain health care to villagers, s/he has to visit and supervise the working of the ANMs at different sub-centers. S/he has to take precautions in preventing different infectious diseases in different villages under his PHC. As such it is required that s/he has to plan and monitor the preventive steps for the infectious diseases under his jurisdiction. As per norms, a doctor will have to tour 20 days at an average in a month and as such a single medical officer working at a particular primary health centre may not be available to the patients as and when they required his presence. As a doctor of a PHC has to attend meetings held at the DM and HO at least for a couple of days in a month, and hence the doctor is not available at the PHC concern. Some times if a doctor in a PHC goes on leave, additional duties are assigned to another doctor working at some other PHC.

Keeping the existing financial constraints in view, the allocations of funds to different hospitals in the state are proportionate to the actual needs of the people in so far as the supply of different drugs and medicines. In spite of the fact that the allocation of funds is proportionate to the needs, some unforeseen contingencies such as supplying of Anti-Robbies vaccine et cetera may cause for the in sufficient supply of medicine to all the people. For example the Government is not providing Anti-Rabbies vaccine at free of cost to the PHCs in the state. It is the reason why the PHCs have to buy the vaccine with in the budget, allotted to them. As the cost of the vaccine is so high that it costs Rs. 1150/- per a patient at the rate of Rs. 250/- per each voile and a patient needs five voiles for completing the treatment. As such it has become an impossibility to provide sufficient medical aid to all the patients at a PHC.

In order to diagnoses the disease, all the tests have to be with in the reach of the people. In most of the PHCs there is no provision for the laboratory facilities. As such patients would go to the nearest town for diagnostic tests and treatment.

There are no Ambulance facilities in majority of the PHCs. Especially the transport facilities are not available to the people living in the remote areas of the rural tribal belt. It has become very arduous for the tribal and the down trodden people to reach the PHCs as there are no link roads and approach roads in most of the villages. As such the people who are far away from the PHCs are not able to properly utilize the medical facilities that are provided by the PHCs. It is the reason why they are depending upon the help of the private doctors mostly Private Medical Practitioners (PMPs) available in their local areas.

Regarding the delivery cases, it is generally held that about 60 per cent of the deliveries are taking place in the hospitals and the remaining 40 per cent are conducted at homes. It is likely that mortalities of women to a larger extent occur in the deliveries held at homes, and this percentage of mortality at the delivery time is relatively more at the remote rural areas where the transportation facilities are scarcely available.

Hence, it is advisable that all the pregnant cases should be brought either to the PHC's or to other Government Hospitals.

There are plans such as '*Janani Sukhibhava*" came in to force since November 2005 introduced by the Central Government for the welfare of the pregnant women in our country. According to this plan a monetary help to the tune of Rs. 1000/- will be given to every patient if the delivery takes place in the PHC. The success of this plan to a large extent is based upon the role of the ANMs and the other NGOs. The responsibility of ANMs is to recognize pregnant women and to educate them by explaining the necessary precautions to be taken by them during the period of conception. Further they are expected to bring the patient to the PHCs for medical checkup and the required tests. If they discharge these duties properly there is every possibility of deterioration in the rates of both the IMR and MMR.

Brief Profile of PHC Gandhampally, Gramapanchayat

The Gandhampally Gramapanchayat is in the *mandal* of Bayyaram, Khammam District which comes under agency area. The population of this mandal is 42,326. The caste–wise distribution of mandal shows that 50 per cent are belong to Schedule Tribe (ST) community (Lambadi and Koya) followed BC community (25 per cent) Schedule Caste (SC) community (10 per cent) and remaining 15 per cent are in forward caste community.

The mandal is 55 km is away from Khammam town. The *mandal* headquarters is well connected with road. The radial distance of this *mandal* is nearly 85 km.

There are two PHCs in this *mandal* one is Gandhampalli and another is at mandal Headquarter, Bayyaram. At present only one female medical officer is working in this center and another medical officer post is vacant. With regard to other staff, except MPHA male post, all other posts are filled. This PHC started in 1995 in a private building, later a permanent building on its own is constructed in 2002. On an average 150 out-patients visit the PHC per day. In this, 50 per cent are female, 30 per cent are male and remaining 20 per cent are children. The reason for relatively more number of female patients when compare to other PHC are due to the availability of female medical officer.

Utilization of Health Services in PHC

- It is observed that in spite of huge expenditure and wide network of the PHCs, the utility in this PHC is below 10 per cent. It is found that a majority of illiterate households, lower income groups, casual labour house holds have been utilizing public health care. Where as the rich economic groups, salaried and self employed and educated household categories utilize the services of the private hospitals available at nearest towns.
- The study also reveals that about 30 per cent of the out patients who visit the hospital on any day happen to be new patients.
- Nearly 70 per cent of the out patients belong to the poor, 20 per cent are from the middle income groups and the remaining 10 per cent are above middle upper cast categories. Mostly the poor patients belong to the agricultural labour. It is observed that 60 per cent among the patients are illiterates and in the remaining 40 per cent, 20 per cent are hardly able to write their names.
- As the PHC is located in the tribal area, 50 per cent of the tribal people take self treatment at the initial stages of diseases by preparing various parts from herbarium roots available from the nearby woods. About 15 per cent of patients who visited PHC, revealed that at initial stages of ailments they would occasionally use some medicine for ailments such as fever, headache cold and the like which is prescribed by a local man who runs a general store. Another 35 per cent disclosed the fact that they would consult a local PMP for treatment at villages. If the disease is not cured or if they could not afford to pay for the treatment, it becomes inevitable for them to turn up to a PHC. No alternative system of medicine is used by the people in this area.
- The major ailments reported at the PHC under out-patient care include arthritis (15 per cent) followed by viral fever and

diabetes gastritis–ulcer and (50 per cent) skin disease, (10 per cent) and the remaining 15 per cent are pediatric problems, (mostly water born diseases like gastroenteritis). Non–communicable disease like asthama, chest TB, allergy fits are also found in 20 per cent cases. The increase of non–communicable diseases in adults is mainly due to smoking tobacco and alcohol consumption.

- The caste– wise distribution of out patients shows that 60 per cent of them belong to the ST and SC Community (Koya , Lambada and Madiga) followed by 20 per cent BC community, (Mudiraj, Yadva, Gowda, Viswa Brahmin) remaining 15 per cent belong to forward community. Mostly the people of the forward caste visit the PHC for blood pressure checkups and taking injections prescribed by the private doctors of near by towns.

IV. Suggestions to Improve Rural Health Care

Increase public health expenditure from present 0.9 per cent of GDP to at least two per cent. Such increases are vital to make public health services more accessible and effective. However, increase in expenditure must be accompanied by better utilization of resources with emphasis on preventive and primary health.

The condition of sanitation is quite unhygienic in rural areas of A.P., only 31 per cent have access to a safe, hygienic toilet. Under the present exigency, the Government has to come forward by providing a low cost material at subsidized rates to low income groups. With regard to safe drinking water, in a majority of villages the availability of drinking water during summer is inadequate and the water available to them is so contaminated that it some times causes diseases like diarrhea. Necessary Steps may be taken by the *Panchayat Raj* Department for continuous supply of drinking water by identifying problem affected areas.

Government control and regulation over private/corporate hospitals is required so that the medical help will be with in the reach of a common man with reasonable charges, that the common man is free from institutional victimization.

Recently, the Government of A.P. announced that the PMP's (about 50,000) working in rural areas with a minimum qualification and some experience at qualified doctor will be recognized as medical practitioners. A periodical refresher course will be provided for them to facilitate the first aid to the villagers. The Government decision is appreciable, for the availability of man power or health infrastructure is either wee or completely naught. In the other hand, provision may be made for the reorganization of PMPs by updating their practitioner abilities periodically by the renowned professionals.

Effective public education, counseling, replacement therapies and treatments should be standardized to suit the requirement of each region and group.

The high reliance on private, out–of–pocket payments in health in India impose disproportionate burden on the poor, hence, radial distance of PHC, sub centers should be reduced, to increase utilization.

Empirical evidence shows that most of the hospitals, PHCs in rural areas are not providing quality patient care. Shortage of critical staff, poor quality maintenance, perpetual budgetary problems, large distance of coverage of hospital is some of the main reasons for this crisis. Hence, the state may take care of these problems to improve the quality of health care.

It would be better if the PHCs are provided with the test for the AIDS as it has become hazardous in the present time. It is also necessary to keep oxygen operator at the PHCs as to meet the needs of the emergency cases.

Last but not the least, it is observed that there is lack of personal attention where the required staff or man power is available, so attention should be drawn to improve this kind of situation in the respective PHCs to improve the credibility and utilization.

References

World Bank (1997): *World Development Report: The State in a Changing World*, Oxford University Press and World Bank, Washington.

Government of India (2002): *The National Health Polity (2002)*, Department of Health, New Delhi.

ICMR (1988): *Utilization of Health and Family Planning Services in Bihar, Gujarat and Kerala: A Task Force Study*, New Delhi.

Narayana K.V. (2003): Changing Health Care system, *Economic Political Weekly*, Vol.38, No. 12 and 13, p. 1230.

Sankar, Deepa (2003): Health Sector in 2003-04 Budget, *Economic Political Weekly*, Vol. 38, No.15.

Government of Andhra Pradesh (Annual Publication): *Statistical Abstract of Andhra Pradesh*, Directorate of Economics and Statistics, Hyderabad.

Index

Index